THE MANY LIVES OF
IBRAHIM NAGUI

THE MANY LIVES OF IBRAHIM NAGUI

A JOURNEY WITH MY GRANDFATHER

SAMIA MEHREZ

Translated by
Eleanor Ellis

The American University in Cairo Press
Cairo   New York

This book has been translated with
the generous assistance of
the Jan Michalski Foundation and
the Shaikh Ebrahim Bin
Mohammed Al-Khalifa
Center for Culture and Research.

This edition published in 2024 by
The American University of Cairo Press
113 Sharia Kasr el Aini, Cairo, Egypt
420 Lexington Avenue, Suite 1644, New York, NY 10170
www.aucpress.com

Text copyright © 2021 by Dar El Shorouk
Illustrations copyright © by Samia Mehrez
Published in Arabic in 2021 as *Ibrahim Nagui: ziyara hamima ta'akharat kathiran* by Dar El Shorouk

English translation copyright © 2024 by Eleanor Ellis

Extract from *In the Eye of the Sun* used by kind permission from Ahdaf Soueif. Copyright © 1992, 1993 by Ahdaf Soueif, used by permission of The Wylie Agency (UK) Limited and Pantheon Books, an imprint of Knopf Doubleday Publishing Group, a division of Penguin Random House LLC.

All rights reserved. No part of this publication may be reproduced, stored in a retrieval system, or transmitted in any form or by any means, electronic, mechanical, photocopying, recording, or otherwise, without the prior written permission of the publisher.

ISBN 978 1 649 03380 2

Library of Congress Cataloging-in-Publication Data

Names: Mehrez, Samia, author. | Ellis, Eleanor, translator.
Title: The many lives of Ibrahim Nagui: a journey with my grandfather /
  Samia Mehrez; translated by Eleanor Ellis.
Other titles: Ibrāhīm Nājī, ziyārah ḥamīmah ta'akhkharat kathīran.
  English.
Description: Cairo; New York: The American University in Cairo Press,
  2024.
Identifiers: LCCN 2023058491 | ISBN 9781649033802 (hardback) | ISBN
  9781649033819 (epub) | ISBN 9781649033826 (adobe pdf)
Subjects: LCSH: Nājī, Ibrāhīm, 1898-1953. | Mehrez, Samia--Family. |
  Poets, Arab--Egypt--Biography. | LCGFT: Biographies.
Classification: LCC PJ7852.A519 Z7213 2024 | DDC
  892.7/15--dc23/eng/20240304
LC record available at https://lccn.loc.gov/2023058491

1 2 3 4 5   28 27 26 25 24

Designed by Adam el-Sehemy

For my mother, Amira Ibrahim Nagui

CONTENTS

Acknowledgments ix

Chapter 1: "What is Dr. Nagui Doing Here?" 1
Chapter 2: 1 Hassouna al-Nawawy Street 15
Chapter 3: All That Remains 33
Chapter 4: Houma and Souma 45
Chapter 5: From N. to A. 65
Chapter 6: *Journal de vie* 87
Chapter 7: Ibrahim Nagui Superstar 117
Chapter 8: My Friend Shakespeare 143
Chapter 9: The Family Doctor 173
Chapter 10: Farewell 199

Notes 225
Appendix: al-Atlal/The Ruins 233

ACKNOWLEDGMENTS

I wish to thank the many wonderful friends who have joined me on this journey—those whom I imposed upon to read a draft of the book, who helped me locate texts that would otherwise have been difficult to find, and who shared crucial material from their personal archives. I would in particular like to thank architect Hassan Abouseda, author Sonallah Ibrahim, critic and historian Sayed Mahmoud, translator Nashwa al-Azhari, my student Dr. Alia Ayman, and Amira Abu al-Maged, director of Dar El Shorouk, for their close reading of the manuscript. They gave me faith in this book, pushed me to continue writing, and did not hesitate to provide honest and insightful feedback throughout the writing process. My friend the historian Hussein Omar shed light on new dimensions of my grandfather's life story which will become apparent to the reader within the chapters of this book. I must also thank Ferial Ghazoul and Mona el-Namoury, who helped me reach Abdel Wahid Lu'lu'a and Mohamed Enani, who generously shared their Arabic translations of Shakespeare's Sonnet 55 with me. I also thank Joy Garnett, the granddaughter of the late poet Ahmed Zaki Abu Shadi, and Michel Hanna and Maggie Morgan, who kindly sent me important historical materials from their personal archives: two photographs that Ibrahim Nagui gave to Abu Shadi (which appear in chapter 10), and photographs of Abu Bakr al-Siddiq Street and Hassouna al-Nawawy Street in Heliopolis (chapter 2).

Special thanks are due to my mother, Amira Ibrahim Nagui, and my son, Nadim Jacquemond. My mother let me read chapters of this book to her and listened carefully with an open mind and remarkable patience. I was glad that Nadim also joined me in visiting his great-grandfather. He even volunteered to work on the preliminary cover design for the Arabic edition of the book, which reflects how thoroughly immersed he became in the twists and turns of this text. My cousin Shahira Abdel Wahed Raineri and her mother, the late Dawheya Ibrahim Nagui, are responsible for this book seeing the light of day; without them, I could not have embarked upon this journey.

Last but not least, I wish to thank Laura Gribbon, managing editor at the AUC Press, for bringing this book to the attention of the Press and for recommending it for translation into English, and Adam el-Sehemy for his work on the book design.

Samia Mehrez

1

"WHAT IS DR. NAGUI DOING HERE?"

I had corresponded with the author Gamal al-Ghitani on various occasions while I was away in the US before we finally arranged a time to meet in 1981, when I returned to Cairo for the summer break. He graciously accepted my invitation to the family home to talk over coffee about my dissertation, which was about his work. That was the first time we had met.

Gamal arrived on time and brought some of his books along with clippings of articles that had been written about them. When I opened the door of the apartment, he asked:

"Is Dr. Samia in?"

I didn't have a doctorate yet, so I just said: "I'm Samia."

He seemed taken aback. "I thought you'd be older," he said. He looked around the *salon* and his eyes settled on a large portrait hanging on the wall.

"What is Dr. Nagui doing here?" he asked me in great astonishment.

"That's my grandfather," I said.

"But your name is Mehrez," he pointed out.

"Yes," I said, "but Ibrahim Nagui is my grandfather. My mother's father."

"Are you serious?"

After the usual torrent of exclamations about my grandfather's work, his poetic prowess, his gentle heart, his wry sense of humor, his role in modern Arabic literature—all the things I'd heard a thousand times over—we began to speak in earnest about my work and why I was interested in Gamal's writing. It was the beginning of a lifelong friendship.

Before Gamal left the house, he took another long look at the portrait of my grandfather and then turned back to me again and said:

"You know, you look just like him."

I was aghast. "*I* look like him?"

"Yes, just like him," he repeated.

Gamal left and I stood staring, as if for the first time, at the portrait of my grandfather that had become inseparable from the house, present and absent at the same time. I'd never really paid attention to the photograph and did not particularly care for it. My mother had enlarged the photo beyond reasonable proportions, and I thought it looked rather out of place in the bourgeois living room.

There was no possible resemblance, I told myself indignantly. To be sure, I was also relatively small in stature, but did I have that balding head, the stony gaze, the enormous nose, the strange thick lips?

As I read descriptions of my grandfather's appearance, I became more aggrieved by the comparison. Dr. Ahmed Heikal wrote in a 1961 introduction to a collection of Nagui's poetry published eight years after my grandfather's death:

> Nagui did not have the best of luck with regard to physique or countenance. He was skinny and short, with a big skull and a broad forehead. He had two wide, round eyes that often stared off into space. Beneath his large nose sat thick lips, which elongated the breadth of his smile. His voice was colorless, and he tended to mumble.[1]

Even those who had good things to say about Nagui, who appreciated his company and were charmed by his poetry, magnanimity of spirit, and quick wit, still had a similar impression. In his 1934 book, *Sawt al-jil* (Voice of a Generation), Ibrahim al-Masri wrote of Nagui:

One stared at him, this scrawny man of middling height and frail physique. He was a balding fellow with a listless gaze and a long chin. Nagui hobbled along in silence, as if he were somewhere else. He'd withdraw to a corner of the coffeeshop, pipe in his mouth, seeming to have drifted off to sleep.[2]

I was still in my twenties and took al-Ghitani's comparison quite literally. I was stunned. But as time passed, once I got over the initial shock of the idea, I began to think over this question of resemblance, and the portrait in the *salon* that I'd long ignored began to take on new dimensions.

1. Ibrahim Nagui in the early 1950s.

I'd grown up in the shadow of this portrait. It had hung in all of the family homes I knew: in my grandmother's home (which had also once been Nagui's) in Heliopolis, in my aunt Dawheya's home on al-Gomhoreya Street in central Cairo, in all the houses Dawheya lived in after she emigrated to the United States in the mid-1960s, and in my own family's home in Zamalek. This same image was printed on the covers of Nagui's poetry collections and many of the books and articles published about him, and even in our school books. Always the same picture. Sometimes it was enlarged and sometimes tiny. It was the portrait of a man I did not know, but who I was told was my grandfather—at once absent and present for many years.

This photograph was likely taken toward the end of Nagui's life. My mother later confirmed it was indeed taken only a handful of months before his death. He was clearly graying around the temples and his eyes were tinged with a quiet sadness and pain. He wasn't looking at the camera and stared off into the distant horizon, indifferent to our presence.

The photo would have been taken in a photography studio in Cairo, although the shot almost resembled a painting. That was why multiple artists had used it as a reference for color sketches of Nagui, on the covers of collections of his poetry or prose, or to accompany articles about his work in the newspaper.

Why did the photographer choose this particular angle, I wondered? Why did he let Nagui turn away from the camera lens, half here and half somewhere else? Why didn't he ask Nagui to smile, even just slightly, as photographers usually do? Did he know Nagui personally and want the shot to reflect his private anguish? I don't know. I only know that I could not get away from this photo, which peered at me in its various iterations at each twist and turn. That was perhaps what drove a wedge between my grandfather and me for many years.

Ibrahim Nagui suddenly died in March 1953, and I came into the world in January 1955. He left my grandmother Samia a widow at forty with three daughters: Amira, Dawheya, and Mahasen. Mahasen was only fourteen; my mother Amira, the oldest of the girls, had only just turned twenty. My grandfather attended her engagement, but death stole him away before the wedding. Despite his early passing, he watched over the ceremony, for the portrait already hung in his home where my mother was wed. On this occasion, as with others, the family made sure that Nagui's image would be present in the background, despite his absence.

2. Amira Nagui and Emad al-Din Mehrez with a photograph of Ibrahim Nagui in the background, 1954.

Nagui had fallen forward suddenly onto a patient he was treating in his clinic in Shubra, without any forewarning. I only realized what a shock this had been to the family when I began working on this book. When I was born, the family was still recovering from this blow. My gradual new appreciation for what had been endured more than six decades earlier spurred me to embark on this long-overdue journey, which I had not expected to ever undertake.

My mother and her sisters always referred to themselves by their full three names: Amira Ibrahim Nagui, Dawheya Ibrahim Nagui, and Mahasen Ibrahim Nagui. They were always immediately asked on social occasions—or even at the doctor's or dentist's—if they were related to the late Ibrahim Nagui, and were happy to confirm that they were his daughters.

This information was always received most warmly and was accompanied by fond recollections of Nagui and what a wonderful poet, doctor, and man he had been. The girls came away from these interactions very proud of their father, whose mantle they now carried after his untimely death.

When my mother and aunts realized that I was studying my grandfather's poetry in school from an early age, they expected me to own up to these family ties just as readily. My mother told me:

"You have to tell the teacher that he's your grandfather. They have to know you're Ibrahim Nagui's granddaughter."

But I wasn't so sure. You're his daughters, I'd explain. Your name is Nagui. It's not reasonable that at every turn I inform people: 'Hello, I'm Samia Mehrez, but I also happen to be Ibrahim Nagui's granddaughter.'

"You should be proud he's your grandfather," my mother would say.

In truth, I was not particularly proud of this fact. One of Ibrahim Nagui's most famous poems, "al-'Awda" (The Return), was assigned to us in school and is still assigned to millions of Egyptian students today. This poem made me the butt of the other children's jokes. Word spread that I was related to Nagui, and my classmates made my life miserable in vengeance for the impenetrability of my grandfather's poem, which we had a great deal of trouble grasping at that age.

The full poem reads as follows:

The Return

> Circled we around this Ka'ba
> > Dawn and dusk devotees to its light

In supplication to the beauty it enshrined
    Returning to whence we came, how can we strangers be?
Where my dreams and love did dwell—
    There now are we greeted coldly
Disavowed by what we held dear
    No radiant lamp to the traveler beckons.
My heart in mortal grasp its frantic wings did beat
    I make my plea: O dear heart, do tarry
Yet stand rebuked by the weeping wounds of the past:
    Wherefore have we returned?
Wherefore have we returned? Would that we had not—
    Wherefore not let love subside
Have done with pangs of longing
    Content ourselves with emptiness?
O aerie, if my paramour takes flight
    Night will no longer have any meaning
The days are yellowed as autumn's leaves
    Keening like the howling desert winds
O! What has fate made of us
    You, this sullen residuum
And I, the bowed heaviness of the mind
    Enough of this bale and sorrow!
Whither went thy voice? Thy chatter and convives?
    My eyes sent forth—ambushed by tears, the path dislimned
Darkness now indwells this place of beauty
    Weariness courses through its veins
Splendor beset by the specters of nightfall
    Witness to decay of cobwebs spun
Wail did I: O woe upon thee that cast thyself
    Where all lived undying, and brought gaiety to grief
On nights that held rapture and torment both
    I hear time's footsteps, a lonely patter on the stairs
O gentle solace, O kindred shelter
    Everlasting refuge beyond earthly miseries—

God alone knows how long this road did run
    To you I've come that I might find my peace
At your door my burdens do I leave
    A vagrant lost in the valley of tribulations
Here hath the Lord brought an end to my wand'rings
    Anchored my boat in the homeland's harbor
From you, my homeland, have I been banished
    An eternity of exile in a world of wretchedness
I return but to this regale of heady confidences
    Only to carry on once more, my brimming cup dry

Even today, the poem is still taught with the same unhelpful explications that we used to be given in school, to memorize and haltingly recite:

Vocabulary:
Tarry: Proceed slowly and deliberately
Aerie, aeries (pl.): The nest of an eagle, or other bird of prey, built high up among rocks
Paramour: Lover
Keening: Crying aloud
O!: Interjection indicating anguish
Residuum: (here) Remnants of an edifice
Bale: Woe and suffering
Convives: Drinking companions
Dislimned: Grew faint
Indwells: Takes up residence within

Figurative Language:
Indicate below whether the following phrases exemplify metaphor, simile, personification, or none of the above.
1. Radiant lamp . . . beckons (line 8)
2. O dear heart, do tarry (line 10)
3. Paramour takes flight (line 17)
4. Days are yellowed (line 19)

5. Keening like the howling desert winds (line 20)
6. Ambushed by tears (line 26)
7. Time's footsteps (line 34)

Explication of Certain Verses in Prose:
1. This house contains memories of love and longing. It once welcomed us fondly when we first met here.
2. The house no longer recognizes us, even though it once greeted us most gladly.
3. My heart jumped eagerly when it saw the house, and I urged it to slow its pace.
4. I shed tears when I remembered those sad days past, and I wished that I had not returned.
5. The poet asks himself why he returned if his love has ended, along with all the pain that went with it.
6. The poet struggles to accept the growing sense of absence and silence in the house.
7. The house lost its meaning once the lovers who lived within it left.
8. The days withered like leaves in the fall and made a wailing sound that resembled wind in the desert.
9. The poet feels afflicted because, with the passage of time, he has become estranged from this sad house.
10. I am a wretched ghost, and these other ghosts cause me great pain and suffering.
11. Where are the people who lived in the house, who once filled it with happiness during better days?
12. I weep when I remember those bygone days.
13. This home was a place of beauty and joy, but now I have found it brimming with sorrows.
14. Night has enveloped the house in a darkness full of terrifying phantoms.
15. I have seen with my own eyes the destruction of this house, which has become a desolate building full of spiderwebs.
16. In an effort to alleviate my suffering and grief, I remarked aloud how everything had changed.

17. Everything in the house has changed: happiness has become grief, and joy has become pain.
18. The days past, and the loneliness and absence since, have all left their mark on the house.
19. O house where we played as children, you were like a heaven to us, and gave us succor when we were weary.
20. God knows that my days of exile were long, and I have come to you at the end of this long journey to rest.

I feel for the millions of students who are assigned this poem buried under such explications. I wonder: What would these students say to me today if they knew I was Ibrahim Nagui's granddaughter?

To be honest, this poem was not the sole source of the problem. There were numerous reasons behind my fraught relationship with Arabic language and literature. My first school was a branch of the École Franciscaines de Marie. I then briefly attended school in the US when my father travelled abroad for his master's when I was five years old. After the family returned to Egypt in 1961, I enrolled in a British school in Cairo. Although British schools had been nationalized after 1952, English remained the language of study for all subjects except Arabic, religion, history, and geography.

We did speak Egyptian Arabic at home, but I learned to read and write first in French and then in English, and thus unfortunately developed a complicated relationship with my mother tongue. From the moment I entered kindergarten, Arabic was pushed to the side. For the most part, I learned Arabic from teachers who understood themselves to be completing a set task, like state employees in government offices. They simply aimed to impart the dull material at hand. Subjects and objects and predicates—it didn't matter whether we understood the text, but only that we could memorize and recite it. Years passed before I'd understand. This approach was at odds with that of our other subjects in English, which adopted a very different pedagogy. All of this propelled me further away from my own culture. I excelled at Arabic anyways, but I understood very little, and such "studying" was painful. I knew I simply had to grin and bear it.

I marveled at the passages set to us for memorization and recitation, from what were considered to be foundational texts in Arabic literature and culture.

"Samia, recite."

I recoiled at those words, but I'd recite anyway, and with each recitation I developed a greater loathing for those texts. Meanwhile, in my English literature classes, we'd read and discuss simplified excerpts from longer canonical texts that were appropriate our age and grade level and encouraged our own creativity.

In 1972, I enrolled in the American University Cairo in the Department of English Literature, against my father's wishes. He wanted me to study economics and political science at Cairo University, where I had already been accepted. My decision to pursue the former path of study was the product of the colonial legacy that had shaped my education: Cairo University was a vast institution with huge numbers of students, whereas AUC was more like the schools I had already attended. It had a small, approachable campus and classes of no more than twenty students. At AUC, I could stay in my cocoon, continuing to read and write in English.

However, as luck would have it, I became a student of Ferial Ghazoul, professor of English and comparative literature at AUC and the supervisor of my master's thesis. Ferial had come to AUC to stake out a space for Arabic. She fought back against the Anglophone focus of the literature department and put me to work as AUC's first master's student in comparative literature. She taught me to love Emile Habibi, Muhammad Afifi Matar, Mahmoud Darwish, Sonallah Ibrahim, Ismail Fahd Ismail, Badr Shakir al-Sayyab, Gamal al-Ghitani, and Yusuf al-Qa'id, among others. These weren't names I'd heard before, because in school, Arabic literature stopped where the classics—including my grandfather—ended. I blamed those classics, so painfully inflicted upon me throughout my grade school years, for my estrangement from my language and culture.

In 1979, I began my doctorate in the US, and had the good fortune of studying with Claude Audebert, professor of Arabic literature at the UCLA, who was responsible for bringing me back to Arabic. Claude was raised in Cairo, where her father had been a superintendent for the French schools at the time. She spoke Egyptian Arabic like I did. She was captivated by Arabic and devoted her life to it, and became a leading scholar in the field of Arabic literature. Claude finally taught me my language, helped me discover the genius of Arabic, continuing what Ferial had begun in Cairo. I eagerly plunged into my Arabic studies and eventually overcame my fears of writing in the language. I produced a dissertation on contemporary Arabic literature, using close readings that drew upon the theoretical frameworks that I had studied in Los Angeles.

That was the context in which I'd come to Gamal al-Ghitani's work. I loved his novel *al-Zayni Barakat*, not only because I was taken with its style and language, but also because it required me to engage with earlier sixteenth-century Arab and Egyptian history. Gamal's entire generation was unknown at the time in the US academy, and even in Egypt they were missing from the map of Arabic literature. As a result, my professors were skeptical of the viability of the project that I had chosen. Still, I stuck to my choice and wrote the first dissertation on Gamal al-Ghitani's work in 1983. Along the way, his remark about my grandfather often came to mind. Sometimes I still steered as far away as I could from engaging with his comment, but now and then I tried to see how it might be true.

The portrait that caught Gamal's attention when he visited me that first time had always loomed larger than life. I don't remember my grandmother telling me about my grandfather. But in my mother's and aunt's stories, Ibrahim Nagui was always the model husband and father, the perfect doctor, a man of unimpeachable character.

Although he was rarely home, Fridays were set aside for family, and they'd invite over friends and relatives—the house was always teeming with guests. They told me about his beautiful twenty-five-year love story with my grandmother. He never interfered in her decisions about the household. Ibrahim Nagui was generous with everyone and open-minded, and filled the house with his good-natured wit. He was a good friend and mentor to his daughters, respecting their decisions about what to study and what to do with their lives, even if he sometimes had a different vision for their future.

The more I tried to disassociate myself from my grandfather, the more Nagui appeared in my life. When I opted to specialize in literature, my family decided that I was the grandchild who had inherited Nagui's talents and would carry on his mantle. I am the eldest granddaughter, and as is the case with eldest sons, I was expected to follow in his footsteps. When they realized I wasn't going to write poetry, they hoped I would study his work and write about it, write about him, but I resisted. I focused on modern novels instead. I never studied or taught Ibrahim Nagui's poetry. I was daunted by the immensity of his legacy. The only time I wrote about him was when I translated one of his poems into English as a challenge.

Ibrahim Nagui died before I could meet him. I arrived two years too late, after he'd left the world in his fifty-sixth year. As I write this now, I am older than he was then. I decided the time had come for my reckoning, to conduct—like Latifa al-Zayyat before me—my own thorough "inspection" of his personal papers,[3] to sift through drafts of poetry, journals, and diaries. I was surprised to find them still there, along with the many memories they unearthed, which I had forgotten, or perhaps simply never understood. I set out to search for what my grandfather and I might have in common, embarking on a much-belated journey, a long-overdue labor of love.

2

HASSOUNA AL-NAWAWY STREET

One Hassouna al-Nawawy Street—that was my grandmother's address. As the eldest grandchild, when I started calling her Tettu, a variant on the usual Sittu, all the other grandchildren followed suit: my brother Mohamed, my cousins, Shahira and Ahmed (Aunt Dawheya's children), and my cousin Samia (the daughter of my mother's youngest sister, Mahasen, whom I called "Nuna"). Like my mother, Nuna had chosen my grandmother's name for her own daughter, so my cousin was known as "little Samia" to distinguish between the two of us. We still call her "little Samia" today, although she is now over fifty. All of us cousins used to say: Let's go see Tettu, we want to sleep over at Tettu's. For the grandchildren, that house bore no connection with my grandfather. We'd only hear his name in passing, when neighbors, servants, or friends would speak of "Dr. Nagui's house."

My grandmother and grandfather moved to Hassouna al-Nawawy Street off Abu Bakr al-Siddiq in Heliopolis after they started their small family. Before that, they lived in my great-grandfather Ahmed Nagui's home in Shubra, which Ibrahim Nagui described in his 1935 book, *Madinat al-ahlam* (City of Dreams):

> Twenty years ago, Shubra was still beautiful, lush and verdant, a gleaming emerald with an ancient charm that had bewitched conquerors of many nations and creeds. Yes, the same Shubra that is now

ruined, overrun with buildings upon buildings. As the city expanded, people were displaced to the area, bought up the beautiful pastures, and built their dense little houses. But it was once a single expanse with homes alighting here and there like white doves spreading their wings, endeavoring to take flight towards some nearby canal or brook. We'd come home from school while it was still light, dump our books at the doorstep, and hurry back out to that quiet haven.[1]

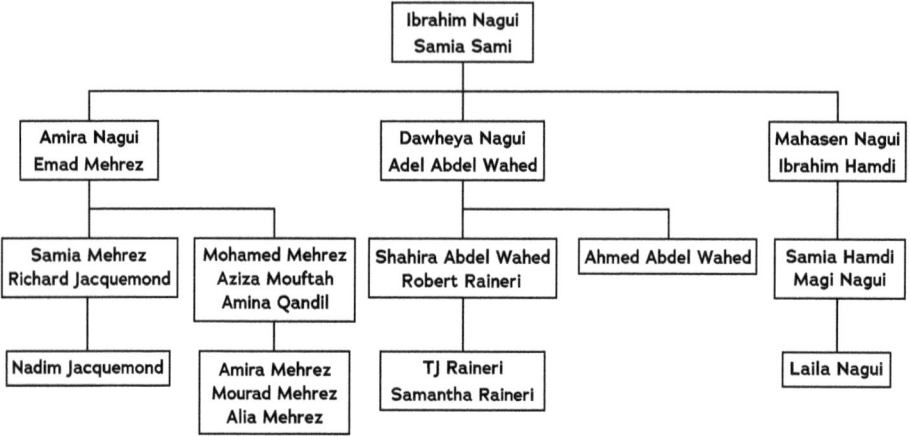

3. Ibrahim Nagui Family Tree

Most of the books that have described Ibrahim Nagui's upbringing include this excerpt on Shubra, which provides a window on Cairo's relentless urban growth. Nagui's "city of dreams" resembles today's desert compounds, although early twentieth-century Shubra was smaller in scope, and had larger homes and a more diverse population. This piece of land was located behind the central train station amid vast fields next to the old Bulaqiyya Canal, which branched off into other irrigation canals.

This was where seven affluent families from Cairo, who had been living in Ghouriya and Sanadiqiya near al-Hussain and al-Azhar, decided to make their home. They wanted to get away from the tumult of the city and decided to head to somewhere quieter—Shubra! These seven families built palace-like homes—the ones Nagui described as doves spreading their wings. The first of these was the home of the politician

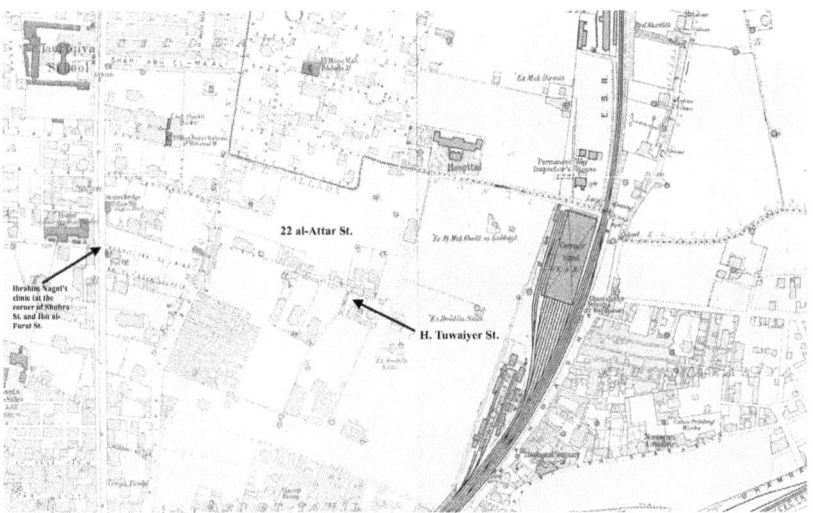

4. Shubra, Nagui's "city of dreams," as depicted in maps of Cairo dating from 1915–1921. Ahmed Nagui's villa was located at 22 al-Attar Street. Accessed via al-Madaq digital archive.

Mohammad Farid, and then the house of Hassouna al-Towayyer, who had Tunisian roots, and who was also related to Nagui's family. This proximity between the Nagui and al-Towayyer families would play an important role in Ibrahim Nagui's life in the years to come. After this came the home of the al-Margushi family, who were prominent merchants in Ghouriya, and then Sobhi al-Attar, a merchant in Sanadiqiya, then Ahmed Nagui, then Sheikh Ibrahim al-Sharqawi, the grandson of Sheikh Abdullah al-Sharqawi, the Grand Imam of al-Azhar, who was also Ibrahim Nagui's great-grandfather on his mother Bahia's side. At the corner of this neighborhood stood the house of Muhammad Uthman Galal, a prominent writer who translated seventeenth-century French writer Jean de La Fontaine's *Fables* into Arabic under the title *al-'Uyun al-yawaqiz fi al-amthal wa-l-mawa'iz* (Eyes Awoken for Parables and Proverbs Spoken).

Ahmed Nagui al-Qasabgui, the secretary general of the telegraph authority, lived with his six children—Mohamed, Ibrahim, Mostafa, Abdelaziz, Leila, Souad, and Hassan—in one of the palaces within this city of dreams. My grandfather Ibrahim was Ahmed Nagui's second son within this large family that continued to grow as grandchildren arrived.

5. Ahmed Nagui with his children and grandchildren at his home in Shubra, 1936.

My mother was born in her grandfather's home in Shubra in 1932. She came into the world five years after my grandfather and grandmother married—spoiling the young lovers' honeymoon, as they would later tell it.

My aunt Dawheya was born two years later, at which point my grandmother decided that the time had come for the small family to set out on their own. They decided to move to Heliopolis and took up residence in a new building near the villa belonging to her father, Mohamed Sami Amin Pasha, a governor-general of Cairo (*hakimdar al-'asima*).

The building was architecturally modern and was located at the corner of the intersection where Hassouna al-Nawawy met Abu Bakr al-Siddiq, with a small and well-curated garden below. The entrance to the building was on Hassouna al-Nawawy Street and each of the four floors contained two apartments. My mother told me that the building had stood alone on that street, surrounded by desert, and that you could even see the Almaza Airport from their balcony. The Bedouin, who were the original inhabitants of the area before

Heliopolis came into being, would pass under the house with their herds of goats and sheep. I remember watching the veiled women and their many children from the balcony, curious and a little apprehensive. As time passed, the original inhabitants of the area began to leave, and had moved on entirely by the mid-1960s, when the neighborhood of Heliopolis became fully developed.

I remember Abu Bakr al-Siddiq as a broad street with a large median full of rows of neatly-trimmed trees. In figure 7 of my mother, which was likely taken in the late 1940s, neither the street nor Safir Square had any trees yet; it was still desert. Eventually, this lone building was joined by many other similarly elegant apartment buildings, villas, and palaces for affluent families along both sides of the street. The map of Cairo was redrawn as families left Shubra, Helmiyya, Abbasiyya, Zeitoun, Hada'iq al-Qobba, and even the countryside in order to settle in Heliopolis. Even after their move, my grandfather kept his clinic in Shubra. Although he lived the rest of his adult life in Heliopolis, he would die suddenly in his Shubra clinic.

Abu Bakr al-Siddiq is one of the most important streets in Heliopolis, on par with Orouba Street. My mother recalled how the king's cabriolet coach used to pass under the house when he'd return home

6a. Amira Nagui, age 2, in the garden of Ahmed Nagui's home in Shubra, 1934.

6b. Amira Nagui on the balcony of my grandfather's home on Hassouna al-Nawawy Street, circa 1950.

from trips abroad. The local residents and their servants would come out onto the balconies, and the shop owners out into the street as the king passed by, standing in his open-top car. Later on, I too would stand on the balcony of my grandfather's house to watch Gamal Abdel Nasser's motorcade as he went back to his house in Manshiyyat al-Bakry in Heliopolis. I'd see Nasser looking up at us smiling, and imagine that he had seen me waving to him from my grandfather's balcony.

As part of urban renovation projects just before the time of writing, the green median and its trees on Abu Bakr al-Siddiq were wantonly destroyed, along with the villas and palaces that used to overlook it, permanently robbing the street of its storied history.

7. Abu Bakr al-Siddiq Street: (1) lined with trees in the 1980s, and (2) after the demolition in 2020. Photos from the archive of Michel Hanna.

My grandmother's apartment was on the second floor, overlooking Abu Bakr al-Siddiq Street and Safir Square. It was a vast apartment, with a spacious *salon* leading onto five other large rooms. Most of these looked out onto a long balcony. There were also two elegant little curved balconies, one off the living room and the other off another room at the farthest end of the apartment, which was variously used as a bedroom or dining room, depending on how many people were living there. Even the kitchen had a pleasant little balcony, where the servants sat, drank tea, played with us kids, and occasionally raised rabbits. The rent for the whole apartment was LE6 per month.

I knew most of the neighbors. They had all come to the building around the same time and were around the same age as my grandparents. They stayed on in the building for the rest of their lives, and after they passed away, left their apartments to their many children. There was Ahmed al-Rifai, who worked for the Ministry of Education, and lived with his wife Zakia al-Shishini on the first floor. They had four children, two girls and two boys: Amal, Nawal, Galal, and little Mahmoud "Bomboni." The last of these was my close friend and liked to tease me, much to my chagrin: *Samsuma wesh al-buma!* ("Samia owl-face!"). Ahmed al-Rifai was obsessed with birds and kept dozens of them in huge cages on his balcony, where they would tweet incessantly all day. We'd wait edgily for him to cover the cages at night, when the birds would finally quiet down. In the apartment opposite my grandmother's lived Ibrahim Farag, a prominent minister and member of parliament, his wife Kawkab, and their daughter Isis (Zizi), who was a friend of my mother and aunts. On the third floor was the apartment of Dr. Ahmed Morsi, who later became minister of higher education, his wife Khadija, and their eight daughters: Camelia, Leila, Fawqia, Samiha, Amal, Nawal, Nadia, and Mona. Mr. Hussain Wahbi and his wife Bahia lived on the same floor, with their three sons Gamil, Samir, and Nabil. All of these children were raised together and remained friends over the years, and in some cases married the children of other families in the building. Lots of comings and goings between apartments. Endless teenage crushes and woes and dramas. It was one enormous family and they were all connected, exchanging visits and niceties, and sharing life's ups and downs. Dr. Nagui was everyone's doctor, going back and forth between the apartments day and night to treat both slight malaise and grave illness, although it was he whom death would first steal away.

I came to know the house of Ibrahim Nagui after his death, as Tettu's house. My grandmother did not change any of the furniture after my grandfather passed away. The house remained a gathering place for friends and relatives, a refuge for anyone facing trying times. The house of Dr. Nagui was a sanctuary for a divorced sister and her girls, for the divorced friend who had nowhere else to go, for traveling female relatives, for female friends from abroad. In my day, the house was still always packed with guests. Many women came and went. I imagined my grandfather trapped at home in this flurry of activity, beset by these ladies and their various problems. My mother would say that my grandmother resorted to filling the house with people to make up for my grandfather's constant absence. For my part, I imagined that the endless crush of people might have been why he always went off elsewhere.

I remember the séances that were held in the *salon*. It was something many families did at that time as a form of entertainment in the evening. They held these séances both during my grandfather's lifetime and after his death. Two people would put their fingers on the edge of a basket covered with a handkerchief, and fasten a pen from the basket so that it hung down toward a piece of paper on the table. This ritual took place under ominously dim light, which frightened us kids. After reciting some Qur'anic verses, the séance began: They would ask whether a particular departed spirit was present in the room. The basket would move and the pen would begin to write, and the word "yes" appeared on the page. The group would then take turns asking questions: What were the names of the people gathered in the room? Was this spirit in peace in its resting place? What did it desire? Was a particular person going to get married? Would someone else be blessed with a child? The evening would pass in this way until they released the spirit from the house. After my grandfather died, they would summon his spirit in this room. They'd ask him: "What are we having for lunch today?" The pen would invariably come up with the right answer: "*Molokheya*."

I loved my grandmother's bedroom. It had art deco furniture, the same furniture that had been there since they first moved to the apartment. My brother and I would sleep in my grandmother's bed, and she'd spread her arm over our pillow as she slept, and we'd hold onto her while we were sleeping. My mother told me once that she and her sisters sometimes used to sneak into my grandparents' room in the morning. They'd open the door and see my skinny grandfather sleeping next to my ample grandmother. She'd monopolize the whole bed and all the blankets, while he looked like a little child curled up by her side in the cold. I remembered how I too had huddled close to my sleeping grandmother for warmth.

My grandfather had his own room in the apartment, which he used as an office. That was his sanctuary away from all the commotion in the building. Although the books and furniture had disappeared from his office before I was born, I heard many stories about it. This was his space alone—no one else was allowed in without his permission. My mother said he'd sit at a desk covered in dead flies, which he swatted expertly as he wrote his poems. I learned about the library he had built from a wonderful article published posthumously in March 1953 in the newspaper *al-Gomhour al-Misri*, immediately after his death. In this article, entitled, "Nagui yu'arrikh hayatihi" (Nagui Chronicles His Life), my grandfather described his libraries in his clinic and at home in detail. They spanned classical and modern literature and poetry in Arabic, English, French, Italian, and even German, as well as books on medicine, psychology, sociology, philosophy, and various encyclopedias. There were even books on playing chess, which he was quite good at. He himself wrote a book with Gabriel Nusra entitled *Kinanat al-shatranj al-ʿasri* (A Guide to Contemporary Chess).

Nagui wrote at the end of that article: "I spent my life reading and might suddenly fall down dead with a book in my hand."

That was indeed what happened to my grandfather twenty-four hours after penning those words.

But why had my grandmother removed everything from that office? Where did his library go? How had everyone possibly agreed to erase his life's work gathering books, leaving only his portrait hanging in a room no one used except on special occasions?

When my grandfather died, he left little behind for his widow and daughters. But even after he passed away, the other members of the household who had been part of his life remained a beloved part of ours. These included Farah, who filled the house with his cheerful energy. Farah had come from a little village near Aswan when he was fourteen to work as a *sofragi* in my grandfather's house. My mother told me that Farah had once been gravely ill, and my grandfather restored him to health. This stayed with Farah for the rest of his life. I remember Farah telling me, tears in his eyes, how kind and generous my grandfather had been. He'd say: "*Sitt* Samia is a bit difficult"—for she was rather harsh with him—"but Dr. Nagui was a good man." He'd say this grinning, in earshot of my grandmother, who would of course reproach him, as he expected. After my grandfather's death, my grandmother lacked the means to keep Farah on as a *sofragi*. They found him a government job to pay the bills, though he continued living in his room on the roof, above my grandmother's apartment. He'd still swing by in the mornings and evenings and during his days off to help her with the cleaning and other tasks. Farah lived in his little room on the roof even after my grandmother died, until the whole building was sold at the end of the 1980s.

I loved Farah. When I was little, he'd carry me on his shoulders and take me around the apartment and up and down the stairs of the building until my head spun, and someone would yell, "Stop—are you crazy? She's going to fall!" He'd laugh loudly at this and pay them no heed. They told me that Farah used to carry me past the chandelier in the living room and ask me in Arabic, "Samsuma, welalambo?"

This was Farah's approximation of the French for "Where is the lamp?" (*Où est la lampe?*), which he'd picked up from one of my mother's friends, who would often ask me this question so that I'd look up at the ceiling before I learned to talk, and point up at the chandelier. After I returned from the US in the 1980s, Farah insisted on calling me "*Sitt* Samia" instead of "Samsuma," as he'd done for all those years. I told him I wanted to stay "Samsuma," but he was firm.

8. Farah, courtesy of Dr. Hisham El Minawi.

Back in the days when I was still Samsuma, I was allowed to go visit Farah in his room on the roof. I was a little taken aback that this strapping young man who was responsible for so many duties around the house lived in such a sparse little room above. He had a narrow bed, a single chair, a small table, and a little gas plate for making tea and cooking. He'd ask me to come up to visit, and I happily stayed until they'd call me back down when I disappeared for too long. Farah died several years ago, to my great sorrow; his health had finally collapsed.

After my grandfather died, the many who had loved him, servants and acquaintances both, continued to regularly visit my grandmother's house, and the homes that my parent's generation moved to, for the rest of their lives. The *sofragi* before Farah, whose name was Mohamed al-Dawi—"Dawwinu," as we children called him—stopped working in Dr. Nagui's house after he asked my grandmother to find him a government post instead. Al-Dawi had been illiterate when he arrived at Dr. Nagui's house, but my grandfather brought in a tutor who taught him to read and write.

My mother and aunts were teenagers during the time al-Dawi worked in Dr. Nagui's home, and they'd have their friends over and speak in French together so as to keep their secrets. When al-Dawi was asked what they had said, he wouldn't say. Instead, he spun bits of their frivolous whisperings into a nonsensical, musical rendition of certain French particles and expressions—*commeçalabastresjoliecestbiendemoi*—which we grandchildren would later repeat around the house like a tongue twister, laughing.

There was also Bashir, who worked as the receptionist at my grandfather's clinic in Shubra. After my grandfather's passing, he too continued to pay visits to my grandmother, and later my mother and aunts. He'd sit in the kitchen and have a cup of tea. They'd give him a little cash to take with him, and when he left he'd wish everyone long life. After Bashir died, his children kept coming. Bashir was a quiet man with an abundance of children and equally numerous difficulties. He was Nubian, and we didn't always understand him when he began talking about his life and the troubles he endured. He too loved my grandfather, and would tell us bits of stories about him that I often couldn't follow, but as a child I'd pretend I understood so he wouldn't begin to tell them again.

Khadra, the *ballana*, stands out in my memory because of her special concoction—*mifata'a*, which everyone looked forward to. She started coming to Dr. Nagui's house in the days when he was still alive. She'd come to sell her rosewater and orange-flower water. In the summer, orange-flower water was the only water my grandmother would drink. The rosewater was for the ladies' complexions. *Mifata'a* was something else entirely: molasses, oil, roasted peanuts, black fennel seed, ground fenugreek, glossostemon root (*moghat*), sesame seeds, lemon juice, and water. It was a remedy for undernourishment, though my grandmother did not suffer from physical frailty. The jar of *mifata'a* looked distinctly dodgy—viscous and vaguely green. I refused to eat it. I wondered: Was this concoction originally intended for my gaunt and sickly grandfather?

Other disciples continued to regularly frequent Dr. Nagui's house, including some of his poorer neighbors and patients from Shubra. They'd come over for dinner or sometimes to stay the night. There was an elderly lady we called Madame Angelle who spoke *shami* Arabic in a strident voice; I think she was the first person I'd heard speak Arabic that way. I didn't understand who she was. She'd show up without warning and sometimes came alone, and sometimes with her unmarried daughter, whom I thought was both insufferable and homely. Madame Angelle had been my grandfather's neighbor in Shubra. She'd come to his clinic sometimes or visit the family at home for reasons that weren't entirely clear to me. When she descended upon my grandmother, everyone would cry out: "Oh no, it's Madame Angelle!"

Madame Angelle was well aware that she was not particularly welcome. They'd ignore her when she came, but she kept coming! She told many long stories which were hard for me to follow. I think that they were stories about the other households she used to visit. My mother explained to me that my grandmother disliked Madame Angelle because she played cards for money, and had taught my mother and her sisters how to bet, which greatly displeased my grandmother.

I don't remember when Madame Angelle got sick or when she died. I only remember that her daughter kept coming for a while after her mother passed away. I mention Madame Angelle, despite her regular unsolicited visits, because she was partly responsible for my own existence: She had been the matchmaker who brought my father to Dr. Nagui's house. Emad Mehrez turned out to be the perfect groom. My mother agreed to his hand in marriage and my grandfather gave them his blessings, although he died before the wedding.

My grandmother took on the expenses for the wedding and all the weddings that came after. She sold her portion of the land she inherited from her father to pay my grandfather's debts, which fell upon her after his death, and to cover the expenses of her three girls: my mother, who was newly married, my aunt Dawheya, for the steep tuition fees at the American University in Cairo, and Mahasen, who had abandoned her studies and turned to painting. My grandmother's brothers also made plenty of sacrifices to look after the girls, and Hassan Nagui, Ibrahim's younger brother, helped support Dawheya's education at AUC, but the daily expenditures were still a lot for my grandmother to handle.

I'd sit beside Tettu during our weekly visits to see her, or when we stayed at her house before traveling to the US and after we came back in the early 1960s. Farah, or the others who came after him, would place the coffee tray before her on the dining room table. The little *kanaka* with its long handle, the finely-ground coffee, the brass alcohol burner on which the *kanaka* was placed, and her particular coffee cup. I'd watch as she carried out this daily ritual, her eyes on the little pot so the coffee wouldn't boil over. The sharp, enticing smell of the coffee beans. We prepared them at home in the kitchen with a manual roaster. I'd sit on the floor of the kitchen watching this process, taking little bits of the roasted beans spread out across the ground. When we sat together, I'd ask my grandmother for a sip, and she'd give me a little on her saucer. Just one sip—that was our agreement.

My grandmother drank her coffee slowly, her cigarette in her other hand. She'd take care of the household affairs each morning, her coffee before her, and I beside her. She made many phone calls, prepared shopping lists, settled with whoever had gone to the market for her, and rebuked them for the rising prices. She'd ask for a sheet of ice for the icebox, and a man would come in with the slab on his shoulders. She'd scold him too because it would drip water on the floor as he went into the kitchen.

Tettu's icebox was an absolute marvel to me, a huge treasure chest. She had insisted on keeping the old box, which was kept cold with ice in the drawer at the top. I remember my grandmother scolding everyone: "Shut the icebox!" "Don't stand in front of the icebox with the top open!" But I would secretly open the ice drawer anyways and take whatever little bits of ice I could break off, and chew on it when my grandmother wasn't looking.

At the insistence of my mother and aunts, and as refrigerators started to become more reasonably priced, that magical icebox eventually disappeared from the house of Dr. Nagui. Although I was happy about the new fridge, I missed the icebox and the ice-seller who disappeared along with it.

I'd stare at my grandmother as she sipped her coffee. How beautiful she was, with her thick, pitch-black hair, with just a touch of white near her forehead. That streak of white appeared when she was still a young woman.

After my grandfather died, it was said that he had various muses, including three Zouzous: Zouzou Hamdi al-Hakim, Zouzou Madi, and Zouzou Nabil. All three were actresses who loved poetry and literature, and all had the same lock of white hair. Was my grandfather chasing some other version of my grandmother? Samia Hanim was a woman from a respectable family who would not deign to take part in the uncouth hubbub of an artist's life. She remained a traditional wife and responsible mother, despite his efforts early on in their marriage to change this state of affairs.

Cigarette smoke always hung over these morning coffee sessions. My grandmother's long fingernails were always painted red, which made her hands look paler. I'd watch her smoking and staring off into the distance. Her cigarettes came in magnificent tins—*Player's Navy Cut*, which had a bearded sailor painted on the front. I always wondered who this sailor was. I loved these tins because they developed various other functions around the house after the cigarettes ran out. Sometimes my grandmother used them as ashtrays, and saved the ash to polish the silver, sometimes they became button tins, and sometimes my aunt Nuna would take the empty tins for mixing colors as she painted.

I don't remember my grandmother laughing much. I remember she was always preoccupied with something, always elsewhere, always thinking. She loved me, loved all of us grandchildren, and spoiled us as best she could, but she was always a little aloof. She never talked to me about my grandfather. She left the telling of these stories and anecdotes to others as they saw fit, and remained silent. I did not ask her about my grandfather either, since I did not know him.

I wasn't aware as a child how many hardships and responsibilities the elegant, forbidding Samia Hanim had borne, especially as the girls grew up. My aunt Dawheya decided to emigrate with her family to the US after the 1967 War with Israel, like thousands of other young Egyptians who were trying to achieve the American dream of a house with a green lawn and a big car. Aunt Mahasen married against my grandmother's wishes, and then fell ill and died suddenly when she was only twenty-eight years old, leaving behind a young daughter who was not yet two ("little Samia"). My grandmother was forbidden from seeing this girl because of her fraught relationship with Mahasen's husband.

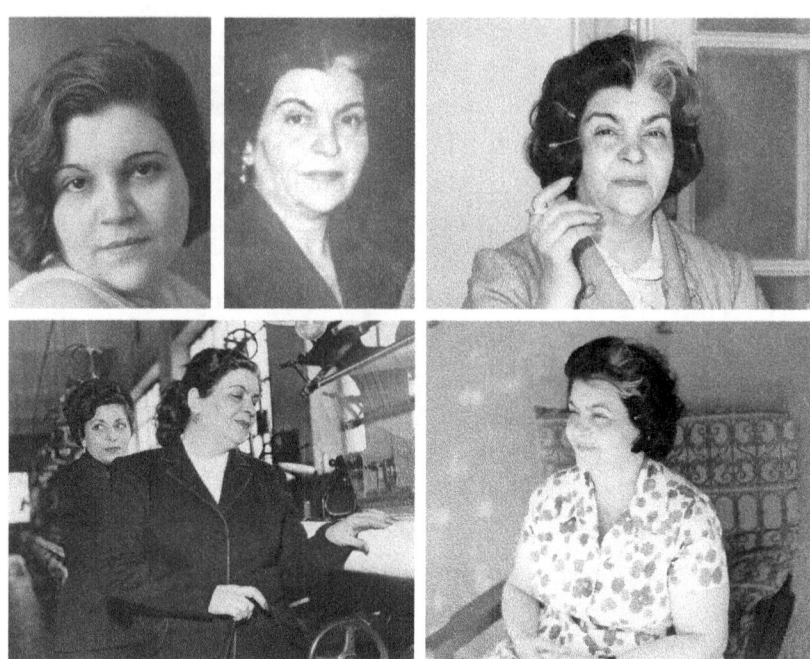

9. My grandmother Samia Sami, at different stages of her life.

My grandmother died of grief after all those years, defeated in spite of her resolve in the face of various crises. She grew frail suddenly after losing Nuna, the spoiled youngest daughter whom we'd all loved. My grandmother died at sixty—younger than I am today, although at the time I thought she was very old indeed.

When I returned from the US in the early 1980s to write my dissertation in Cairo, I asked my parents if I could stay by myself at Tettu's house, since I'd become used to living on my own while I was abroad. My parents agreed (rather reluctantly, since we were "in Egypt not America") and I took up residence in the house of Dr. Nagui. I closed up my grandparents' room, and left behind the bed where I'd slept as a child. I also closed up Nuna's room, where I also once used to spend the night—the same room that had been Dr. Nagui's office. I decided to get away from these ghosts and also changed the furniture in the other rooms.

Farah still lived in the little room on the roof, and he'd ring the bell as he went in and out to ask after me and to see if I needed anything.

He was uneasy about me staying there alone, not only out of concern for me, but also for the house itself. I could understand why he felt this way, since he had been the guardian of Dr. Nagui's legacy all those years. Nevertheless, I felt I was under constant scrutiny.

"The light was on very late yesterday, *Sitt* Samia."
"Why didn't you ask me to come help with the washing up once your guests left, *Sitt* Samia?"
"You know you aren't eating enough, *Sitt* Samia."
"When are you going out today, *Sitt* Samia?"
"When are you coming home, *Sitt* Samia?"

Eventually this well-meaning concern drove me out of my grandfather's house, and I packed my bags to return to my family home. I closed up Dr. Nagui's house, which was later sold along with the rest of the building, once all its residents had left.

10. 1 Hassouna al-Nawawy Street, formerly al-Arin Street, in 2021. Photos from the archive of my friend Maggie Morgan.

3

ALL THAT REMAINS

My aunt Dawheya died in 2012 in San Diego, after living a small slice of the American dream, which unfortunately fell apart at the end of her life. Dawheya got her name from my great-grandfather Mohamed Sami Amin Pasha's second wife. He'd married a young woman his daughter's age after his first wife died, so my grandmother Samia and his young wife Dawheya became close friends, and my grandmother passed on the unusual name to her second child. Since her birth name was a mouthful, everyone called her "Douha" at home, whereas her college friends at the American University in Cairo, and later, her colleagues in Egypt and abroad, simply called her "Do."

Do had been my lifelong friend and confidant since I was a child. Her life seemed magical and very different from the world inside my grandmother's house. Lobna Abdel Aziz was a friend of Do's from college, and she'd take me with her to the studio where Lobna would be recording her famous children's show *Auntie Loulou* as part of what was known as the European Program on Egyptian radio. I went to Do's graduation ceremony at AUC when I was five years old and dreamed of wearing the same robes when I grew up. After she left to the US, we wrote to each other regularly. Do was forbearing with my long letters full of the details of my teenage life; she always paid attention to the little things and wrote a nice response back. We were still very close when she died.

11. My aunt Dawheya Nagui in the family home.

Shahira, Do's daughter, was on her own abroad after her mother died, so I went to be with her. Shahira had already dealt with the lonely labor of burying her father, whose idea it had been to emigrate to the US.

I washed Do's body, and we all buried her together—Shahira and I, her children TJ and Samantha, and a friend of Do's from California. Then we got to work going through Do's apartment—the furniture clothes, and photographs. We donated nearly everything and kept only a few things for the family.

As we were sorting through her many papers, we found two sealed envelopes. When we opened the envelopes, we found a journal full of Arabic script, which we realized were our grandfather Ibrahim's diaries. In the second envelope we found various old papers and notebooks, some in Arabic and some in English. Shahira suggested that I take these two envelopes since she didn't read Arabic well. Like many immigrants of her generation whose parents had wanted them to assimilate into American culture, she'd never studied her mother tongue.

I was happy to keep the envelopes as a token of remembrance. I sealed them again and said to myself: I'll find time once I'm back in Cairo to look through these more closely.

These two envelopes had a long and arduous journey and had narrowly missed being thrown away. The documents had been in Do's possession since her father died when she was seventeen—more than sixty years before. When she got married, she brought the papers with her to her new house in Cairo and then took them with her when she moved abroad. Once in America, she moved several times between states, each time taking the papers with her until we found them in the two envelopes after her death. Do had never told me about the envelopes during the course of our long friendship, even after I began to study literature at university. Did Do leave them sealed because she wanted to go through them herself later and publish the contents, or because she was afraid of bringing my grandfather up with me, since I had always made clear I wanted nothing to do with him?

When Shahira gave me the envelopes, they returned again to Cairo after more than fifty years in transit abroad with Do. I knew, as she must have known, that these envelopes needed to be looked after. For almost ten years, I carried them with me as she had done as I moved between three different houses before I finally opened them again. I wanted to go through them properly, before it was too late for me, too.

When I opened the first envelope, I discovered that the little notebooks contained smaller, carefully-folded papers. I opened one of these to find a facsimile of a deed of sale for my grandfather's library for LE70. It was dated 13 April 1955—two years after my grandfather's death. My mother got married in 1954, and I was born on 1 January 1955. I had been three months old when my grandfather's library was sold. I later often wondered why I had never seen any trace of my grandfather at 1 Hassouna al-Nawawy Street. I thought his books had disappeared from the house as a result of carelessness or lack of interest on the part of my grandmother, mother, or aunt, but I realized when I opened the envelopes that the truth was harsher than I was expecting.

The deed had been drawn up by a lawyer named Mohamed Hossam al-Din Sami, my grandmother Samia Sami's younger brother. It was signed by my grandmother (the seller) and Mohamed Nagui (the buyer), who was my grandfather Ibrahim Nagui's older brother, in his capacity as the head of the Modern Egyptian Literature Association (Rabitat al-Adab al-Hadith), which Mohamed had taken charge of after his brother's death. The deed stipulated that my grandfather's

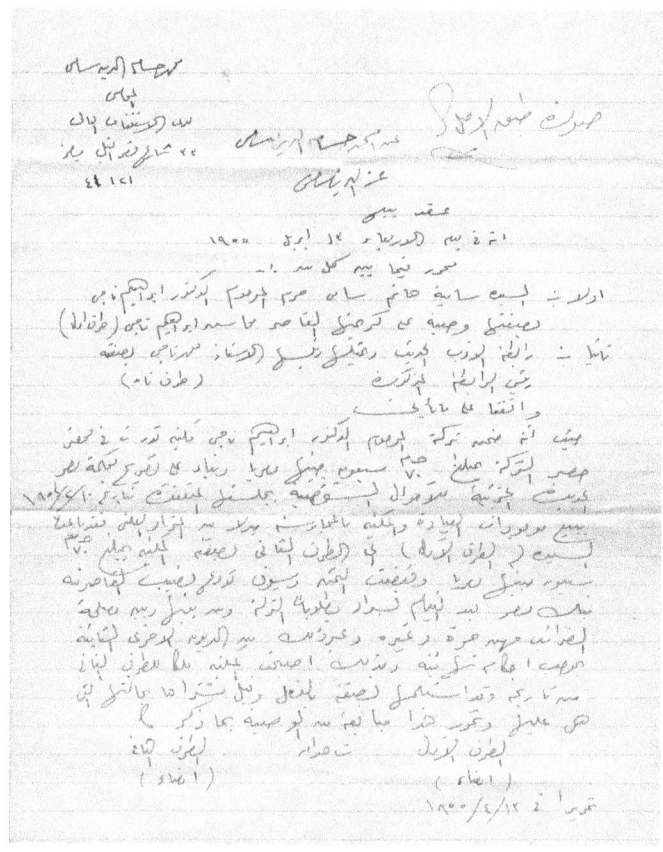

12. The deed for the sale of Ibrahim Nagui's library to the Modern Egyptian Literature Association, 1955.

libraries (from his clinic and home) would be sold for only LE70 to the association, where it would be preserved as part of Ibrahim Nagui's legacy, in lieu of holding a public auction. The agreed-upon sum would be brought to the court to pay my grandfather's debts, for which a final judgment had already been entered.

So, it had been kept in the family: My grandmother and her girls had little say in the deal. Her younger brother and my grandfather's older brother had agreed that this was the best way to pay off Nagui's debts and save the library at the same time. My grandmother had signed the contract to avoid the scandal of a public auction of family possessions, and to get the LE70 to settle some of his debts. But this plan to save my grandfather's books would not succeed in the long run, since the association that bought the library later fell apart. No one knows what happened to the books after that.

I'd asked my mother about what had happened to my grandfather's library on several occasions, but she'd never given a clear answer. She only knew that the books had been sold or given away to some institution. The three girls—my mother and aunts—were not party to these arrangements. Here I was with this paper that held the definitive answer on the fate of that wonderful library, which I had once read about in an article my grandfather had written, entitled "Nagui Chronicles His Life."

My poor grandfather. I reread the article and lamented what had happened to that legacy which had constituted, as he put it, "his life's work":

> My library grew up with me. I started to seriously gather books as a young man, but before that my library was jumbled stacks, with branches to visit next to and under the bed and strewn across the chairs, tables, and couches. Sometimes there were so many books on the bed that there was barely space left for their reader. This was also the state of affairs when I opened my clinic, until one of my patients, who was a carpenter, suggested we put in a little bookcase. And so he did: He built something one meter long and two meters high. I didn't argue. I laughed and said: That's

not bad for a start! We'll build more shelves on top of it and add more cases just the same size and if we're lucky we'll end up with an entire block. The library grew little by little. Whenever we had too many books we added a new home for them using the same design.

I didn't set out intending to buy books, but rather to see what was inside them. You can't buy books at random or for the sake of buying books. I picked my books as carefully as my friends [. . .]

I let my library grow of its own volition, to serve as a record of what I had read and thought: a medical text beside a piece of literature alongside a history book, and plenty of philosophy. I didn't sort them out and put the same kinds of books together as they do in bookshops. Once I finished a book, I'd just inscribe it with a number and the date, and maybe write a little note inside about what I'd thought of it. Then I'd add the title and number of the book to the catalogue for my library.

It really had been his life's work—now sadly blotted out, although not by fickle custodians who took the job too lightly, as I had imagined. Instead my grandmother's hand—and her brother and brother-in-law's—had been forced by unhappy circumstance to sell this city of books that my grandfather had spent so many years building.

I looked through the envelope again and found another little folded-up piece of paper. I opened it and found an attestation notice dated 7 May 1960, more than seven years after my grandfather's death. The note indicated that the signatory, whose name I did not recognize, had received a court statement from Nagui's heirs via my grandfather's brother Mohamed Nagui regarding his bequest. The "right to sell the publishing rights" had been transferred from the current heirs, that is, my grandmother, her daughters, and my grandfather's brothers, to "Miss Dawheya Nagui." What did this mean? What was "Miss Dawheya Nagui" intending to publish that had required this formal permission from all of Ibrahim Nagui's heirs?

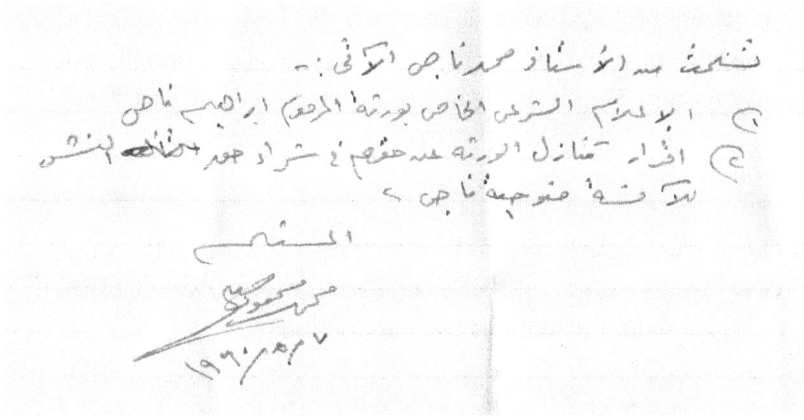

13. Attestation of the transfer of publishing rights from Ibrahim Nagui's heirs to Dawheya Nagui.

Among the other papers I found a text that Do had written—an unpublished introduction to the circumstances and the contents of those two envelopes. Here she explained what it was that she had been thinking of publishing from among Nagui's work. Do wrote:

> When my father died, I was only seventeen years old, my younger sister fifteen, and my elder sister not yet twenty. We had no brothers, so my uncles were responsible for going through the contents of my father's office in his clinic and his office at home. They found many manuscripts and poems that had not yet been published. The Ministry of Culture had set up a committee that included Ahmed Ramy, Saleh Gawdat, Mohamed Nagui (my uncle), and Ahmed Abd al-Maqsud Heikal to compile all the collected poems of Ibrahim Nagui. Beyond that, there was still a lot of material in my father's own handwriting that we had found at the clinic. My older sister and I asked to hold onto some of these handwritten works as a keepsake. They gave us his diary and various letters and personal papers as well as some of his unmetered verse [. . .]
>
> I found that the diaries were intensely personal, and I felt that my friendship with my father (even though I was quite young)

required me to guard his secrets well. So I asked that the diaries and unmetered poems written in his own handwriting be left in my care. My older sister, ever generous and self-sacrificing, agreed, and decided that she would hold onto the letters and personal papers.

I cherished these keepsakes from my father and decided that one day I would publish the diaries after removing the more personal sections and translating the rest into English.

As for the unmetered poems, I was not sure what they were until I read them one after the next. I noticed that there were numbers at the top of each page, but I didn't understand this numbering until I ran across a sheet with the inscription "from Shakespeare to his love." I realized that the numbers were not in fact page numbers, but rather the numbers of Shakespeare's sonnets! I tried to figure out which sonnets they were and began to line up the English and the Arabic. The numbers he had written on the pages helped with that. I felt that I had stumbled upon a treasure: all Shakespeare's sonnets, translated into Arabic!

In fact, not all 154 sonnets were there. I didn't know where to look for the missing ones since I had not realized what they were until four years after my father had died, while I was still a student at the American University in Cairo. There were forty sonnets total missing from the collection.

Do had signed the introduction to this never-published book, but there was no date. Do explained later on in the introduction that she had taken the diaries and translations of the sonnets with her to the US in hopes of going through the diaries and finishing the translation of the missing sonnets herself. She subsequently changed her mind about translating and decided to publish the incomplete collection that Nagui had translated. She had written the introduction above as she got ready to publish them. Yet she had never published either the translations or her selections from his diaries. Now they had been passed on to me, and I finally began to read these papers that had been tucked away in various drawers and shelves in each Cairo flat I lived in. What was I supposed to do now?

I reread the introduction. Dawheya had written that she felt obliged to keep her father's secrets because of the friendship between them. I paused on this sentence. It is true that Do had been the closest of her siblings to my grandfather. They had had many things in common: She was a voracious reader of Arabic, French, and English, and loved theater, music, and film. She read a lot of poetry and wrote her own in French and English, always excelled at school, and like her father, suffered from poor health. He'd shown a special interest in her, and they developed a different kind of relationship than he'd had with his other daughters.

Had that friendship foiled her efforts to publish his diaries and translations of Shakespeare? Why did she feel the need to "guard his secrets well"? Why had she decided that his diaries contained material better left unpublished, even though he'd already put pen to paper? How does one pen secrets, anyway—isn't all writing inherently revelatory? In any case, the question was: Had my grandfather actually disclosed certain secrets in his diaries, or was it my aunt who read them as secrets, so that when she tried to take out the "personal sections," as she put it, she found that what was left did not amount to enough to publish? We might ask: Did Do change her mind about publishing to protect the secrets of Ibrahim Nagui—a man who had no great secrets to speak of—or to preserve the unassailable image that she and her sisters had created of my grandfather, whom they called "papa" as in French?

After all these years I sit here now asking myself: Do I, as the granddaughter who doggedly eschewed any association with him, have the right to divulge the secrets that my aunt carried with her to the grave? I try to conjure up my grandfather, the open-minded intellectual, the vagabond poet, the people's doctor. We too—he and I—have our similarities, and if he had lived a little longer, I would have competed with his girls for his friendship.

I think back to what my grandfather wrote in his article, "Nagui Chronicles His Life": "Whosoever might wish to chronicle my life, if it has had any meaning, should take a good look at my library, at the dates inscribed in the books, and read the comments and notes I left in the margins." In other words, the titles of the books that packed the shelves of his two libraries were only his public face. So he had left a directive: to reconstruct his life from those margins.

Ibrahim Nagui's diaries, which Do had kept secret, contained some of the margins of his more public life. If we were to remove these "personal sections," as my aunt had put it, we would distort him just as we have distorted other political and cultural figures, transforming them into infallible beings, immune from fear or regret, impervious to love and life. These erasures were the main reason for my estrangement from my grandfather. Was I supposed to put down my pen and drive the wedge in further?

Diaries are their own literary genre, transforming everyday life into public spectacle. This requires very intentional choices about how to frame personal narratives that might complicate or challenge a public persona. Writing a diary is also an historical act of critical importance and provides space for professional, political, and personal sagas that exist outside official histories. Should we expunge these private histories from the record? For whose benefit are we engaging in this censorship? Who decides that diaries contain material better left unpublished, as Do had said? These are crucial questions that merit further consideration.

Do had set aside my grandfather's diaries and decided not to finish the translation of the sonnets. I understand that she was afraid of imposing her own choices as a translator among those of her father in a collection he had already translated. She writes in her introduction:

> I present these Shakespearean sonnets to the Arabic reader in Ibrahim Nagui's translation. I will not begin with a literary critique of this opus since I lack the training to do so; I will only say that Nagui's translations evoke all the beautiful sentiments and music of the Shakespearean originals. No other poet could have rendered these sonnets with the lyricism you will see here: Nagui

is the only poet of love capable of capturing the cadence of these sentiments so aptly in Arabic.

Therefore, I have not attempted to translate the missing sonnets. This is also why these sonnets have not seen the light of day until now, and for that I ask the reader's forgiveness.

My aunt recused herself from translating alongside such an illustrious translator as her father, or even from commenting on his work, because she felt she lacked the training. Now that I had become the literary critic in the family and, indeed, a literary translator and scholar of translation studies, I wondered: Could I in good faith turn away from Ibrahim Nagui's overlooked legacy in translating both poetry and prose?

I went back to my grandfather's personal papers, which were now in the care of my mother, his eldest daughter. She had kept the collection of letters that my grandfather had sent to my grandmother at the beginning of their married life when he was still a young doctor in Mansoura. Unlike my aunt, who had shielded her portion of his legacy from the public eye, my mother had often shared selections from these letters to defend my grandfather against claims that his marriage with my grandmother had not been a happy one, or whenever someone emerged claiming to have been his poetic muse. I went through some of the interviews my mother had given with the press and learned that she had provided copies of some of the letters to the journalists who pestered her with the usual questions each year on my grandfather's birthday or on the anniversary of his death. When this happened, she'd send them away with letters that demonstrated her parents' love for each other.

My mother said in an interview with *al-Shabab* magazine (issue 311, June 2003): "My mother and father lived the most romantic of love stories for twenty-five years, and he dedicated his most beautiful poems to her." She added: "My father had many muses, but he loved only my mother from the day they were married." In an article in *al-Ahram* dated 11 April 1995, Sameh Karim had launched various accusations against an unnamed actress, most probably Zouzou Hamdi al-Hakim. Zouzou had previously claimed she had not been Nagui's lover and only exchanged verses of poetry with him. In this article, Sameh Karim referenced the letters my mother shared with him: "Nagui's eldest daughter Amira has kept his private letters to her late mother in her possession in Cairo to defend her father, the renowned poet who was both a model father and a model husband."

In another long interview on 13 February 2000 with the magazine *Nesf al-Donya*, my mother explained that "my father expressed his love for my mother on every page set before him: doctor's prescriptions, forms, the covers of notebooks, even dinner receipts. He wrote to her every day that he loved her and worshiped her, that she was his life."

The interviews with my mother continue until this day, and she continues to call upon these letters to weave the tale of a twenty-five-year love story between my grandmother and my grandfather.

But when I sat down to read the letters one after the next, I realized that these letters had another story to tell, beyond the love of Ibrahim Nagui for Samia Sami, although they were certainly full of affection. I want to revisit these letters now in a different light than my mother, journalists, and previous readers have done.

4

HOUMA AND SOUMA

Ibrahim Nagui was born on 31 December 1898, and married my grandmother Samia Sami in December 1927. He was not yet thirty; she was still about twenty. The young doctor had begun his working life in 1923, commuting between Sohag and Minya. Immediately after he was married, the Egyptian Railway Authority appointed him as a physician in Mansoura, and the newlyweds moved to the Delta city together.

My grandmother had lost her mother when she was only fourteen years old, and her father Sami Pasha had married his cousin Dawheya, who had been orphaned and was about two years older than my grandmother. He told his children—Ezz, Samia, Zeinat, and Mohamed—that he had brought them a sister, and Dawheya indeed became like their older sibling. My grandmother and her sister Zeinat were studying at the École Franciscaines de Marie in downtown Cairo (at a branch of the same school I later briefly attended). They were boarding students, as per the wishes of their father, who wanted to protect them from having to go out every day to commute to school. My mother told me that after her grandfather's first wife died and he married Dawheya, Sami Pasha withdrew my grandmother and her sister Zeinat from school, one after the next, so that they could prepare for marriage. As a result, they did not continue their education past middle school.

A suitable husband was found for my grandmother: Ibrahim Nagui. However, he was not a traditional groom, because he refused to marry a woman he hadn't met. His sisters Leila and Souad, who were friends with the bride-to-be, helped him concoct a plan to see my grandmother in her father's villa, even though this was not supposed to be done. Nagui was smitten with the young lady even though he had already been grievously wounded in love—an ache he'd carry for the rest of his life. He had, in his mind at least, been on the verge of marriage once before—with a childhood friend and neighbor from Shubra who was also a distant relative, but who had chosen another man whom her father deemed more suitable. Although Nagui's first love married someone else, she remained present in his poetry, which was often dedicated "from N. to A." or "to A. M." He married Samia Sami, after initially postponing their union.

At first, Mansoura seemed to be the perfect city for this stage of Nagui's life, both personally and professionally. He settled there in 1927, the same year he married my grandmother. The poet Saleh Gawdat, who was still in high school in Mansoura when Nagui arrived, described the city in his book *Nagui: His Life and Poetry*. Gawdat wrote:

> Mansoura was lush and beautiful, a fertile ground for poetry and love. The riverbank there was the childhood playground of Egypt's most prominent poets, writers, singers, and musicians: Mohammed Hussein Heikal, Ibrahim Ramzy, Mohammed al-Asmar, Lofty el-Sayed, Ahmed Hassan al-Zayyat, Ali Mahmoud Taha, Mohammed Abdullah Annan, Mohamed al-Hamshari, Umm Kulthum, Abdel Wahab, Riad al-Sunbati, and dozens of others, from every field of literature, poetry, music, and art.
>
> I cannot fully capture the spell that they cast on this sleepy city on one of branches of the Nile. Suffice it to say that the air itself was enchanting and every man you met on the street was a poet. There was a spectacular renaissance of art and literature and a breadth of romantic expression unparalleled in any other city in Egypt.[1]

Although Gawdat's description is not inaccurate, it also brushed over much of Mansoura's history. The city had long been celebrated as a haven for artists and musicians as well as the foreign merchants who had become part of its social fabric, and imbued it with the effervescent spirit that Gawdat had described. Mohamed Ahmed Ghoneim, a professor of sociology and anthropology at Mansoura University, wrote in his book *Troupes of Singers and Musicians: An Anthropological Study of the City of Mansoura* that the city had been home to prominent families in the arts for generations and had always been a vibrant gathering place for musicians, vocalists, and composers, among others. Since the 1920s, the city had also been famous for its belly dancing. Siyam Street had different sections known for various kinds of belly dancers, singers, oudists, violinists, accordionists, keyboardists, *qanun* players, and other musicians.[2]

In his book on *souq al-khawagat*, Ghoneim writes that Mansoura had initially had a street market in the city center, which lasted until the 1950s, and might have been the original impetus for the city. It was known as *souq al-khawagat* ("the foreigners' market") because 95 percent of the stalls were run by Greek, Jewish, or British merchants, who became actively involved in these commercial networks during the British occupation of Egypt.[3] Mansoura also experienced a major architectural transformation during the mid-nineteenth to mid-twentieth centuries. In the introduction to his master's thesis on historic buildings in Mansoura, Hani Saad Salem Ahmed illustrates this shift from Ottoman Islamic to Baroque and Rococo architectural styles.[4]

The city of Mansoura underwent this cultural, artistic, and architectural renaissance at the same time that my grandparents were beginning their married life there. Their love story unfolded in the letters that my grandfather penned to my grandmother, most of which were written after they were separated by her illness, when she was obliged to return to Cairo on the doctor's orders. My mother inherited these letters after her father's death and used them to refute any skepticism that emerged about her parents' affection for or commitment to each other.

As I write this, I have before me twenty-eight letters of varying length, dated between 1928 and 1929. Some of these were written on prescription sheets from my grandfather's clinic in Mansoura, and others on the letterhead of the medical department of the Egyptian Railway Authority where he worked. Nearly all of the letters were written by my grandfather to my grandmother: There is only a single letter in her handwriting, sent from Ras al-Bar on 20 August 1928. The first question that came to my mind was: Where are the other letters from my grandmother? But as soon as I took a closer look at their "correspondence," it became clear that she was not writing back.

Although my mother always described these missives as love letters, the most important material within them is not the affection my grandfather expresses toward my grandmother. We might instead read these letters as a window onto the social history of that era and as illustrative of my grandfather's writing style.

I reread the single letter that remains from my grandmother. I remind myself that she was only twenty at the time. She hadn't finished her education and had been raised in a traditional household with an exceptionally strict father. She writes from Ras al-Bar as a young bride recuperating her health while on summer holiday with her family, away from her husband. In her letter, she is clearly responding to another letter of his.

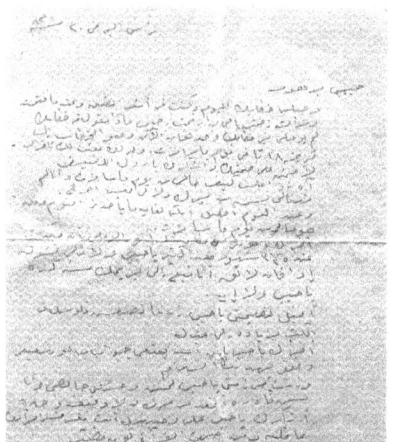
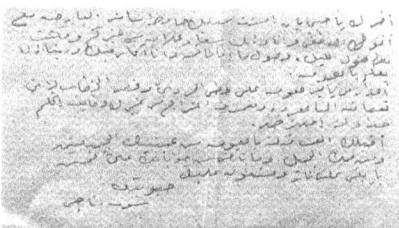

14. The sole letter from my grandmother to my grandfather.

The first thing I notice about this letter is how much worse her handwriting is compared to his—even though doctors are supposed to be the ones with impossible handwriting! She is self-conscious about her penmanship in the letter: "Forgive me, dear Barhuma, for my poor handwriting and the brevity of this letter; I'm very tired today and I miss you, I don't feel like taking [sic] with anyone."

It is indeed a very short letter but full of affection for him. She calls him "my love" at least eight times over the course of the letter, and sometimes more than once in the same sentence. She uses various terms of endearment ("Barhuma," or "my Houma") and signs the letter "your sweetheart, Souma Nagui." This was all very well—they were newlyweds, after all—but I also wondered if the lack of variety in her word choice was because she was unable to write more expansively in Arabic. It seemed that way because the language in the letter was very basic:

Dear Barhuma,

Your letter arrived today when I was in a right state. When I opened it and read it, I felt much better. My love, what are you talking about in your letter? I have only received one letter as of yet, dated the 18th of this month, the day after I left. So I sent you a telegram to ask after your health. I thank you for your lovly [sic] reply.

She then goes on to apologize for the brevity of the letter, as described above. He had written her, in a letter dated 22 August 1928, about the books he had bought in Mansoura while she was away. To this, she replies: "Take my advice, my love: don't waste your money on too many books"—a prelude to the rift that would later arise between them.

If there is only one brief and halting letter from my grandmother, my grandfather sent her a deluge of letters—the first two of which were written in French.

The first letter from my grandfather read:

My dearest Sooma,

Here is my first letter to you in French. You can write me back in Arabic, but no mater [sic] the language, you must write. I am lonely and lost; it is agony to be away from you. You are expecting me Wednesday, tomorrow, but I am obliged to stay here until Thursday because there are patients I must see to. Do you remember that you promised to write me every day?

The first day has already passd [sic] without a single word from you. How will I bear tomorrow without your sweet nothings, without our bewitching conversations? How can I fill my long monotonous days and the dreary hours that drag on? I will surely die without you. As soon as you see me next you will understand how much your faithful husband misses you.

Ibrahim Nagy[5]

P.S. Your friends here all send their greetings.

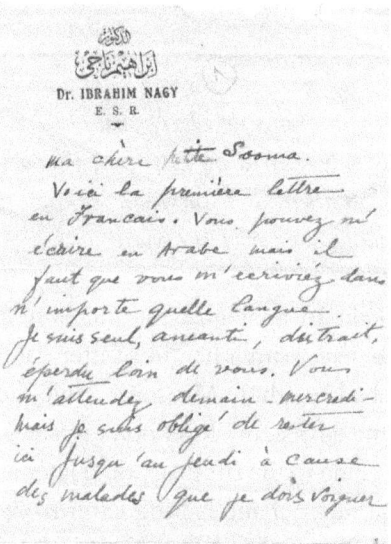

15. The first page of the first letter, written in French, from my grandfather to my grandmother.

This seems to be the letter which my grandmother says has not arrived. This first letter to her in French was followed by a second. In the latter missive, my grandfather explains that the clinic is struggling, but that he still spent everything he has on buying new books on medicine. Her response to the second letter arrives in Arabic rather than French, as he expected.

In his second letter in French, sent from Tanta, we can see the beginnings of my grandfather's misgivings about whether their budding love story might fall short of his dreams.

Dearest Souma,

I sent you a telegram yestirday [sic] at noon. I spent the rest of the day in considerable [sic] anguish. Why have you not written to me? Have you not time? How do I find the time? I am lonely, worn down, overwhelmed with work, but when I sit down to write you, your dear face appears before me, and that is my only moment of joy.

Don't you feel the same way when you write to me? I love you and I am waiting to hear anything at all from you to get me through the day. What will become of me without any word from you? You are the star in my heavens. Are you not writing because I have told you a thousand times that I love you, that you are everything to me? Don't you want to know what is happening in my life? But my dear little angel, you must know that I am as bereft and frantic as a lost child.

Everything was amiss yesterday. I had a long face all day, buzi shibrayn. I was really in a state.

Things were bad at the clinic—I was arguing with people and didn't make any money. I spent what little I had on some books of medicine.

I hope that I will be able to come tomorrow, but you must write to me. Yestirday [sic] evening Dr. Ramly tried to cheer me up a bit and took me to the house of a friend of his, where someone was playing the violin.

I am writing you now from the clinic. I send you a kiss and I love you, a thousand times I love you.

Ibrahim

One might wonder: Why did Nagui write to her in French? Did he think that she was proficient in French because she'd studied briefly at Les Franciscaines de Marie—even though in all likelihood she had never written a letter before? Was it to show off his third language, which he'd taught himself to communicate with his childhood sweetheart? Nagui makes all sorts of errors in French that show he's new to writing in the language, yet he's also developed a fairly expansive lexicon by these two letters. It almost seems as if he's lifting expressions directly from novels he's read in French: His sentences are cumbersome and his elaborate vocabulary seems out of place in a simple love letter.

I imagine my grandmother receiving that first letter. She doesn't respond, claims his letter never arrived, and sends him a telegram instead of keeping her promise to write every day. My poor grandmother! The traditional young bride, appropriately reticent, and uncertain of her French, with a poet-doctor husband pouring out his lonely longing. Even if she had been proficient in French, how could she possibly reply?

The most surprising thing about these letters and telegrams from a contemporary perspective is that they arrived, and on time. At the beginning of the twentieth century, the postal service was a reliable enough institution that my grandparents could depend upon it for this intensive correspondence. My grandfather never wondered if my grandmother's replies had been lost in the mail; he is quite certain the lack of a response from her simply meant that she was not writing.

After these first two letters, my grandfather gave up writing in French and switched to Arabic. He continued to regularly send my grandmother effusive love letters over the next two years.

My mother told me that later on, after the couple settled in Cairo, my grandfather found two tutors to come to the house to improve my grandmother's French and Arabic, based on what he had realized about the gaps in her proficiency from their correspondence.

It is clear from the letters that Nagui was quite concerned with educating his wife and encouraged her to read and engage with literature. He personally read to her sometimes, told her about what he was reading, or taught her about meter through the poetry he was writing. These letters shed light on what he was reading and how he spent his time away from her. In one letter dated 9 December 1928, Nagui wrote:

My dear Souma,

I left you this morning, not knowing how I'd go back home without you, my guardian angel. You keep me company in my solitude, and your face lights up this dreary world. I was sitting alone on the train wondering how I'd bear everything now that I've gotten used to you being beside me, your head on my shoulder, falling asleep as I read to you or told you about what I'd read.

The funny thing is that he seems happy she was falling asleep as he read. Perhaps this sounds romantic at first glance, but she also doesn't seem to have been very interested in listening, and he doesn't seem to have realized this. Love is blind, I guess.

The next letter, written in Arabic, also spoke to Nagui's persistent efforts to win my grandmother over to reading. I found this letter, dated 10 December 1928, particularly fascinating.

To my heart, my dearest Souma,

I am writing you a second letter. God only knows whether you think of me as I think of you. Yesterday evening when I went home, the house felt terribly empty and desolate without your charming presence. Whenever I saw any of your clothes hanging around the house, I kissed them and wept. I didn't go out that evening because I was really tired and 'Amm Ali stayed over. I only had tea for dinner. Everything was in the kitchen cabinet but I realized you had the key, so I gave him some money yesterday to get what we needed and again today so we could have a small lunch.

I've been really restless and couldn't settle on a book. I kept putting one down and picking up another until I began this wonderful Italian short story by Grazia Deledda, "Two Men and a Woman."[6] *The protagonist shows a nobility of character that reminded me of you. In the story, a man falls in love with a woman and commits forgery for her sake. He is sentenced to prison and when he goes to jail, the prison warden, who is a harsh man, turns out to have the same name he does. When the girl writes her fiancé a series of sweet letters, the warden opens them. And since she is pretending to be the young man's sister in the letters, the warden falls in love with her. He is inspired by her gentle spirit to try to get the young man released. He does all this hoping to marry the prisoner's "sister." One day the girl sends a photo of herself to the boy, her imprisoned lover. The warden is astounded by her beauty and doesn't give the prisoner the photo. Eventually the warden summons the young man and tells him he's received orders to release him and then reveals his love for the girl and explains that he wants to marry her. The young man is afraid to say that she's his fiancée but promises that he'll try! He also figures it would be better for the girl if she married the warden anyways because he—the prisoner—is a poor chap without the kind of standing that the warden has. So the next day he goes to the warden and tells him the whole story and explains that the girl is his fiancée but that he still wants to ask her opinion and see if she'd rather marry the warden. It's important to him to let her choose because he owes the warden a debt for his release and also because the warden is a better choice for marriage. The warden is taken aback by this chivalry and says: My boy, don't write that to her, because if she agrees to marry me after all this, she won't be the lovely noble person she was in the letters. Anyways, it's only fair she marries you after you've been imprisoned so long on her account. May God grant you all happiness, and bring me fortune!*

It's a nice story, right?

Kisses and hugs to you, dear Souma. I love you, I love you, I love you!

Ibrahim

Houma . . . and Souma! They were kissing before they came down for lunch with everybody.

To hell with Sami!

In this letter, my grandfather uses simple language to summarize what is in fact a very profound piece of literature—Grazia Deledda was the recipient of the Nobel Prize in Literature in 1926. It surprises me that only two years later, her writings were already available in Mansoura. Had Nagui read Deledda in the French translation? Had her work already been translated into Arabic? Or had he read the story in Italian, which he'd also taught himself? In "Nagui Chronicles His Life," he explains:

> A doctor asked me to translate an important Italian article on a case involving a medical professional and the government. I began to read Italian with an Italian friend until I could accurately translate the report in question to help the case. In the corner of my library is a small handbook for learning Italian, which my friend's daughter gave to me. What a strange creature fate is! I wonder where Olga, the book's former owner, is now?

Whichever translation Nagui had read, the fact that he was reading Deledda in 1928 is important because it demonstrates that he was engaged with international literature; he would later go on to translate various works. It is also revelatory of the broader linkages between cultural and literary spheres in Egypt (including in Mansoura) and elsewhere, and the circulation of these European books in Egypt.

The curious thing about Deledda's story is that it was a story about letters, and specifically about the power of letters to elicit strong feelings and shape fates. Meanwhile, Nagui was living his own epistolary relationship. The difference of course was that my grandmother scarcely wrote to him—she does not seem to have taken any hints from the comparison Nagui makes with the story's protagonist in his letter.

My mother explained to me the final lines in the letter ("Houma... and Souma! They were kissing before they came down for lunch with everybody. To hell with Sami!"): My grandmother's half-sister Nelly, the daughter of her father's second wife Dawheya, was still a little girl when Ibrahim Nagui married my grandmother Samia. Nelly would often sneak into the newlyweds' room whenever they visited Samia's father's house. Little Nelly was always tattling about their personal affairs. She'd overhear them in their room and tell other members of the household about the nicknames they had for each other (Houma and Souma), the kisses they exchanged, and the private moments they

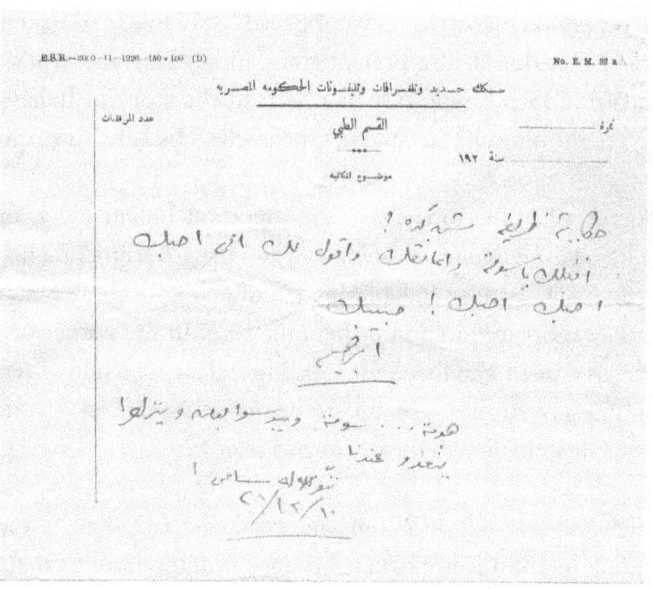

16. The last page of a 10 December 1928 letter from my grandfather to my grandmother.

shared. The couple were obliged to join the extended family for lunch at a particular time. The last line of the letter was something my grandfather had said in reference to Sami Pasha's severity, which forced the young lovers to steal away for quick moments together before making their formal appearance at these family occasions.

This postscript is also perhaps an indication of a certain nostalgia for the early days of their love. Perhaps he reminds her of those giddy moments in hopes that she might yearn for him too, and finally write. Moreover, it sheds light on the inevitable circulation of secrets and rumor in such households during that era, in which circumspection was seen as central to social decorum. No one had any privacy in these extended family contexts, to the extent that Nelly's tattling has now become a part of family lore that continues to be passed down even to my generation.

In a letter dated 21 August 1928, we also get a picture of the economic parameters of Nagui's life and his excessive expenditures, which later became a nightmare for him, both personally and professionally:

To Houma's heart and soul:

I thank you from the bottom of my heart for your telegram and hold your sentiments in the highest regard. But where are your long letters and your news and your sweet nothings? Today is Tuesday, my dear Souma, and still there is no letter from you, even though you promised to write every day, just as I promised to tell you all my daily happenings. I hope you've received my letters.

Light of my eyes, let me tell you about something that happened yesterday:

I was working in the clinic in Mansoura until 1:00pm and then my uncle came over so we played chess together for a while. I caught the train without having any lunch. I had meant to eat something on the train but I fell asleep and didn't wake up until we got to Mansoura. Then I went to the clinic. Work was alright and at 6:00pm I decided to go home and change my clothes. It was only after I got home and undressed that I realized you had the key to the wardrobe. I thought, well, what now? My suit's all wrinkled from traveling. It looks like a grocer's shirt with its extra layer of grime, so what's to be done? The only solution was to buy a new white shirt to cover up how filthy the suit was. I also polished my shoes and wiped my cap clean and no one noticed how dirty my pants were. In any case, I bought a new white cotton button-up shirt for 25 piasters. I couldn't buy any other kind of shirt because you have all the spare buttons!

I ate on the train on the way back—a bit of cheese and grapes—and slept until Tanta where I discovered that Ramly and my uncle Abdullah were waiting for me. I introduced them to each other and we went to sit in a coffeeshop. After a while my uncle got up to leave because he had to travel early in the morning today. I went to have dinner with Ali and his wife. We played backgammon until midnight and then I fell asleep. Ali's wife sends her regards and wants you to know they have two rooms that are ready for us if we're interested in taking them. What do you think? You'd be at home there, chez vous.

I'm writing you now from Ali's clinic where I'm helping see to his patients. I just finished one examination and the patient gave me a whole riyal!

Souma, I've been spending too much for no reason. It's all gone to cups of coffee, shining my shoes, buying newspapers, all that fluff. I added it up and realized I'd spent 8 pounds!

My dear Souma, my beautiful angel. I miss your companionship and your voice. I can't live a moment without you. Everything is such rubbish when you're away.

Souma, hopefully I'll be able to come on Thursday evening on the Delta train, which gets to Damietta at 6:30pm and to Ras al-Bar at 7:00pm.

I send a kiss and a hug and whisper in your beautiful ear: I love you, Souma, and await your letter.

Give my best to everyone—

Ibrahim

In this letter, the young bride does not sound equipped to handle married life. She accidentally takes the key to the wardrobe and leaves him without clothes! He makes light of the situation and finds reasonable solutions without reprimanding her. But this incident was neither the first nor the last time such things happened. In the earlier letter discussed above, my grandmother had also taken the keys to the kitchen cabinet and left him without anything to eat.

We can see from the letters that my grandmother sometimes visited Mansoura but then quickly returned to Cairo or to one of their families' summer homes. She was very forgetful during all these comings and goings, and my grandfather's response was to treat her almost as a child. In another letter, he writes to her: "Don't forget to get your ticket stamped at the counter when you get to the train station, and to pay the quarter fare for you and the servant." He adds, "I sent you two copies of your ticket, one to show at the ticket window and the second to keep with you for when the ticket inspector asks."

In this letter, dated 21 August 1928, Nagui elaborates on his earnings and extravagant daily expenditures. It's clear he's trying to expand his income sources: He works with patients in his friend Ali's clinic in Tanta in addition to maintaining his own private clinic and serving in the medical department of the Egyptian Railway Authority in Mansoura. But the riyal about which he is so excited in the letter was only equivalent to 20 piasters! When my grandfather calculates his expenses over the course of the day, he realizes he has far overspent his income. This profligacy and poor financial management would plague him throughout his life and prove a constant source of anxiety.

It's interesting that his expenditures remained a regular feature of his letters. In a letter dated 15 July 1929, my grandfather writes, "everything was going just fine, I'd sent 10 pounds to Mohamed Hafez [Nagui's sister Souad's husband]. After I'd paid all the bills I realized I only had 7 pounds left, plus 10 pounds in the drawer. I paid the water bill which was 80 piasters for 2 months. Then it was 2.5 piasters for bread (*baladi*, I never get *shami*)." In another letter on 9 December 1930, he writes that "I'll ask about the fabric and send it when I've bought some, fortunately I have enough at the moment—LE4." It's clear that they had a limited income and that Nagui's management of his pocketbook left something to be desired.

Nagui's letters are laden with frustration about my grandmother's extended absences from Mansoura. At first, she is gone for medical reasons; the doctors had ordered "a change of air," and while disappointed and lonely, he is sympathetic. Later, however, he becomes irritated as he begins to feel he is being neglected. In a letter dated 25 March 1928, addressed only to "Souma!", Nagui reproaches her for being so often elsewhere:

> *I didn't call or write yesterday the way I usually do. You know I can't bear to be away from you for even an hour. But I gather from what you said on Friday that you're staying on in Cairo. I said to myself: Maybe she's caught up in the diversions of being with family and has forgotten me. Maybe she doesn't realize how I spend my time here. It's a living hell. Yesterday I sat up in bed all night, my head exploding from anguish and worry. The day*

before yesterday was the same. I'm glad you're happy in Cairo, Souma, but your poor Ibrahim cannot find any companionship or peace without his dear Souma. Will you spare any of your affections for him? Yet I realized it's in God's hands. Souma takes pleasure in being in Cairo. Let her stay there until she understands how I am suffering. I said to myself: God give me the patience to endure the intolerable torment of this separation.

Ibrahim

This anguish over my grandmother's prolonged absence and her apparent preference to remain with her family escalates further in later letters. Meanwhile, she also seems to have become irritated with the sheer number of letters he has sent, his insistence that she write every day, and his romantic outpourings. This is apparent from his letter, dated 25 April 1929—which he addresses to "Ms. Souma," for the first time, abandoning his earlier terms of endearment.

What you wrote in your letter really stunned me. You reminded me that love isn't in what we write or say; love is in the heart. Imagine if I stopped writing and calling and made do with the fact that I know that you love me. What would you say about me then? You'd say I've forgotten you or loved you less because I've stopped writing and asking after you, and kept it all inside! I can't do that, Souma, please don't ask me to. [. . .]

I want to remind you of something, Souma. Remember when you used to tell me you loved me with tears in your eyes that you could scarcely hold back? That's love and nothing else. Love isn't something superficial, it can't just be pushed under the rug, if you really love each other. [. . .]

I'll do the same, hold it all inside and not send any letters, and if you reproach me for this, I'll tell you I wrote it all inside my heart!

Come when you can, Souma, I can't manage to get away to Cairo.

Ibrahim

Later in their correspondence, in a letter from March 1931, my grandfather begins with a similarly tepid salutation to "Ms. Souma" after she has apparently sent a particularly brief letter.

In your last letter you said I seemed annoyed with your chatter, but you haven't written me anything! You haven't given me any of your heart or your time, as is due to me. I thought perhaps you were just writing in a rush but wanted to offer what kindness you could. [. . .]

But when you called me, you didn't say when you were coming back. It didn't feel like you'd missed me. No matter—these are all trifling things. But where then shall I find proof of your love?

Unfortunately, these silly little things are what love is made of. I don't know what you'll make of this letter. Do as you please, Souma. Still I must tell you I am ill at ease because you don't share anything with me about your day or what you're thinking. I'm also miserable because I don't have enough work for all my expenses during these wretched days.

I don't understand what's happened. I often help others with their sorrows but I myself am at my wit's end.

I wish I could find a way into your heart. You never tell me what you are thinking about and you don't ask how I'm doing. Is the sewing that gets you up at seven more important to you than I am? Do your siblings and family deserve to hear your thoughts more than I? Have you been writing pages and pages to Khairiya and Zeinat and Zainab, yet I only get a few lines? And then you tell me I seem frustrated!

Enough, I don't want to go on and on. Come back when you can, when you remember there is a poor man over here who happens to be your husband.

Ibrahim

And so their love story began to unravel. I feel for the two of them as they dealt with this crisis. It's evident from these letters and from my grandmother's absences that they had quite divergent views of the relationship. My grandmother had married a young doctor who suddenly showered her with passionate love letters instead of acting the part of a husband. She moved with him to Mansoura but found herself alone all day while he was at his office and clinic, so she returned to Cairo to be with her family and enjoy all the enticements of the city. He didn't force her to return to Mansoura right away, but instead made a more difficult request: He implored her constantly to write. He asked her to be beside him even from Cairo, to proclaim her love for him every day. However, her opinion on this was clear: Love was in the heart. That was the traditional view of married life. Nagui had a more romantic vision of love at this point in his life, especially since they hadn't yet had children. He was lonely in Mansoura and felt her absence every night. He sounds juvenile, and she eventually becomes exasperated with him. She doesn't want a whining child—she wants a husband. Meanwhile, for Nagui, writing was his craft: He wrote poetry, articles, stories, gave lectures, translated literature. How could they understand each other when she had such a traditional upbringing and comparatively limited access to education?

In the last letter quoted above, my grandfather ends on a rather glum note. This letter is also the first time he refers to himself directly as her husband, which heralded difficult new dimensions to come in their relationship.

I read and reread these letters. It is strange that episodes from this romantic melodrama have primarily been used to cement a narrative about the strength of the bond between my grandparents. In fact, these letters tell a much more nuanced story about the beginnings of the married life of a romantic poet-doctor and a bride ten years his junior in a provincial city in the Delta in the early twentieth century.

My mother, the steward of his carefully-curated legacy, chuckled when I first read her this chapter. But she became more wary of my efforts to rummage through their history when she realized I intended to unravel her and my aunt's version of my grandparents' love story. Still, I reminded her that the only way that I could make my peace with my late grandfather was to begin to piece together a fuller version of that tale.

5
FROM N. TO A.

O my better half, beyond compare
Your wish is my heart's only desire
You who witnessed my sorrow profound
and cured my pain with a fresh wound
—Ibrahim Nagui, "From N. to A."

Everyone who has written about Ibrahim Nagui has mentioned his enigmatic "first muse," who is usually identified only by her initials. Nagui never publicly revealed the name of his childhood sweetheart, whom he cherished all his life. Although he poured the joys and torments of this attachment into many of his poems, the love story between Nagui and "A. M." was largely opaque, even to those close to him, and the identity of his beloved muse remained a matter of guesswork and speculation.

Nagui's friend, the poet Wadie Filastin, wrote in his book *Nagui: His Life and Selected Poems* that this first muse had preoccupied my grandfather his whole life:

> Nagui buried the secret of this love deep inside him. He kept this so close to his chest that we don't even know whether this was a real love affair or a figment of his imagination that became larger than life in his poetry.

Illusory as she may have been, this first love stayed with Nagui the rest of his life, and continued to plague him. She was the love of his life, and gained a steadily greater hold on his heart and mind as the years passed.[1]

The poet Saleh Gawdat claimed to have been personally acquainted with Nagui's first muse—but I looked into this and found that his claim had no basis in fact, as I will explain later. Gawdat held that A.M. had only liked Nagui's poems, but that my grandfather's love remained unrequited. Gawdat writes:

> The object of Nagui's love was the source of his yearning in his poetry. He refers to her in a poem entitled "From N. to A."—the "N." refers to Nagui, and "A." was the first letter of her name. Her first initials were "A. M." I knew Nagui's first muse personally. She had a very sweet personality, a poet's disposition. Whenever she spoke to me, to us, about this poet, she said that she knew how much he loved her, but she felt only a passing affection, little more than pity, for him. If she had once loved him, it was as a poet who moved her imagination, but not as a man who might fill her days.[2]

Gawdat appointed himself as an unofficial spokesperson on this matter, and the details he circulated appeared in numerous news articles over the years. For example, Lam'i al-Muti'i wrote an article about their love story in *al-Wafd* on 23 March 2000, more than forty years after Gawdat's initial claim. Al-Muti'i drew on information relayed by Nagui's anthologist, Hassan Tawfiq:

> Hassan Tawfiq wrote that he had published an article in the Qatari newspaper *al-Raya* (issue 28, June 1984) entitled "Ibrahim Nagui, al-ashiq' alladhi mat hubban" (Ibrahim Nagui, the Poet Who Died for Love). At the end of the article, Tawfiq wrote, "Now his real-life muse has left us, the one to whom Nagui wrote all his life through his poetry, we can make her name public: She is Ms. Anayat Mahmoud al-Towayyer."

This fiction about Anayat became more deeply embedded the more it was passed around, until it took on the veneer of truth, particularly after my grandfather's younger brother allegedly confirmed the veracity of the story himself.[3]

Another fanciful version of this history, more far-fetched than the first, appeared in an article by Ibrahim Khalil Ibrahim, "Remembering Dr. Ibrahim Nagui," published in *Donia al-Watan* on 23 March 2018:

> Dr. Ibrahim Nagui had a single muse: A. M. T., one of his distant relatives, and his first love. She married someone else before he finished his studies and he continued to lament her loss in his poems. Other women only reminded him of her. His poems are often dedicated from "N." to "A." [. . .]
>
> Ibrahim Nagui traveled abroad to study medicine and when he returned, he learned that his love had married another. One night he heard a loud knock on the door. He got out of bed to see who was there and found a man looking for a doctor to help his wife, who was in the midst of a difficult labor. Nagui took his doctor's bag and went to the man's house, where he found the woman in grave condition . . . When Dr. Nagui approached her, he recognized his sweetheart.

There is plenty of facile description and narrative embellishment here, to the extent that this account bears little relation to the facts of Nagui's life. Nagui did not study medicine abroad as the writer of the above article claims, so he cannot have returned to Egypt to find his sweetheart suddenly married. A reader familiar with Nagui's poetry will also know that Nagui had many muses, to whom he dedicated various poems. He did not spend his entire life as a Qays grieving his Layla, as the article would have us believe. As for the story of the husband who descended on Nagui's house by night—this is an extremely improbable tale, since Nagui's medical work never involved midwifery of any kind; that was not his area of specialization. It's also unlikely that a man who did not know my grandfather at all would come to him personally with such an urgent issue as an obstructed labor. Such tragic melodramas suited the image that Nagui's critics spun of the "delicate, sensitive poet" (*sha'ir al-riqqa al-'atifiyya*) as Abbas Mahmoud al-Aqqad once disparagingly called him.

The grain of truth in all these stories was that the young Ibrahim Nagui was determined to spend the rest of his life with this first muse, but fate robbed him of the opportunity. In the introduction to his book *City of Dreams*, dedicated to his father Ahmed Nagui, Ibrahim writes that his father was his first teacher and had introduced him to Charles Dickens's *Oliver Twist* and *David Copperfield*. My grandfather writes:

> Dickens made me love literature, but David Copperfield made me a poet. He sent me looking for a Dora of my own to teach me the secrets of existence, but my Dora tormented me and my soul was rent in two.
>
> My father had his designs, and Dickens and Copperfield had theirs. As for me, fate had something else in mind entirely. Woe is fate![4]

In a later article, "Kutub aththarat fi hayati" (Books That Shaped Me), published in *al-Gomhour al-Misri* in February 1952, Nagui recounts the impact that Dickens had on him when he was only eleven years old:

> [David Copperfield] doesn't call Dora his love, but rather his "dear life." This is the most eloquent description of tenderness that I've seen. She wasn't just his lover, but his whole existence and inspiration.

So it was with Nagui's first muse, A. M. Or at least, that was how he saw her. But the mysterious A. M. shows up in other contexts, in a different guise than Dora. Nagui dedicated his first collection, *Wara' al-ghamam* (Behind the Clouds), to her, with a short poem at the beginning of the volume, which opens:

You are the fount of genius and the splendor of eternity,
Mercy's infinite melodies for the wretched earth.

This is the volume that contains the poetry of Nagui's youth, the first verses that he penned to his love. He also dedicated his second collection *Layali al-Qahira* (Cairo Nights, 1950) to her. In the Arabic, he conceals her identity by referring to her in the masculine:

To my dear friend, A. M., who bedewed the wilted bloom in yesterday's grove, and sowed seeds in the gardens of today, blossoms brushed with vitality and anguish. To him I dedicate the verses he has inspired.

In his 1952 article, Nagui also details how his attachment spurred him to learn French as a young man:

I learned French so that I could read the great writer [Paul] Bourget's book *The Disciple*. At the time I only knew English because my high school's science track didn't teach French. However, I needed to learn the language in order to communicate with the most important creature in the world, who only spoke French and loved Bourget. She thought that *The Disciple* was his very best work and hoped we might read it together in French!

It was a nice idea, but how could I? I was going to have to learn quickly so I could read with her before the moment passed.

In this case, necessity was the mother of diligence. I said to myself: Well, I'll learn French like a child does—memorize words and learn to say them and then string them together, words first and then sentences. And so I did. In the first month I began to memorize French words and practiced saying them aloud using a pronunciation dictionary. Thirty words per day, and soon I had a thousand words fully at my disposal.

During the second month I began to study grammar and learned how to connect the words I knew together, and in the third month I attempted to apply this knowledge to reading *The Disciple*. I read it through on my first try and didn't understand a thing. The second time I understood a little bit, and the third time a little more, and the fourth more still. By the eighth time I felt I had a full grasp of its contents. I went to my friend and we read Bourget's story together and she could scarcely believe it.

A. M. had inspired my grandfather to learn his third language, from which he would later translate various works of literature into Arabic. She wasn't just his muse, but also significantly shaped his professional trajectory. Yet she remained enigmatic. Who was she?

When I began writing this book, my mother gave me a draft of a television screenplay on Ibrahim Nagui's life written by Enas al-Assal. Enas was a distant relative, although I hadn't met her before. She'd written the script in 1993 but the project never came through. My mother gave me Enas's phone number and I called her to find out why she was interested in Nagui's life and what sources she'd used to write the script, especially the parts that dealt with A. M. I discovered during this conversation that Enas and I had gone to high school together at Port Said School in Zamalek. I had been two years ahead of her in school. She had gone on to become an IT specialist and then changed careers, and had started writing the screenplay after studying at the Cinema Culture Palace for a while. Enas said that Nagui was her favorite poet. That was why she had focused on Nagui's life for the screenplay, which allowed her to incorporate both fact and fiction.

I was mainly interested in the part of the script that dealt with A. M., whom Enas decided to call Effat. Here follows a small portion of the script that Enas al-Assal wrote, in which she imagines Ibrahim and Effat meeting again after a long time apart:

One day, as Ibrahim is examining a particular bone, he hears a woman's voice.

EFFAT
Tired of studying?

He looks up and sees Effat, his childhood sweetheart, who has now become a lovely woman. He hasn't seen her for three years. He calls out in greeting.

IBRAHIM
Is it really you, Effat?

FIFI [EFFAT]
Here I am, flesh and blood. Is medicine tiring?

IBRAHIM
I don't really like it.

FIFI
What's a poet doing with these bones then?

IBRAHIM
That's how the world works, the poet's a doctor and the doctor's a butcher.

FIFI
It's a hard path, to see people in pain. But you can help them. My father, God rest his soul . . . I wished there was something I could do to help when he was ill, but I couldn't do anything. The doctors wrote their prescriptions and left. To them he was just a case, but to me, he was my life. *(Begins to cry.)*

Ibrahim feels that he wants to hug her and help her bear her sadness but he can't. He decides to try to make her laugh instead.

IBRAHIM
Please don't cry. We don't come to cures for weeping until next year. I'll cure you then. But I heard laugh-cetamol's quite good medicine.

FIFI
(Giggles.) Ok, I'll put it off til next year. But promise me you'll study well because I'd love to know how to stave off sadness.

IBRAHIM
Whatever you like.

FIFI
(Blushing.) It would be good to see you again. Don't you miss my brother Aziz?

IBRAHIM
Aziz? Isn't he at the Sorbonne?

FIFI
No, he came back to Egypt so we wouldn't be left on our own.

Ibrahim realizes that they are about to go back to talking about her father and wants to keep things cheerful.

IBRAHIM
So when would Aziz be around?

FIFI
This afternoon. *(In a hurry.)* Bonsoir! My mum's waiting for me.

After this magical meeting, Ibrahim imagines he'll be able to make his dreams come true and marry Effat. He feels he can do the impossible and is full of goodwill. He wants to be the doctor that Fifi needed when her father took ill. Ibrahim's friend Sabri asks him why he is suddenly much more interested in his studies.

IBRAHIM
Love.

SABRI
You love studying?

IBRAHIM
I love medicine and doctors and patients. I love the whole world. I even love studying. I love everything because I love her. With a single word she makes the driest medical text into a love poem.

SABRI
Who are you talking about, man?

IBRAHIM
That's my secret until the day we are engaged.

In the screenplay, Effat tells Ibrahim that she loves the book *The Disciple*, and would like to read it with him. Nagui is embarrassed to tell her he doesn't know French and says that they'll read it together during their next vacation. Ibrahim buys the book and a French dictionary and begins to teach himself French, as in real life.[5]

Enas draws these scenes and dialogues from Nagui's writings and poetry from his youth, especially the introduction to his book *City of Dreams*, including his description of searching for Dora. She was also working from the introduction to his short story collection, *Adrikni ya duktur* (Cure Me, Doctor), in which he explains his perspective on the medical profession:

> I have never seen patients as "cases," as doctors often say, but as people. Treating someone is not a matter of prescribing the right medicine but rather understanding the whole human being.[6]

The screenplay was also based on the article, "Nagui Chronicles His Life," in which he talks about learning to read in French, which he sees as a great turning point in his education. Nagui writes:

> A day came that I shall never forget, a revolutionary day. That day I met a *litteratrice* skilled in French. She enticed me away from my doctor friends and introduced me to new companions: Bourget, Anatole France, [Émile] Zola . . .

In Enas's screenplay, A. M. is transformed from David Copperfield's Dora into Effat, who falls into a trope we have seen in dozens of other Egyptian novels and films—the young middle-class woman, newly come of age, who dazzles her childhood sweetheart.

Enas was not necessarily responsible for imposing this trope, since she drew much of the detail in the scene between Ibrahim and Effat from "Safhat gharam" (A Tale of Love), a short story from Nagui's book *Cure Me, Doctor*. In fact, the dialogue is taken almost word-for-word from this story that Nagui himself wrote, so it is really he who reimagined his love story with these narrative dimensions.

In Nagui's story, the adventures of protagonists Fakhry and Leila closely resemble what we know of the story of my grandfather and A. M. Fakhry is a doctor and poet who suddenly runs into his old neighbor Leila: "She appeared again, coy and elegant, having blossomed into a charming woman in every way."[7] Fakhry then proceeds to learn French with Leila. This version of the story goes beyond their relationship itself to shed light on the protagonist's anxieties regarding whether he is sufficiently handsome or otherwise qualified in the eyes of his love. Nagui writes:

> She knew that Fakhry loved her and she tried to love him. But her heart said no. She could see that Fakhry had left medicine and had an uncertain future. He was not very handsome, neither tall nor strong nor in robust health. Practically speaking, marriage wouldn't do.
>
> And she was right. Fakhry was a poet and a selfish man who thought she should love him because he loved her with all his heart and soul. Poor fellow. Did he think that what he felt in his heart carried the same weight as the ability to pay a good dowry?

Leila always thought things over very deeply. This tortured Fakhry because he knew she was conflicted inside, and would be for many years [. . .]

Fakhry was tormented because if he asked her whether she'd return his love she wouldn't be lying if she said she didn't know, and that she didn't dislike him but perhaps also didn't love him the way he loved her, tempestuously, completely, without rhyme or reason [. . .]

Hadn't he started writing poetry ten years before? Wasn't his heart breaking? Didn't he cry when she approached? Didn't he go to the station to see her coming and going? Didn't he speak her praises, write of seeing her and leaving her, of her laughter and her sadness? She had married someone she didn't know. But *he* knew her and loved her and would go on composing poetry and weeping.[8]

Fakhry also recounts a nightmare about Leila that stirs him from sleep:

He saw Leila beside him in the operating room. He was reading, and she was holding a scalpel. Finally, she turned to him and said, "Where is your heart?" "Here on the left," he said. She took the scalpel, and cut through his clothes, and then his skin, and then his muscle. With a single thrust she reached into his chest cavity and took out his heart, and said cheerfully: "See? Your heart is in my hands." Then she flew into an inexplicable rage and threw the heart on the operating room floor, where it got all grimy and another medical student stepped on it. Fakhry cried out in anguish. Then he woke up, trembling and sobbing and dizzy. He turned toward Leila, Leila who had cut out his heart, and found that she had already gone.[9]

Beyond Dora who rent his soul in two and Leila who cut out his heart with her own hands, the identity of Nagui's first muse remained a puzzle. I asked my mother, but she knew only fragmentary bits and pieces. She said this wasn't something that was talked about at home. My mother knew, of course, that Nagui had a sweetheart named A. M. before he was married. She said she knew the initials but didn't know any more than that. Even when she had been asked about Nagui's first muse in interviews with the press, my mother would take A. M.'s name from Enas's screenplay, and call her Effat.

I too had almost accepted this account, but as fate would have it, I stumbled upon more of the story, years after both my grandfather and A. M. had passed away.

In September 2019, I invited the historian Hussein Omar to AUC to give a lecture, entitled "Revolutionary Genealogy: Family History and 1919." Hussein Omar was a grandson of the revolution by blood and also worked on the diaries of figures such as Saad Zaghloul as a scholar. I knew that Hussein and I had some kind of family connection. Several years before, Hussein had sent me a copy of a 1953 obituary for Ibrahim Nagui in *al-Ahram*, which detailed our two families' genealogical links. However, I had not paid attention to this aspect of the obituary at the time. Hussein has encyclopedic knowledge of many family trees going back at least two centuries, but years passed before we sat down to properly talk through this.

Hussein and I met at my home after his lecture, along with Hassan Abouseda, who had introduced us several years before. It was a family gathering in which Hussein was going through the genealogy and expertly filling out the family tree starting with our common forebear, my great-great-great-grandfather Sheikh Abdullah al-Sharqawi. I gradually began to understand the connection between the al-Towayyer family (the family of Hussein Omar's great-grandmother) and the Seoudi family (the family of Bahia, Ibrahim Nagui's mother).

It turned out that Hussein Omar was the son of Mona Sabaa, the granddaughter of Alia Mahmoud al-Towayyer. They were both descended from Sheikh Abdullah al-Sharqawi, who had been the Grand Imam of al-Azhar in 1793, at a particularly crucial juncture of Egyptian history. He was among the most important leaders of the resistance during the French occupation of Egypt. Later, his descendants—the al-Towayyer, Seoudi/Nagui, and al-Sharqawi families—would move from Fatimid Cairo to neighboring homes in Shubra, and grow close to one another in their idyllic "city of dreams."

During that evening, Hussein told me the secret that my grandfather had hidden from everyone on our side of the family: Ibrahim Nagui had asked for Alia al-Towayyer's hand in marriage—not her sister Anayat's, as Saleh Gawdat had claimed—and been turned away. If this had happened, it would have been in 1921 or 1922, when Nagui had either just graduated from university or when he was studying medicine. Alia would marry Mahmoud Sabaa in 1923, although Hussein said that Alia became depressed at the end of her life and that her sisters had often said they were sorry that Alia had not married Ibrahim Nagui, especially after he became a prominent poet and physician.

Hussein told me that Alia al-Towayyer's daughter was called Amira, like my mother, and that the two Amiras got to know each other through Aziza Wahby (Zouzou, as everyone called her) at the Gezira Club in Zamalek. Zouzou was good friends with both Amiras. I asked my mother about this encounter and she confirmed that it had taken place. However, she added that Amira Sabaa did not tell her during this meeting that she was the daughter of my grandfather's muse, that is, she hadn't mentioned her mother's name. Perhaps she was embarrassed to talk about the subject with Ibrahim Nagui's daughter, since it was only the first time they had met. She just told my mother how much she appreciated my grandfather's poetry, and my mother gave her some of his books. That is how the two Amiras met without discussing the secret that bound Alia to my grandfather.

Many years after this brief encounter, Hussein and I sat down to write our respective family histories and untangle these threads. Hussein graciously gave me a photo of Alia al-Towayyer, with an inscription in French to her mother. The photo was taken in Paris in 1923, the same year she was married. Finally, I saw her, after all these years, smiling faintly: Alia Mahmoud al-Towayyer, A. M., the elegant young lady whose passion for books and quiet charm had so captivated my grandfather. Her clothing and hairstyle marked her as part of the Europeanized elite, and she wrote neatly and fluidly in French.

I took another look at the photo. Did Alia resemble my grandmother at all? Not really. Maybe the hairstyle wasn't far off, the reticent comportment, the gentle smile. But my grandmother never traveled to Paris and would never have given anyone photos with French inscriptions! Was Alia more like David Copperfield's Dora or Leila in Nagui's "Tale of Love"? Looking at this photo, it seemed she was a different character entirely.

I filled out the rest of the picture of Alia al-Towayyer's life with the help of her daughter Amira Sabaa, who now lives in Canada. Her nephew Alaa Sabaa had passed along her phone number during an evening at the house of Hassan Abouseda, who was also his relative.

17. Alia al-Towayyer, 1923, from the archive of Hussein Omar.

When I called Amira, I discovered she was expecting my call because Alaa had kindly informed her that Ibrahim Nagui's granddaughter wanted to ask her some questions about her mother Alia.

I could hear Amira Sabaa's voice clearly on the phone, warm and welcoming: "Ahlan Samia." My initial hesitations vanished and we spoke for about an hour during this first call, which took place in mid-November 2019. I was impressed with her presence of mind and precise memory, for she was older than my mother, who is herself over eighty-eight. She remembered my mother, and said that they'd had a very nice meeting several years before.

I came to the matter at hand. I asked her: Did Nagui really ask for Alia's hand in marriage but was turned away? Amira didn't think so. She took me back through the family tree: Hassouna al-Towayyer, a leading Tunisian merchant (*shahbandar*) had come to Egypt, settled down, and married the daughter of Sheikh Abdullah al-Sharqawi. Amira said that Alia's father, Mahmoud al-Towayyer, was a judge (*qadi*) in the Mixed Courts, and that he loved books and encouraged his seven daughters, including Alia, to read and develop themselves. His palace in Shubra was right next to the palace of Ahmed Nagui, my grandfather's father. According to Amira, the al-Towayyer family later moved to a villa next door to the American University in Cairo in downtown. In the 1950s, their villa at the corner of al-Sheikh Rihan and Falaki streets became a school, the al-Qarbiya Secondary School for Boys, as happened with many old villas from that era. The family later settled in Zamalek.

Amira told me that her mother Alia was born in 1900. She was slightly less than two years younger than my grandfather, who was born in December 1898. I thought to myself: Yes, that always happens, childhood neighbors close in age who fall in love. The Nagui and al-Towayyer families were already connected with each other, and remained close even after the al-Towayyer family left Shubra for al-Sheikh Rihan Street. Alia studied at the Lycée in Bab al-Louq. She loved French literature and would memorize poems by heart. Amira said that Mahmoud al-Towayyer had brought a French governess for his daughters Alia and Atiya, and the governess lived with the family. French was integral to the girls' daily lives: They studied it in school and spoke it at home. The family also travelled frequently to France where they owned a place they could stay each year. Hence the French inscription on the portrait Alia gave her mother would have been something normal in the al-Towayyer family, and indeed expected in correspondence between family members.

Amira said that her mother Alia helped Ibrahim learn French when he was young, and that they'd shared a passion for reading and literature from an early age. I asked whether Ibrahim's love for Alia (not, as was previously thought, Anayat) was really unrequited, as Saleh Gawdat had claimed based on "personal knowledge" of Nagui's first muse. Amira said she didn't know Gawdat, and that she and her siblings (Hassouna and Amir) knew all their parents' close friends. So Gawdat had not in fact been a close confidant of the family.

I wondered: Why had Gawdat made the claim about Anayat in his book on Nagui, which is considered one of the main sources of reference on Nagui's life? Had he just appointed himself the custodian of the facts of Nagui's life, or was there perhaps some sort of jealousy or rivalry involved? Gawdat's book begins with an introduction by Abbas Mahmoud al-Aqqad, who, like Taha Hussein, had attacked Nagui during his lifetime for allegedly lifting verses from his poems and stealing his spotlight. In that introduction, al-Aqqad dismisses Nagui's poetry as sentimental fluff in the tradition of the Abbasid *zurafa* ("elegant") poets—a critique that echoed Taha Hussein's comment that Nagui's sensitive verse would "catch cold if it went outside." It's odd that a "friend" like Gawdat would have chosen al-Aqqad to write this introduction after Nagui's death. Gawdat also expressed doubts about the provenance of Nagui's poetry and suggested that certain poems attributed to Nagui had actually been written by Gawdat himself. He also had strongly criticized some of Nagui's other work. When I read what the eminent poet Ahmed Abdel Muti Hijazi had written in the introduction to his book on Ibrahim Nagui, my fears and suspicions were confirmed. Hijazi explains after an extensive discussion of my grandfather's work:

> I think that this image of an erudite poet engaged with the issues of his time is very much at odds with the notion of the hapless vagabond that Saleh Gawdat had conjured. Gawdat had claimed to be a friend of Nagui since the latter had worked as a doctor in Mansoura around 1929. But by that time, Nagui was thirty-one years old and Saleh Gawdat only seventeen![10]

In any case, my conversation with Amira Sabaa shed new light on my grandfather's love story with A. M. and helped bring the picture into clearer focus on both sides. Amira told me that Alia al-Towayyer was married in 1923 to Mahmoud Sabaa, a highly suitable groom, who held the post of Egyptian consul in Liverpool, England. The photo from Hussein Omar with its French inscription was taken the same year. Alia married at twenty-three—relatively late for girls of her generation. It was a traditional marriage, to a man she did not know, while Ibrahim Nagui was still a medical student unable to provide the material guarantees that her husband could. Nagui's future had not yet taken clear shape. The closeness of age between Ibrahim and Alia, which had brought them together as children, now became an obstacle to their potential future together. In Nagui's story, Leila kept her head and married a man she didn't know instead of marrying Fakhry, the man she loved.

Alia traveled with her husband Mahmoud to England after their marriage, where he took up his post in the consulate in Liverpool. However, they quickly returned to Cairo after little less than a year after Alia became gravely ill following complications with medical treatment, or so Amira told me. She said that Alia's parents had gone to England after receiving news of her health crisis, despite the difficulties of the journey. Mahmoud Sabaa was obliged to resign from his post in the foreign ministry, return to Cairo, and take up a new professional life in the judiciary. Amira said that Alia was happy with her married life with Mahmoud, a voracious reader whose library was later acquired by the Rare Books and Special Collections Library at the American University in Cairo.

I said to myself: What a strange story this is. People usually travel *to* England for medical treatment. And why did the newlyweds return to Cairo so quickly, especially when their move had such serious implications for Mahmoud's future and for their family? I didn't press Amira about this. Families have their secrets and stories, and the book I was writing was part of that. Still, the question hung in my mind and I tried to come up with possible answers about what might have happened.

I did ask: Did Alia just pity my grandfather? Was he imagining their love? Amira said: No, I think she really cared for him. She said that Ibrahim Nagui remained close with Alia after her marriage and even after she had children—Hassouna, Amira, and Amir. She said that

Nagui would come to visit Alia at her father's house. I asked, "How was this allowed when she was already a mother and wife?" She said that Nagui wasn't a stranger to the household. He was a relative, a friend, and an old neighbor, and it was normal for him to pop by and see the al-Towayyer family along with his younger brother Hassan, or even to sit alone with Alia. The house of Mahmoud al-Towayyer was always open to friends and family. She said that her older brother Hassouna remembered those visits because he'd sit with them too. Amira remembered the visits of Hassan Nagui (the most handsome of the Nagui brothers) to her grandfather's home, which had been full of girls—seven daughters! I was surprised that Amira already knew about al-Muti'i's account, which incorrectly identified Anayat, Alia's sister, as Nagui's first muse. She said the family had been quite annoyed that Anayat, who had no special connection to Ibrahim Nagui, had been caught up in this story.

Amira said that Alia's connection to my grandfather was "romantic" but platonic. She was glad of his visits and so she continued to spend time with him at her father's home. I wondered what they said to each other during these visits. Did he read her his poems? Did they talk about literature? Did they reminisce about their childhood in Shubra or lament how things had ended up?

Alia married in 1923, but my grandfather didn't marry until 1928. He continued to visit her in the intervening years, even after she became a mother. Why did Hassouna Sabaa remember my grandfather's visits, and tell his sister about them? Was it because Ibrahim Nagui had become an eminent poet and doctor? Or because they knew about their mother's connection to my grandfather, especially once he became well-known after his death as the poet who wrote "al-Atlal" (The Ruins), which was then performed by Umm Kulthum? In any case, the relationship between Ibrahim and Alia did not end with their childhood, but remained a crucial part of their lives for many years.

I looked through my grandfather's diaries—which I will come to in more depth in the following chapter—and was particularly taken by an entry from 10 December 1946. Here it is not only my grandfather who provides evidence of continuing affection, but Alia who calls him:

18. An entry in Nagui's diary about A. M., dated 10 December 1946.

The most important thing about today is that I saw A.! She called me on the telephone, which I was not expecting at all. She invited me to visit her so that we could go to see her sister. I went the following day and she was agonizingly sweet. She asked me to recite poetry I had written for her. Her son was also there.

We went to visit her sister, and managed to talk the whole way there. She blamed me for leaving her. I was stunned and said: *My fault, you —?* But time will be our witness.

Nagui refers to her by her full name—Alia—just once in his unpublished diaries, in an entry dated January 1947. In all his other writings, he calls her A., A. M., or occasionally A. T. Only in this entry does he slip up after seeing her:

Kazima al-Towayyer [one of Alia al-Towayyer's sisters] fell sick on the houseboat where my brother Mohamed lives so I went to check in on her there. We then moved her to the Sednawy Hospital where she died several days later. During this time, I saw Alia again. Time is strange. She was sweet but so infernally reserved. It was as if no time had passed . . . she looked exactly as she always had. I imagined kissing her hands, her feet, every part of her, and was engulfed by that yearning again . . . a sweeping wave of desire.

Nagui's diaries end suddenly on 4 October 1949 with a brief paragraph after an entire year without writing. He sums up that year in two vague lines without further detail. This unusually brief entry stands out from the rest of his entries, but is characteristically opaque.

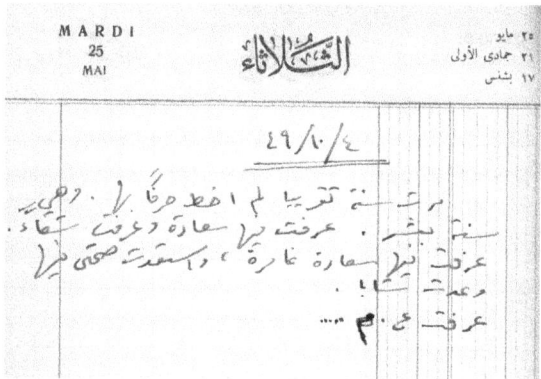

19. A later entry about A. M., dated 4 October 1949.

> Almost a year has passed in which I have not penned a single line. It felt like a decade. It has been a year of tremendous happiness and misfortune both. I regained my health and felt like a young man. I came to know A. M. . . .

Hussein Omar told me that Alia al-Towayyer died in the late 1970s, about twenty-five years after my grandfather passed away. She outlived him, for he had died young when he was only fifty-six. Alia lived into her late seventies. Did she grieve his passing, or speak of what she felt?

According to Hussein, Alia was stricken by depression in the latter years of her life and became like a ghost, wandering through the halls of her house, speaking very little, watching the others in silence. She'd tell the women of the family that Nagui's famous poem "al-Atlal" was written about her—for her—and they'd make fun of this apparently preposterous claim.

Learning all this about Alia made me feel fond of her, although I had only come to know her through a series of coincidences and the stories I was told. I loved that she had been with my grandfather all through his childhood and had given him so much, despite the impossibility of their love story. The enigmatic A. M., whose name he had been so reluctant to reveal, was now known to both of us. Alia had come to life before my very eyes, an unexpected guest on my journey toward my grandfather.

6

JOURNAL DE VIE

That was how my grandfather titled his diary—or to be more precise, his handwritten entries in a daily journal from 1943. This journal, which he actually began keeping on 5 March 1944 and continued through 4 April 1949, was among the papers that my aunt Dawheya inherited after Ibrahim Nagui passed away. The diary spanned almost five years of his life and ended about three years before his death in March 1953. These scattered entries—as Do had observed in her unpublished introduction to some of his work—touch briefly on personal, political, romantic, financial, and family affairs without going into much detail.

It's curious that my grandfather chose to give this diary a French heading: *journal de vie*. One might imagine that Nagui would have continued writing in French, but he did not. He writes his entries in English for the first ten months until 4 December 1944, after which he switches to Arabic for the rest of the diary. The reader might wonder, as did I, why Nagui moves between languages in this way. Was he reluctant to write in French? Did he have second thoughts after those first three words? He might have felt less capable of expressing himself in his third language, even if he had translated French literature into Arabic. Or had he intended to write more solemn, grandiose memoirs in English or French until life overtook him and he fell back into Arabic to jot down what was happening? I don't know. Still, even after he switches back, he continues to intersperse some English and French within his Arabic.

20. The cover of Ibrahim Nagui's diary.

Because the diary entries are so hurried and brief, Nagui's English and Arabic are equally spare. The diary feels like an oral account in which he is mainly talking to himself, trying to keep up with what's happening around him. He is keen not to leave anything out and writes on multiple occasions, sometimes in Arabic and sometimes in English: *Nasitu an adhkur . . ./*"I forgot to mention . . ." He is writing for some future reader, making sure to relate the full story, including these bits that initially slipped his mind. In an Arabic entry dated 28 November 1944, he recounts reading a female friend what he'd written about her in his diary:

> When she was here, I read part of this *journal* to her. She didn't read English but I told her what I'd written about her so she'd know what she meant to me . . . Do you think she'll be assured of that now?

Nagui begins his diary with an entry dated 5 March 1944, in which he writes, in English:

> Full three months without a single line. Have had nasty dark times. Had no appetite no tendency no whim to write down anything.

Last year ended v. bad. Began excellent, contained several glorious events. Ended unexpectedly in failure. Everything was at stake. Today only some ray is seen.

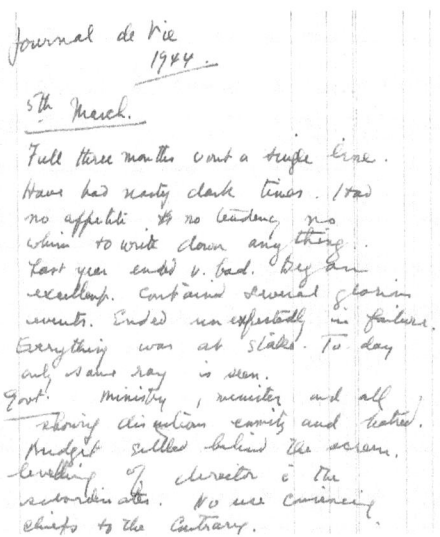

21. The first entry in Nagui's diary, dated 5 March 1944.

The telegraphic style of this initial entry is characteristic of the rest of the journal. This first entry is divided into several separate sections: his government job, matters of the heart, finances, work. His English feels as if it's been translated from Arabic, his mother tongue. It sometimes feels as if he's writing Arabic in English.

The first line of this entry ("full three months without a single line . . .") makes clear that this was not Nagui first's diary. There seems to have been another diary before this 1943 notebook that I had found in the envelope from my aunt Dawheya. But this earlier volume was nowhere to be found: it must have been lost along with many of his other papers. I wondered if Nagui had written a previous *journal de vie* in French, and had meant to continue in that vein. Or maybe it was full of the same hurried notes as the diary passed down to Do, as if he'd been thinking aloud to himself on the page. Did it recount his dejection about being attacked by Taha Hussein and Abbas Mahmoud al-Aqqad after publishing his first poetry collection, *Behind the*

Clouds? Did Nagui expound on his conception of poetry and how it diverged from Taha Hussein's? Did he vent about the crisis between them, which ultimately led my grandfather to abandon poetry and turn instead to translations, short stories, and articles?

It's a shame that this earlier diary was lost, if it did indeed exist, because the period it would have covered was one of the most important of his life. During this time, he solidified his standing as a Romantic poet within the new Apollo school of Arabic poetry, which challenged the conservative school of al-Aqqad and Taha Hussein. It was a particularly prolific period for Nagui, who produced books, translations, and lectures across many different spheres of knowledge: medicine, psychology, sociology, literary criticism, translation, short stories, and of course poetry. An exhausting variety of fields which consumed his time and energy.

The diary I hold in my hands bears witness to other "dark times" in Nagui's life over this five-year period. After his initial entry, there are various other entries from 1944: 15 April, 23 May, 18 June, 13 August, 12 October, Eid al-Adha (which fell in late November that year), 28 December, and New Year's 1944–45. The early 1944 entries were written approximately monthly but by summer had become less frequent, and Nagui began to sum up two months or more in a single entry. Most of the time, the occasion for writing was one of the various professional, political, financial, or personal crises he endured, although he also recorded his romantic, professional, and literary triumphs in these pages.

I understand why my aunt Do decided not to publish his diary or to put off publishing until she had redacted the "more personal" material. However, it honestly seems that the diary as a whole was not meant for publication. The entries are often vague, unchronological, abrupt, and inattentive to style. They are just a space for him to vent, and can be a bit impenetrable for anyone else. Nevertheless, the diary remains important because it is my grandfather's own account of the tragedies that befell him.

No doubt this version of Nagui's life weighed heavy on his daughter Dawheya, who had considered herself to be close to him, the trusted guardian of his legacy. Nagui's depiction of himself was at odds with the image of the model father that his daughters had held up their whole lives. He paints himself instead as a man who is struggling—psychologically, professionally, financially. Since he has no one to talk to about these crises, he writes to himself in his journal. My poor lonely grandfather. And my poor aunt, who must have stumbled upon these revelations and then put the diary away in the sealed envelope, where it remained for almost half a century.

Despite my initial impressions of an abrupt and scattered diary, I realized it was also a very illuminating document. These brief entries shed a clear and steady light on Nagui's relationship with all the institutions he was connected to: the professional institutions where he worked, the cultural institutions that he was part of, and the social institutions of marriage and fatherhood with their corresponding financial burdens. I decided to follow some of these interwoven paths through his diary.

My aunt Do had chosen to keep quiet about what she found in my grandfather's diary, and did not even share this with her sister—my mother—who knew the diary existed but had never seen or read it. My mother was apprehensive about me writing this chapter, since it was full of revelations for both of us, stories she too was hearing for the first time, or which she had perhaps heard long ago but tried to forget. Throughout the writing of this book, I read drafts of each chapter to my mother as I went along, and she became a keen audience. Our visits turned into reading sessions. In the morning she'd say to me, "So, where have you gotten to now?" or "How much've you written?" or "When are you coming to read?" I became a Shahrazad, delivering the story in episodes. She'd tell me, "We had no idea—he never let that show," or "We were little and didn't realize what was happening." It was hard for her to come to grips with all this. She had to acclimate herself after all these years to what her sister had hidden, but she took it in her stride.

I spent a long time going through the diary—reading and rereading it, tracing different threads through recurrent themes: work, home, romance, accomplishments, finances, etc. I'd ask my mother from time to time about particular names or incidents my grandfather described. Sometimes she had answers, but often our conversations just raised more questions. She'd add to what my grandfather had said, elaborating on certain details, or remembering what was happening at the time. Occasionally she was surprised by what he'd written. The wonderful thing about this journey with my mother was that she was open to these new dimensions I was introducing to her father's legacy from his own words.

I now saw the portrait of my grandfather that hung on the wall of the *salon* with new eyes. I wondered: What do I do with this diary, and how can I reconcile it with that present-absent image?

Let me begin as Nagui himself did, with his professional travails during the period from 1944–1949, which he describes in English in his first entry as "disastrous":

> Ministry, minister and all showing disastrous enmity and hatred. Budget settled behind the screen. Levelling of director and the subordinates. No use convincing chiefs to the contrary.

The ministry here is the Ministry of Endowments, where Nagui was the head of the medical department. He was plagued by this sense of ill will and lack of transparency, and the situation remained fraught even after the minister changed. In May 1944, my grandfather wrote:

> Got nothing. This year – no increase – no promotion. Our section is awfully wronged.

Instead of climbing the professional ladder, my grandfather found himself in perpetual freefall. In his Arabic entry from New Year's 1944/1945, he indicates that he wasn't getting along well with his doctor colleagues, or anyone in the ministry for that matter, and decided there was "a conspiracy afoot." For all his meetings with and memos to his superiors, there was no hope of getting a foot in the door. He seemed not to grasp how institutions work, that ministries are enduring but their ministers short-lived.

It is also clear from these entries that this was not his first such ordeal. His troubles at the Ministry of Endowments evoked earlier challenges with the Railroad Authority, where he had worked in the 1930s. He continues in Arabic in the 1944–45 end-of-year entry quoted above:

I was not keeping a diary during the crisis with the Railroad Authority. But it was the same story: I was threatened with being transferred to Asyut. Thank God I was saved from that fate. Providence came to my aid in the guise I expected least: Ibrahim Bey Abdel Hady and his superior [Ahmad] Maher Pasha.

However, things quickly went downhill again after Ahmad Maher Pasha—then prime minister—was assassinated. On 3 March 1945, Nagui writes (in Arabic):

> It happened as I had feared: They really booted me down. I was demoted to the fourth rank, from director to inspector. A technical inspector, of all things! [. . .]

> Ahmad Maher Pasha was shot in parliament. He was killed by the lawyer Mahmoud el-Essawy, a horrific crime. Maher Pasha had been fond of me and I depended upon his help. Now he's dead and the knife's at my throat next [. . .]

> My salary was reduced from LE52 to LE36. When I started at the Ministry of Endowments I was earning LE40 but now I'm making even less!

My grandfather locks horns with the ministry and asks for his retirement pension since he is unwilling to continue under such "despicable circumstances." He writes on 17 March 1945: "I am free now and can breathe a sigh of relief. I am searching for work where I'll be free." However, he soon gives up on this plan when his efforts to find "free" work prove unsuccessful.

On 15 May 1945, he writes:

> It's over. I'm not free. I've gone back to work and penned the writ of my humiliation myself. I'm back to being a fourth-rank technical inspector. No office, no space, nothing. These have been the most miserable months of my life. But the lesson's learned.

Journal de vie

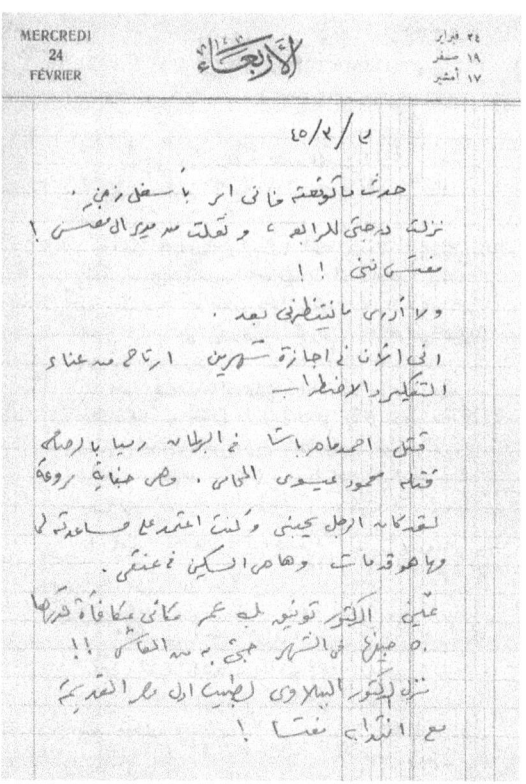

22. From Nagui's entry dated 3 March 1945.

My grandfather continued to be sidelined and pushed around by the ministry until he fell ill in 1947 and was taken to the hospital. He recounts at various points throughout his diary that he is coughing, and sometimes coughing up blood. At the hospital, he is diagnosed with tuberculosis.

On 10 July 1948, after getting through this difficult period and taking the Ministry of Endowments to court, he writes:

> Now it's Ramadan 1948 and it's been almost a year and a half since my last entry. The last entry I wrote was in January 1947. During Ramadan 1946 I'd written that I was coughing and coughing and didn't know why. I was taken to the Khazendar Hospital in April 1947 [...]

It was a grim illness. Very trying. It's a miracle that I survived. I don't feel like I've been cured—my chest still is teetering on the edge. I know I'm at the brink of a precipice. But I have to fight for my life, keep up with my obligations, pay my debts, overcome my adversaries, and raise my children. It's too much. I'm an unfortunate fellow [...]

I write now from the clinic. I've changed the hours so now I only work during the day. I'm taking a break from the hospital. The hospital is like the ministry or the government—the pits. I feel unsettled even thinking of it. I don't have a single friend in the ministry or the hospital even though I've done everyone a good turn, never offended anyone [...]

I won't forget that the ministry gave me some streptomycin [for treating TB] and paid for it, and then changed its mind. They ruined everything by wanting it back, spoiled the kindness with their base deceit.

I wrote the court filing myself. It's quite venomous. Desouky Pasha[1] didn't stand up for me. He hasn't treated me like a friend, may God forgive him.

Inside the diary, I found a copy of a typewritten letter to the prime minister (Mahmoud al-Nokrashy Pasha) on 8 April 1945, laying out Nagui's grievances with the Ministry of Endowments. He explains what has happened to him throughout his professional career in order to demonstrate the extent of the ministry's wrongdoing.

My grandfather opens the letter by saying that he's had a life "full of struggle," in which he constantly had to prove his true colors. He describes how he finished his medical studies in 1922, graduating second in his cohort, and then delved into diverse fields of knowledge including psychology, sociology, and literature, which he sees as key to his success. By his own account, these multidisciplinary engagements enabled him to better fulfill his professional duties as a doctor of internal medicine, as evidenced by the many patients who frequented his private clinic.

Finally, we come to the crux of the letter, namely, my grandfather's dual identities as doctor and poet. He writes:

> I have mentioned literature and sociology because some have faulted me for these endeavors in fields unconnected to medicine. They feel that this diminishes the medical profession—if only they knew the opposite is true. This knowledge complements internal medicine, where diagnoses rely upon isolated symptoms, all of which are more profoundly shaped by the patient's psychology than by the illness itself.
>
> I draw upon literature and sociology in writing to Your Excellency because I have no doubt at all that you are at the forefront of promoting a cultural and literary renaissance for the betterment of Egypt. You must know how much everyone attacks Dr. Ibrahim Nagui on this account and how much he has unjustly endured as a government physician.
>
> In conclusion, I offer a final example from my present government service. They are saying, now, at the end of my long career, that Dr. Nagui won't do as head of the medical department in the Ministry of Endowments because he is a doctor and a poet. They don't say this directly. There are only murmurs, since they cannot find any actual failings in his performance as a physician [. . .]
>
> When His Excellency Abdel Hamid Abdel Haqq took charge of the Ministry of Endowments, all of the department heads were promoted to second rank.
>
> But when His Excellency Mustafa Pasha Abd al-Raziq took over I am sorry to report that he saw me as someone without merit who had risen by chance, and decided I'd been put in a position

I wasn't qualified for. I think he had heard the same old story about literature and psychology, and that was why I was removed from my position. His Excellency did not have the kind of comprehensive vision that abided even a single exception, whatever that law might say.

My grandfather was let go by the Ministry of Endowments in 1952. Neither his defense of his medical accolades, nor his tale of struggle and multidisciplinary forays proved convincing. Even the extensive list of patients from his private clinic could not overcome the accusations of having divided himself between poetry and medicine.

I'm surprised that my grandfather, so well versed in sociology and psychology, would have written such a letter, which seems to me the final nail in the coffin! He pays no heed to the defined scope of particular disciplines or fields and wrongly assumes that the field will meritoriously reward his prowess and promote him based on the unique contributions of Ibrahim Nagui. He does not seem aware that working between medicine and poetry meant that he was operating outside the parameters of the medical field and challenging its boundaries. Power depended upon the capital derived from maintaining authority and the perpetual conflict between actors within the field who were always expected to comply with and conform to the status quo. Maintaining the status quo allowed the gatekeepers of the field to maintain its boundaries and values and cast out all those who tried to unsettle them.

My grandfather studied sociology before French sociologist Pierre Bourdieu came onto the scene. Bourdieu became a key figure in modern sociology starting in the 1960s, and his interdisciplinary theory on forms of social domination and reproduction fundamentally reshaped the humanities. Bourdieu argued that the social world was characterized by struggle, and that each social field relied upon classificatory schemes that constituted various forms of symbolic violence and resulted in the exclusion of those outside particular social domains. As a result, perpetual conflict occurs between those who control the field and those who lay new claims to this symbolic power and challenge established values. I cannot do justice to the full scope of this theory here, but these particular elements of Bourdieu's work helped me understand my grandfather's diary, particularly the end of his saga as a government physician with the Ministry of Endowments.

My grandfather's grievances and letters went unanswered, his merit as a doctor overlooked, and his poetry cast aside by ministers who came and went. His fleeting ties with some of these figures brought him only brief moments of acknowledgment or temporary promotion, because that wasn't how the field worked. Personal relationships or individual achievement could not overcome the structural constraints that served to perpetuate the established order and exclude outsiders. Hence, my grandfather was demoted and then dismissed a year before his death.

In addition to detailing this professional ostracization, many of his diary entries also attest to the nightmarish collapse of his finances. In his first English entry on 5 March 1944, he writes:

> Money. Same L.E. 100 post. No increase. Same extravagance some expenses even worse. Car sold yesterday for L.E. 70.

He continues in this vein in an Arabic entry from the end of that year, on 28 December 1944:

> I don't know where I'm headed [. . .] Government service has taught me cowardice, that I should be afraid to stand on my own two feet. But why am I afraid? These affairs are in God's hands. Who knows, maybe this ordeal will provide a way out of the woes that I have borne. What's to become of these two years? One blow after another.

On 25 January 1945, he writes:

> Finances a muddle. Expenses going up. Always just barely enough. I don't know what to do. Foolish—spending far too much.

Things are still not going well by 17 July 1946:

> Financial situation: utter rubbish. I've overspent and I'm nearly penniless. I can't reconcile my income, which is good, with the exorbitant expenses.

By January 1947, the situation has become even worse:

> I'm going through a huge crisis. I haven't paid the girls' school fees. For the first time in my life I didn't pay the two bills at the grocery shop. I didn't pay the telephone bill either. I'm squandering it all.

In his second-to-last entry on 10 July 1948, after he recovers from the tuberculosis, Nagui writes:

> My finances are very bad. I wanted to put a little money toward settling things with people, loans and such. Unfortunately, I couldn't pay off anything. I still can't.

My grandfather died leaving all these debts for my grandmother Samia. It seems like a bleak ending, but there was a silver lining. Bourdieu argues that something is gained from loss, particularly with regard to symbolic profit, which can be more important and more enduring than its economic counterpart. Ibrahim Nagui slips down the professional ladder of governmental rank and salary, and is defeated in the eyes of those controlling the field, who felt he didn't fit in with his doctor colleagues at the ministry. But symbolically, Nagui gains something else: the people's support. He became known as the poor man's doctor (*tabib al-ghalaba*). In 1953, the syndicate of newspaper sellers posthumously reissued his 1950 short story collection, *Cure Me, Doctor*, at their own expense, in thanks for having treated some of their members for free.

The decision of the newspaper sellers' syndicate to republish a collection of Nagui's stories, and this collection in particular, had important implications. The stories were a testament to Nagui's dual legacy as doctor and poet. The protagonist in this collection was also a poet-doctor, and all of the stories dealt with human moments between the doctor and his patients. Nagui begins this collection with an introduction that I see as his riposte to the ministry on this matter. He writes:

> I know that many of my doctor colleagues have literary inclinations, but they compose their poetry quietly and write in secret. I have always said to them: Doctors make good writers, and if they shared what they knew they'd cause quite a stir and alter how we live. [. . .] If you look through literary history, you'll find works by famous doctors, not too many, but timeless and enduring. No doubt many of you have read the works of famous Swiss doctor Axel Munthe, [Georges] Duhamel's *Salavin*, or [A.J.] Cronin's novel, *The Citadel*. [. . .]
>
> I was driven to write this book out of pressing personal need, which I could not ignore, because I am a doctor surrounded by the people. I work among them, young and old. My patients are my friends, and those who frequent my clinic are no strangers to me. They are an integral part of my life. I have never seen patients as "cases," as doctors often say, but as people. Treating someone is not a matter of prescribing the right medicine but rather understanding the whole human being.[2]

This introduction draws attention to how some of Nagui's doctor friends did in fact produce literature in private, since—as he was told at the Ministry—this was seen to "diminish" the medical profession. Unlike Nagui, they abided by the limits of the field and didn't dare to openly trespass its boundaries. The introduction mentions various leading European doctor–writers, all Nagui's contemporaries, each guilty of the same charge that the ministry leveled against him. Finally, my grandfather closes with his compassionate understanding of medicine: that the patient is first and foremost a human being, and not a clinical "case." Nagui had also developed an interest in psychology, which his superiors in the Ministry of Endowments likewise regarded as beyond his field of specialization as a doctor of internal medicine.

I wondered: Why hasn't anyone who has written about Nagui mentioned this short story collection or its introduction? Why has it been relegated to the periphery of his literary production? Still, my grandfather's struggles were not in vain. In 1986, I invited the late Yusuf Idris to give a lecture at Cornell University, where I was teaching Arabic literature at the time. Idris had been a student of my grandfather while he was still in medical school. Idris said that my grandfather was the reason why he chose literature over medicine. He gave my grandfather a draft of his first short story collection, *Arkhas layali (The Cheapest Nights)*. After Nagui read it, he said to him: "What on earth are you doing studying medicine?" Those fateful words changed the course of Idris's life. My grandfather helped Idris steer clear of the not-so-symbolic violence that he had himself experienced as a doctor between two worlds.

Beyond these professional woes, Nagui's journal is also filled with his literary accomplishments. Nagui chronicled his interdisciplinary endeavors in incredible detail and kept track of the books that he was reading, which he'd summarize in his diary. He recorded the lectures and poetry readings he was invited to give and how the audience reacted, the works that he translated, the books he published, the money he earned, the publishers he squabbled with. In general, he was keen to capture that his literary life soared even as his professional life collapsed. He carefully recorded the symbolic capital he accrued through literature, despite his material losses in the fields of medicine and literature alike. He was well aware that literature would not materially sustain him, but as Bourdieu put it: he who loses, wins.

I pored over these five years of literary undertakings Nagui documented and wondered at how my ailing grandfather found energy for all this writing and creative production. I cannot enumerate each of these endeavors in this chapter, but I will touch on some examples and spend a little longer on his trip to Palestine in 1946, which was particularly heartbreaking to read almost seventy-five years later.

Nagui was a *nahdawi* who read, lectured, and translated across disciplines, complementing his equally interdisciplinary perspectives on medicine. It grieves me that Abbas Mahmoud al-Aqqad reduced my grandfather to a "delicate, sensitive poet." In the midst of all this, Nagui was also working at the Ministry, the hospital, and his private clinic. Reading, writing, translating, and giving lectures became his refuge during the other ordeals he underwent.

In his 1 March 1945 entry in Arabic, my grandfather lists what he's accomplished that month:

> A lecture at [the communist group Iskra's] research center tonight on political psychology, a lecture at the clinical association on the psychology of sex *(jins)*, and the same lecture at the medical school. I was also invited to the British Institute in Minya to give a lecture on Shakespeare.

He continues on, primarily in English:

> Forgot to mention that last month I lectured by invitation in Mansourah on *saykulujiyyat al-mar'a* [the psychology of women] at the society of *nashr al-thaqafa*.[3] It was a magnificent reception. I recited too from *Layali al-Qahira* [Cairo Nights]. In short a memorable night.

In an April 1944 entry, he writes (also mostly in English):

> *Principes du succès, Psychology of Character, Psychoanalysis*—Ernest Jones. Finished "What is Man?" by Mark Twain. V. impressive. Will never forget what he said—'We only do what pleases us, what pleases the "master" in us, what makes us avoid pain and find peace, tranquility [...] The *principes du succès* is very impressive too. For success there must be audacity based on thinking, aims, etc. It is a fine book [...] Have been reading Arabic, *fi al-rawa'i'* [From the Greats], finished Amru ibn Kulthum, al-Mutanabbi, Hassan ibn Thabit. Very good revival of study and worth continuing.

He continues on in January 1945, in Arabic:

> I wrote a thorough study on Tawfiq al-Hakim and gave it to Sami al-Kayyali the day before yesterday. Now I am embarking on writing a book on family medicine as I agreed upon with Omar Abdel al-Aziz, who writes pocket novels.

In March 1945, he continues, mostly in Arabic:

> I'm getting a breather doing some writing. I finished part of the family medicine book and part of the book on psychology. I began working through the A.B.C [sic] of Psychology.

He continued to lecture widely: a talk at the medical association in Minya about strides made in the field of medicine during the war; another on the meanings of *al-adab* (including but not limited to literature); five lectures about various schools of literature and literary criticism; and weekly lectures every Sunday at the publishing house Maktab al-Sahafa al-Dawli (all of which he records in his Eid al-Adha entry from 1945). In another entry from July 1946, he mentions a lecture at the Faculty of Arts on directions in modern literature, a debate on women and society, and a lecture on Dostoevsky at the British Institute in Minya. He also describes the Literature Association that he founded and the literary festivals at which he read his poetry, including various storytelling, spring, and moon festivals. In a January 1947 entry, he describes the Literature Association's festival for which he wrote a stage script for *Ragul bayna imra'tayn* (A Man Between Two Women), and readings at the Doctors' Club.

He writes about publishing in the same entry:

> I've put an enormous amount of effort into helping the magazine *Musamarat al-jayb* (Pocket Conversations). I published "Junun al-gharam" (The Madness of Love), "'Awdat al-gharib" (The Stranger's Return), "al-Hiqd" (Malice), etc., with them. The main thing is that I made LE30 in a single month from writing. This is the only time that I have had a literary income. I was writing for

al-Hilal for free so I stopped. Mustafa Bey Abdel Hadi also had me write for *Nidaa al-watan* for LE15. I think this is going to ruin things with *Musamarat* if it hasn't already. That's mainly what I've been up to, along with various articles in newspapers and magazines. These days I have pretty decent literary standing.

In January 1947 he writes:

Mamoun el-Shenawy published a poem I wrote in *Kilma wa-nuss* magazine. The poem is called "Ya's 'ala ka's" (A Glass Half Empty). Mahmoud al-Sharif put it to music and Umm Kulthum will perform it.

However, the income from his writing remained unpredictable, and Nagui continued to need to work the government job that he loathed:

Hassouna suggested I translate some stories, LE3 for each story. He gave me a book by Tolstoy called *Hadji Murat* which he wanted me to translate from the French. He said he'd give me LE20 for that! When I visited him I learned he was planning to snatch up Said Abdou from the magazine *Akher sa'a*. So I gave that up and I don't intend to ever go back. All of this literary business has failed to result in anything solid. I will put this aside—at least for now—because I can't seem to make a living from it.

In a Ramadan 1946 entry, he writes:

If I resign from government service I'll get LE22.5 as a pension. I've left *Musamarat al-jayb* where I made LE30 in a month plus the LE15 from Mustafa Bey Abdel Hadi who runs *Nidaa al-watan* along with the money for the translated stories, LE5 each. But is this going to last?

Nagui's entries on his literary endeavors demonstrate that it was not only an unsteady source of income, but indeed a financial drain on him.

104 *Journal de vie*

My grandfather describes his experience with the Literature Association, which he founded in 1945. He continued to chair its board until the organization folded in 1952. Wadie Filastin, deputy head of the board, wrote in his book on Nagui that he had wanted it to be a space for learning, to "refine the younger generation's tastes and guide them toward the sources of Arabic and Western thought, to give them a foot up in the field of literature, and to get people used to freedom of thought."[4] The association relied upon contributions from its members, "not to exceed 25 piasters per month," which was of course insufficient to sustain it. They were forced to find a cheaper office space to rent, and eventually found a place they could use free of charge. The association continued to move around between different locations in Shubra, Hada'iq al-Qobba, Sayeda Zainab, downtown Cairo, Giza, and Dokki.[5] Despite these troubles, the association lasted almost seven years at significant cost to my grandfather's health and meager income. He wrote, on 10 July 1948, during the early days of the association:

> The Literature Association has really worn me down, financially and physically. That is because of Abdel Hamid Shehata. He ran things badly when I was ill and I was forced to hold the association's reception myself at great personal cost. God only knows how exhausted I've been.

One of the most important literary episodes in my grandfather's diary is his 10 December 1946 entry about his trip to Palestine. This entry also gives a detailed impression of the cultural and literary scene in the region prior to the 1948 Palestine war:

> The British Council invited me to travel to Palestine. This brought about a welcome change in my state of mind—the trip was a great success. I flew for the first time in my life from al-Maza Airport on a morning the week before Eid al-Adha. It took two hours to get to Jerusalem, where the British Council's car was waiting for me. We drove to Jerusalem, where I met with Mr. Jardine and Mr. Livingstone.[6] I stayed at the Claridge Hotel.

Journal de vie

I did two broadcasts for the Jerusalem radio and was paid LE20, including LE10 for al-Atlal which was also broadcast in Egypt, where I think I made 150 piasters [. . .]

I lectured in Palestine in Jaffa, al-Khalil (Hebron), al-Nasira (Nazareth), and Haifa. I did radio broadcasts in Jerusalem and Jaffa. I spoke on the psychology of crime and directions in modern literature and both were great successes. Jardine told me that it was a "phenomenal" success but I was paid very little, only LE16. The British Council paid me. No doubt the most important part of the trip was Haifa. I saw Jacqueline and we had a very nice time. I gave a lecture at the Council and another at the Catholic Club. I met many poets including Wadie al-Bustani. We made up a poem for Jacqueline at an unforgettable literary gathering [. . .]

In Jaffa I stayed with Abdel Rahman al-Khamisi. He's married now and works for the radio. His life has settled down a bit [. . .]

The time in Jaffa was very memorable. I did a radio broadcast, gave a lecture in English in Tel Aviv at the Rotary Club, and in the evening spoke to the Muslim Brotherhood. Then we went to a musical concert as arranged by Mr. Clayton, the secretary of the British Council. We stayed up late with Amid al-Imam, Akram al-Khalidi, and the others and eventually went out to sit in a *qahwa*. Amid al-Imam told me that he was going to start publishing his newspaper again. He promised we'd do it together. I went to Amman by car and spoke at the al-Hussein Club. I didn't have the fortune of meeting King Abdullah although I'd composed a poem for him in case of such an encounter. I went back to Jerusalem and saw Prince Nayef's wife, so I read her the poem instead. Mustafa Wahbi [Tal] had written me to tell me she'd arrived.

My grandfather's account of his trip to Palestine comes near the end of his diary and differs from the other entries—here, he's keen to spell out all the details. It's apparent how important the trip was to him, proof he was becoming known throughout the region as a doctor-poet and intellectual, whatever the Egyptian Ministry of Endowments might think. It solidified his standing in the literary world as a pioneer of modern Arabic poetry, even if he only made about LE20 from the whole trip.

Nagui's account of this trip is also important because of his description of the various connections among literary figures in the region and how knowledge production circulated across regional borders in ways that would be impossible today. Looking back at these possibilities is both exhilarating and rather grim.

The British Council played a very prominent role in this story as the organization hosting my grandfather in Palestine and Jordan—the same role that Western cultural institutions continue to play in the Arab world today. This raises crucial questions about why my grandfather was invited in the first place. Was it because of his close ties with the British Council and British Institute in Egypt, where he had given an annual lecture at the Institute's Minya branch? Or was he invited as a Romantic poet who would steer clear of the political conflict? There is virtually no mention of politics in his diary—with the exception of a quick reference to changing prime ministers in Egypt—even though he was writing during a historic turning point in the region and world in the wake of World War II.

In any case, Nagui's careful documentation of his literary endeavors demonstrates that he was fully aware of his symbolic capital in the cultural field. These entries also capture how even "modern" poets continued to play very traditional roles, improvising poems in coffeeshops, competing against each other, and composing poetry for leaders and dignitaries.

Another topic Nagui covers in his diary are his many "small crimes," as he calls them, which earned him a reputation as a "vagabond" poet. Presumably these romantic exploits were related both to his floundering relationship with my grandmother and his rising star in the literary world. The protagonists of these stories generally remain unnamed—he mentions these women only by their initials except in specific cases. Due to the brevity of the entries, the nature of these alleged romantic infractions remains unclear, somewhere between interest, attraction, literary collegiality, friendship, and desire, which is to say it is not always clear if there is necessarily an actual liaison. In the case of "foreign women"—a term he uses for both non-Egyptian women (usually Syrian or Palestinian) and those belonging to religious or ethnic minorities (including Egyptian Jews and other Jewish communities in Egypt)—he writes their full first names: Germaine, Jacqueline, Falak, Henriette, etc. These women were not seen as part of the Egyptian bourgeoisie, which left them open to scandal (if there was anything to expose), should the diary fall into other hands. And sure enough, my aunt Do and I came along and tried to riddle out who these characters might be.

My perspective on Nagui's romantic escapades is very different than that of his daughters. My aunt had wanted to remove these "more personal sections" that could reflect negatively on him or on the family as a whole. My mother was likewise worried about including these stories in this book and kept asking me to "tone it down a little" or simply not to mention certain parts. But I found the material amusing. I was also honestly surprised that my grandfather had wanted to record these anecdotes even though they were cryptic fragments that fell short of full-on love stories or physical relationships. In most—and perhaps all—cases, they are just narcissistic reflections of how he wanted to see himself. I was taken aback that he saw these encounters as conquests, while also fashioning himself as a "modern" man writing on topics like "women and society" or "the psychology of women." At the same time, he was the father of three girls whom he raised to express themselves freely and make their own choices about their personal lives and futures.

I call my grandfather to task here in light of his own "modern" commitments and from a feminist perspective: What on earth were you up to?

What's the point of these stories? Why the constant need to prove his masculinity? Are these just desperate attempts to compensate for his diminishing virility as he grew older, especially given the constant specter of illness and the isolation of family life amid his financial and professional misfortunes? My grandfather describes his declining health in an early English entry from 13 August 1944:

Lost much wt - 4 ½ kilos! Tried afterwards to give up smoking, fed myself forcibly regained wt quickly. It is just ten years sharp now since I had that cough and loss of wt. Will never forget those times. Also stopped now sexual business—any. Seems to have let me down. Of course [with] the food, long irregular hours of reading, late hours, little sleep—what can be expected! Some days ago I had a terrible feeling of pessimism.

It indeed seems plausible that his "small crimes" aimed to make up for these challenges as his health declined. These women became "little morsels"[7] for Nagui, as Kamel al-Shenawy once described Nagui's numerous escapades.

But I also take a step back and think about the psychology of Arab modernity in relation to my grandfather—which is really a section my grandfather should have written, given how obsessed he was with psychology. We are witness to a festering modernity, to paraphrase what Algerian writer Waciny Laredj wrote about Lebanese-Palestinian feminist and writer May Ziadeh. Laredj's novel reflects on Ziadeh's ties with leading figures of modernism (including Taha Hussein, al-Aqqad, al-Rafi'i, and others). Although she initially hosted such men at her literary salon, they never treated her as an equal, and despite their claims of being modern, she remained the target of their masculine desires. I am very sorry to say my grandfather also fits into this mold. But I remind myself not to judge him too harshly—it's not my place.

Many of my friends who know I am writing this book imagine that I will reveal all my grandfather's romantic exploits, and magically produce definitive evidence about all his muses. But unfortunately, his diary will not live up to those expectations: It contains only quick sketches of various women who I never imagined had been part of his life.

Some of the more amusing, unusual, or daring entries caught my attention. For example, in Ramadan (July) 1948, Nagui writes:

About a year ago I met S. H., who I have mentioned before. We've kept up our acquaintance and I ventured to meet her again. She gave me everything. Last time we met in Helmiyya Palace. She was getting ready for her wedding and came in her dress. But we got cross with each other and had a difficult evening. Then she got sick and left to Alexandria.

This anecdote is melodramatic, but is also emblematic of deeper social contradictions. This girl (who was probably much younger than my grandfather if she was just about to be married) pursued him in her wedding dress, which is a quite daring infraction of social codes.

Then comes Falak, who appears on 5 March 1944, in a short entry written in English:

No news from Falak.

She appears again in late 1944 and early 1945, in an entry in Arabic:

Falak stayed with us for a while. Now's she gone and I don't know where she went. While she was here Samia got into a tizzy. It wasn't because of Falak, it was something that had been brewing for a while that came to a head that morning. That was because I deserted her in bed. I mean yes, I was fed up with her. Often I went out in the evening and came back to a darkened house—no one welcomed me home or listened to my aggrieved tales.

Naturally I asked my mother, "Mom, who was this Falak? The one who stayed with you, who Tettu was up in arms about." I read her the fragments from my grandfather's diary.

My mother remembered her and filled in the rest of the story. She said that my grandfather had come to the house with a young "Levantine" girl, who had stayed over for several days. Falak slept with my mother in her room and shared a bed with her, and he would bring Falak breakfast in his oldest daughter's room.

I think this young woman might have been Falak Tarzi (1912–1987), a Syrian writer who had come to Cairo. She later wrote about her trip to Egypt, and was known in literary circles in Syria and Egypt in the 1940s as a translator of French literature and a progressive writer especially regarding women's issues. Why did my grandfather invite her to stay with them when he knew this would provoke my grandmother's ire? Was he trying to retaliate against my grandmother for (allegedly) ignoring him? Although my mother remembered Falak, she didn't remember exactly who she was—my mother was not yet twelve at the time. She remembered the incident with Falak because it was unusual for their household and because my grandmother had been so furious.

Falak reappears in my grandfather's diary on 15 May 1945 in an entry in Arabic that alludes to the end of their brief story:

> Falak sent me a letter I have not yet responded to. What shall I say to her? She was lacking something. I'm more or less ready to move on.

My mother did not remember Germaine, Jacqueline, or any of the other protagonists of these stories, and the women referenced only by their initials remain even more obscure. Even in the case of Alia al-Towayyer, my mother found out who she was for the first time through the chapter in this book. Strangely enough, the diary contains none of the numerous self-proclaimed (or otherwise rumored) muses whose stories filled the papers and magazines. These characters all claimed Nagui had written them verses of poetry on the pages of his prescription book. All these stories started to circulate after the incredible success of the song "al-Atlal" in 1966. They all emerged at once, years after Nagui had died in 1953, and my mother and aunt had to handle this as best they could.

However, these other women, whether they are mentioned in the diary or not, played an important role in my grandfather's life. They filled a gap left by my grandmother, who had told him at the beginning of their relationship that love was in the heart. Some of these women wrote to Nagui for years, exchanged books or articles, attended his seminars, and came to hear his poetry, occasionally proclaiming their love for him or even declaring that they wanted to marry him.

It is difficult to follow even one of these stories properly because they are so opaque, and because there are so many different names and initials—especially since this was all seemingly happening at the same time! In the following entry, he provides one such list:

> Just a lot of emotion. Nothing worth mentioning. Jacqueline left—we had a misunderstanding. Then she came back and we had another quarrel. Finally we got together. Her love came first, and I put great hopes in it. I thought she did too. But things didn't go as we'd imagined.
>
> Henriette appeared again. It turns out she has a husband and children. He is Muslim but they say he's Jewish. May God curse her deception.
>
> Bahija is going to marry the doctor tomorrow. I look back at what I wrote about us and think: What a fool I was.
>
> Germaine sent a long letter a week ago and enclosed a photo of her husband. That photo pierced me like a dagger and I can't look at it. In her letter she wrote a lot about the two of them. Whenever I look at her letter I ask myself: Why did she send this? What was the point? Does she think she's kept her promise? A fool again.
>
> Farida showed up and then left again. The way she appears and disappears is very curious. She brought up the past and then slipped away, and became nothing but a faraway voice on the phone!
>
> Hakam came back too. She's studying for her matriculation exam and asked me to help her. I didn't think twice. I will visit her later on and provide my assistance.
>
> Z. J. – The syndicate held an opening for the new season and I saw Z. J. and recited part of al-Atlal for her.

To be honest, I am not particularly interested in chasing down all these unfinished stories. The important thing is that all of these brief anecdotes indicate he was in the midst of a real crisis. So many unfinished tales, in which it is often already clear that the relationship couldn't go anywhere.

His constantly-threatened masculinity is perhaps the source of all these would-be love affairs. Why did he come to this in middle age, as he began to become known as a literary star? Was this his way of cheering himself up from an unhappy married life? Or are these anecdotes indicative of certain kinds of social openness from someone who wanted to act the modern man and conduct himself outside the traditional institution of marriage? We might say that recording these fragments in his diary attests to the contradictions of a modern society conflicted about what should be public or private. Others might claim writing was therapeutic for Nagui. In the end, I can't reproach my grandfather—he kept his own diary as he saw fit. In any case, these entries provide a diverse sketch of human relationships in Egyptian society during the first half of the twentieth century.

By this time, the days of Houma and Souma were long over. With one exception, Nagui never uses any term of endearment for my grandmother in his diary. He merely calls her "Samia" or "the wife," often accompanied by some kind of biting remark, that she doesn't love or understand him, etc. He doesn't like coming home to a "darkened house" each evening, only to find her already asleep. This rift in their relationship is apparent from the beginning of his diary, following his sisters' accusation that my grandmother was having an affair with a distant relative.

He writes at the beginning of his diary on 5 March 1944 (in English):

The wife is fine. Eternal quarrel with my sisters. They accuse her of going with . . . It cannot be without basis. She likes him and she had times with him. I forgive her. God forgive me.

In an entry dated 15 April 1944, he writes, also in English:

Quarreled with wife to-day. She was nasty and sulky yesterday just because I said I got no enough [sic] money today. I had L.E.

20 to spare. I put them all under the service of her and the children. She is looking ? & forwards for a check of L.E. 70 in my pocket. Why should she not have it and squander it all?? That is what she's thinking of! They said she is *kharaba!* She is! She only thinks of her own points of view. Seems she deserves what bad luck she has met. Some of these scandals might be true. No crime without retribution. I have had mine but I have tried to aquit [sic] my conscience.

The love story between my grandmother and grandfather that my aunt and mother had always embraced was collapsing. My grandfather's romantic vision of life with my grandmother had faded under the brunt of financial pressures and divergent perspectives, dragged down by rumor and allegations on both sides, not to mention jealousy and spite.

Despite the marital strife depicted throughout the diary, my grandfather remains confined within the institution of marriage. We don't ever see him turning against it. He picks fights with it and flouts it—but he also stays the course.

Nagui's relationship with his daughters was one of the most important reasons that he remained married to my grandmother. His daughters show up often in his entries. He calls them his "flowers," and describes their studies and their health, as well as the expenses he foots to make them happy.

He writes on 15 May 1945, in Arabic:

My children! Amura the beautiful and delicate has grown up and blossomed, Douha is verse upon verse of brilliance, and Suna is sweet and lovely. I am so happy to see them before me every morning. Nothing is too much for them. I went back [to the job in the ministry] for them, I impoverish myself for them. I haven't saved anything because I spend everything I can to spoil them.

Nagui's stormy relationship with my grandmother temporarily grew calmer during his illness. He would later reconsider his

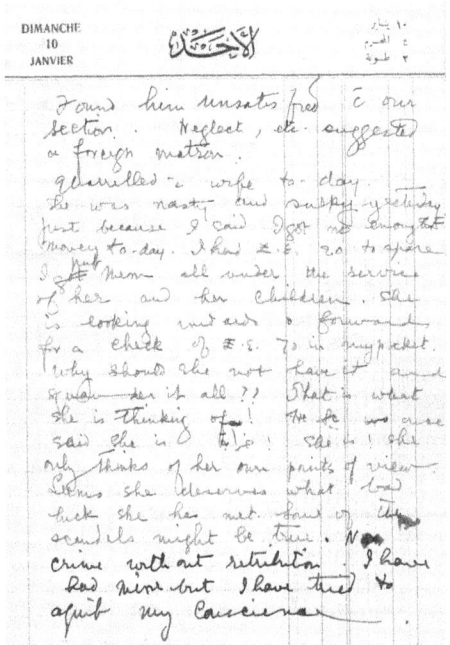

23. From Nagui's diary entry from 15 April 1944.

perspective on their relationship after she stood by him through his financial and health ordeals. He writes on 10 July 1948, the second-to-last entry before a very brief note in 1949:

> Samia has done me the greatest of services. She sat up with me when I was ill, and helped me financially with the children's expenses. I now rarely go out in the afternoon and I stay in with her. I've done her wrong in what I've said. She has a very kind side too. There is beauty that was hidden from me. That is why I had been distant before. But now I feel I love her very much and I really regret my harsh words.

Reading my grandfather's diary was a very important part of this journey for me. I confronted the legacy my mother and aunt had inherited and allowed myself to divulge what they had not wanted to reveal. I came to know Ibrahim Nagui the doctor, the intellectual, the man, the

Journal de vie 115

husband, and the father—for better and for worse. I began to understand some of the dimensions of my grandfather beyond the portrait that had once loomed over my life. The most pressing question for me after this intimate visit to my grandfather was: What do I do with this diary now? Do I donate it to a research archive—perhaps the Rare Books Library at AUC? Do such brief, opaque sketches really count as archival research material? Should I stick it back in the envelope that I inherited from my aunt, close it again, and put it in a drawer as Do had done? Or should I leave it to my son, who barely reads Arabic, to pass along to some future grandchild, as Dawheya's daughter Shahira had passed it on to me? If I did, who, perchance, might those future readers be, and what would they make of it? What countries would they live in, what languages—likely not Arabic—would they speak? Did my grandfather realize when he was writing these entries that we would find his diary and face this predicament: What shall we do with this *journal de vie*?

7

IBRAHIM NAGUI SUPERSTAR

7 April 1966

Good evening, ladies and gentlemen.

Greetings from Cairo to everyone listening tonight. Whenever I am in the studio at a moment like this, I find myself transported to the pulsating heart of Cairo, to Alexandria and Aswan; to Khartoum and Omdurman; to Sanaa and Taiz; to Oman and the south;[1] to Mecca and Riyadh; to Kuwait, Qatar, and Bahrain; to Baghdad and Mosul; to Damascus and Aleppo; to Beirut and Tripoli; to Amman and Jerusalem; to Gaza and Khan Younis and the stolen land; to Benghazi and the Tripoli of the west; to Tunis and Bizerte; to Constantine and Algiers; to Rabat and Casablanca—to all these far-flung cities across Africa and Asia, to the east and west, north and south, throughout this great nation, this homeland with its towns and villages, mountains and plains, valleys and deserts; to the denizens of hovels and palaces alike, to workers in the factories and the fields. We are all brought together tonight for an evening to remember, another one for the books, broadcast to you from Cairo, where all our hearts have gathered.

I said to myself: God, how boring. Is this a lecture on Arab nationalism or geography or what? Wasn't this supposed to be music? I sat alone in my room beside the radio with the door closed. I was eleven years old and listened to this long introduction with great foreboding, waiting for the important part:

> *Umm Kulthum sings to all of the Arab peoples in Egyptian ammiya. Although our dialects differ, millions have sung along. From time to time, Umm Kulthum chooses the most exceptional of poems, literary masterpieces—both traditional and contemporary—that unite all the Arab peoples in every region, and bring our luminaries in all their glory to the masses. Umm Kulthum sings about all that is good and true in this world: She has sung many religious songs, songs that express human faith in the Creator, songs that bolstered the ranks of the Arab nationalist struggle and raised its banner high. She sings to the human heart, besotted, and of the tortures and pleasures of love. Nothing is truly virtuous and noble until Umm Kulthum has blessed it with her voice.*

I said to myself: Okay, enough of this lesson already, let's get to the music! In the time that had already elapsed I could have listened to at least four songs by the Beatles or the Rolling Stones.

> *Tonight, ladies and gentlemen, we have a new performance of a new song by one of our poets, the late Dr. Ibrahim Nagui. The melody is composed, as you may not be surprised to hear, by the distinguished, reclusive musician Riad al-Sunbati, who dips deep inside his soul to bring to thousands of listeners Umm Kulthum's timeless masterpieces. It is no accident that tonight's composer is responsible for setting most of the poems that Umm Kulthum has previously performed to music.*

At last the announcer said my grandfather's name! But who was this Riad al-Sunbati? I felt another rush of apprehension. His name had an older ring to it, like the names of sheikhs and Qur'an-reciters.

I had been anxious about this evening for a while, ever since my mother had happily informed me that Umm Kulthum was going to perform my grandfather's poem. This was a disaster, as far as I was concerned.

My mother and aunt Do adored Umm Kulthum and learned all her songs by heart. They both had beautiful voices and would sing around the house with the radio on. We kids would get annoyed with all this mournful wailing and would beg them to stop the racket or sing more quietly. But they paid us no heed and went on singing. Umm Kulthum's songs continue to be heard around my mother's house today. Every morning, my eighty-seven-year-old mother sits in her chair in her room and sings along with great enthusiasm. This has persisted to such an extent that I am convinced Umm Kulthum has prolonged my mother's life, bringing her joy each day and reminding her of all that is beautiful in the world. My mother's voice resembles *al-Sitt*'s and when she was young, she used to put on performances of Umm Kulthum songs for family friends—and sometimes still does!—to a keen audience.

Yet sitting in my room that evening of 7 April 1966, I did not love Umm Kulthum—not the length of the songs, nor the gloomy lamentations, nor the endless repetition. I couldn't understand why the audience always demanded an encore. I had grown up with fast-paced Western music and upbeat love songs like Abdel Halim Hafiz. But Umm Kulthum I just could not understand: Why did she have that handkerchief in her hand? Why did she need so many other musicians in the little orchestra behind her? She'd fix them with her terrifying gaze and they'd go back and repeat the line again. I did not love Umm Kulthum—I was afraid of her. That was why it was such a nightmare when I found out she was going to sing my grandfather's poem. Indeed, as I listened, my worst fears came true.

The *al-Ahram* newspaper usually published the words to each of her new songs on the first Thursday of the month, the morning before the "star of the East" *(kawkab al-sharq)* would perform on the radio—and later, on TV. This meant her listeners and acolytes could learn the words, often by heart (as my mother did) before *al-Sitt* sang that evening. As far as I could tell, Umm Kulthum played no insignificant part in getting the audience to memorize the songs so fully, since she kept repeating each line until you really could not forget! The audience was always ready to sing along: practice makes perfect.

The first Thursday of each month, life stopped except for the voice of Umm Kulthum. A select few attended the actual concert, but every living creature who could watch the performance did—from the coffeeshops, streets, shops, and clubs, regardless of socioeconomic class or political affiliation. Bourgeois families like mine gathered in their homes with friends to stay up with *al-Sitt* until the early hours of the morning. Families would sing, discuss the performance, debate the merits of different songs, and decide which were their favorites.

I would breathe a sigh of relief when my mother told me that the first Thursday gathering was to be held at a friend's house and let out a groan when it was at ours. On this particular occasion, the festivities were of course held at our house. My mother was beside herself with joy. This was something she had never imagined: Umm Kulthum, the crowning glory of all Arab music, was going to sing one of her father's poems, thirteen years after his death. My grandfather had always hoped Umm Kulthum would sing one of his poems, but she never did during his lifetime.

My mother failed entirely to persuade me of the importance of this occasion, especially since Umm Kulthum (whom I did not like anyway) was going to sing a poem (written in formal Arabic, which meant that it was going to be impossible to understand, like my grandfather's poems in school). I was as nervous about facing my peers as my mother was eager to tell her friends about the occasion. I imagined my classmates taunting me mercilessly with what the radio announcer was now saying: "The poet Ibrahim Nagui, who excelled at smoldering sentiments of passion and yearning," who "gave a most delicate voice to lovers' hopes and sorrows."

I hid away from my family and their friends in my room to listen to the words of the song, which the announcer was now reading out:

The Ruins
by Ibrahim Nagui[2]

Oh heart! Ask not where love has wander'd to;
'Twas Fancy's labour then today all lost.
Drink us together to this ruined woo;

Tears have long remembered, heart retell,
How such a love a memory has become,
Among the tales of true adoration.

Seduced I was, so how can I forget.
A mouth so delicate, how sweet it breath'd.
Forget a hand which was stretch'd out to me
Across the waves to save my shipwreck'd soul?
A glitter driving high-soul'd men to thirst,
Where in thine eyes is now such glittering?

Your hiding place I have once visited.
I flew in longing singing my own pain.
With gracefulness you strode, benevolent;
How cruelly powerful and obstinate!
Compassion burns my chest; it yearns for you;
Instants consume my blood with wild fire.

Oh end my bondage! Set these poor wrists free
I gave you all; withheld nothing from thee,
Your chains oh how they cause my wrists to bleed!
Why should I cherish? You've forsaken me.
Why live on oaths and promises unkept?
World's arms are stretch'd out there inviting me.

Such an enchanting lover have I lost
Of rarest majesty and bashfulness.
In glory strides she so assuredly
Cruel beauty walks in mighty haughtiness.
Perfum'd bewitchingly like mountain breeze
With slumb'ring gaze as that of nightly dreams

Where can I hope to see you once again,
Sublime enchanting beauty so complete.
A loving, roaming heart do I possess,

A restless butterfly towards you draws.
Sweet messenger has Passion 'tween us sent,
Companion who to us presents the wine.

Has love e'er seen drunkards like us,
Around we spun our fancy, oh so well!
We walked along a path in moonlit nights,
Our happiness skipp'd on, we fell behind.
Our laughter rang like that of babes at play;
We raced ahead our shadows we outrun.

The morning came the choicest scents had gone
Conscious of time, would unconscious remained,
A wakefulness that swept away our dreams.
Night turned away and Night was our sole friend.
Gave way to Light who warned us and threatened.
A dawn upon us shone like fir'y blaze,
Once more we saw life empty as before;
Lovers depart each in a path, a maze.

Oh lover sleepless nights have slumber'd thee
Remembrance of the oath awaketh you.
As soon as one wound healeth gradually,
Old wounds, old pains reopen painfully.
So now learn thee oh heart how to forget;
Erase old memories, learn but that art.

Oh dearest one we're in the hands of Fate,
Our stars foretold we'd be unfortunate.
Perhaps one day our destinies shall meet,
Sometime when no reunion is decreed.
Till one ignores the other when we meet,
As strangers unfamiliar, cold receit.
Depart we then, and each pursue his path;
We wanted not but fate desireth.

It was just as I had feared. I had no idea what half the words meant. And why was it so long? This was going to take all night to sing!

The orchestral introduction began—lugubriously slow and monotonous. Why so depressing? And it lasted more than a quarter of an hour. When was it going to actually start?

Finally, *al-Sitt* began to sing, to much cheering and applause. Very grim. I knew that Sunbati name could not bode well! Was this even music?

My mother came to my room to make sure I was listening, and found me crying. She couldn't understand why I felt so distant from everything. She was giddy with the song and the evening and didn't stay with me long. She went and found Uncle Nabih, a family friend, who along with his wife was a regular part of our Umm Kulthum gatherings. My mother knew that I liked him—he was the father of my closest friend at the time, and he was open-minded and understanding to his daughters. My mother thought he was a positive influence and might be a helpful third party in this situation—maybe he could help me stop crying. Uncle Nabih tried to convince me that this was a fabulous song, that my grandfather was fabulously creative, and that Umm Kulthum was absolutely stunning, but I kept on crying. So he just said to me, "You don't have to understand it now. You'll understand later, and when you understand, you'll love it too."

God bless his soul—how right he was.

"Al-Atlal" quickly became one of Umm Kulthum's most famous songs, and a cornerstone of her performances to support the war effort after the 1967 defeat against Israel. Viewers marveled at Umm Kulthum's unprecedented performance in November 1967 in Paris before an enormous audience, and then in Morocco, Tunisia, and elsewhere across the Arab world. Suddenly my grandfather too was thrust into the spotlight, the many avenues of his life overshadowed by this single point of fame. For better or for worse, from that moment on, he became "the poet of al-Atlal."

Newspapers and magazines flocked to interview my mother and aunt Dawheya. Meanwhile, they began their battle with the newly-declared "muses," who filled the pages of these publications, wanting their share of the glory and claiming that "al-Atlal" had been written for them. Some of these women would apologize to my mother and aunt for tales the press had concocted. My mother became close friends with Yvonne Madi, the daughter of Zuzu Madi (one of the "Zuzus"—the various women who had allegedly inspired "al-Atlal"). My aunt also developed a wonderful friendship, later cut short by ill fortune, with the late TV broadcaster Salwa Hegazi, who had covered Umm Kulthum's concert at L'Olympia Theater in Paris. Salwa Hegazi and Dawheya shared an interest in writing French poetry. My aunt also met Jehan Sadat, who had included some of Nagui's work in her master's thesis on how the English Romantic poet Percy Bysshe Shelley had influenced Egyptian poetry.

"Al-Atlal" became Nagui's bestselling work, and after the song became well-known, his poetry collections were republished in Cairo and Beirut. Poems erroneously attributed to Nagui were circulated in his name, either by accident or to capitalize on his fame. The stage was set, and everyone had to perform their part. As for me, I would begin to make my own peace with "al-Atlal" after I became more open to matters of love once I grew a few years older.

24. Dawheya Nagui with Jehan Sadat (right); Dawheya and the late TV broadcaster Salwa Hegazi (left).

Some readers might be aware that the version of "al-Atlal" that Umm Kulthum performed is not the same as the original poem that Nagui wrote. The song is actually a significantly abbreviated mix of two poems, "al-Atlal" (The Ruins) and "al-Wada'" (The Farewell), although it primarily draws upon the former poem of the same name. Nagui had hoped his whole life that Umm Kulthum would perform those words. According to my mother, Umm Kulthum always replied, "Your poetry isn't the kind that can be sung, Nagui." In many ways, she was right: Nagui did not write poetry with music in mind, as is very evident from the poem "al-Atlal" itself. The original poem is vast, consisting of a total of 134 verses—far too long to be sung, and also extremely flowery and repetitive. Such repetition can work fine in a written poem but would be nearly impossible to reasonably fit within the parameters of vocal performance. Umm Kulthum concerts usually involved two or three long songs, but nothing of this length. Hence my grandfather died with his wish unfulfilled.

It has been said that Umm Kulthum wanted to "reconcile" with my grandfather after his death and therefore decided to perform one of his poems. That seems strange to me—why would she have wanted to reach out to him thirteen years after his passing? I find this version of events unconvincing and I think that another story is more likely: Umm Kulthum's choice of "al-Atlal" marked a return to more classical love poetry (*qasa'id*) in her work after a period in which she had sung in ammiya with more contemporary melodies as part of the modernization of her image and expansion of her audience. In 1965, she had just sung "Amal hayati" ("Hope of My Life," with words by Ahmed Shafiq Kamel) and "Enta el-hubb" ("You are Love," with words by Ahmed Ramy and music composed by Mohammed Abdel Wahab). The same year she also sang "Ba'id 'anak" ("Far From You," written by Mamoun el-Shenawy, with music by Baligh Hamdi). Umm Kulthum chose "al-Atlal" because it was written in more classical Arabic, in order to showcase the full scope of her vocal capabilities.

But why did Umm Kulthum choose "al-Atlal" in particular? There are also several different tales about how this came to pass. One story goes that Umm Kulthum asked the journalist Kamal al-Mallakh to form a committee to choose a poem for her to sing. I don't know if this story is true, but it doesn't necessarily make sense that she would have chosen a journalist for this task, even a prominent one whom she knew well. Another explanation appears in an eponymous TV series on Umm Kulthum's life. In the twentieth episode, Umm Kulthum, played by the actress Sabreen, and Ahmed Ramy, played by Kamal Abu Raya, sit down together in the *salon* of her home. He takes a handwritten page out of his pocket, and when she asks him what it is, he tells her it's Ibrahim Nagui's poem "al-Atlal," which he found in an old chest in his house. He begins to read the beginning of the poem to her and Umm Kulthum runs to call Riad al-Sunbati (played by Ayman Azab) to come hear the poem. This is also a pretty improbable tale, since "al-Atlal" had been in public circulation since the mid-1940s after it was published serially by Ahmed al-Sawi Muhammad in his *Majallati*, beginning with the 9 May 1937 issue of the magazine. It had also been published serially in *al-Risala* magazine starting with the 13 October 1941 issue. The poem was then published in full in 1950 in Nagui's second collection, *Cairo Nights*. Nagui had also given readings of the poem on various occasions, including on Egyptian and Palestinian radio, as he recorded in his diary. So, it is not plausible that the poem was discovered later in an old chest.

However, Ahmed Ramy (1892–1981) did indeed play a crucial role in choosing "al-Atlal" and adapting the original into verses to be sung. Ramy was among Nagui's closest friends and was one of the few who also knew the family well, such that my mother and aunt called him "Uncle Ramy." My mother said that Ramy, who was about six years older than my grandfather, used to affectionately call Nagui *ya waladi* ("my boy").

After my grandfather passed away, Ahmed Ramy wrote a eulogy for him:

> Last February, before death snatched Dr. Ibrahim Nagui away from us, the distinguished *al-Hilal* asked me [to write about] the friend I most depend upon and with whom I would hope to live out the rest of my days. Immediately I thought of my friend Ibrahim Nagui because he was the model of a good and loyal man [...]
>
> I [first] had the opportunity to meet him at a gathering. I heard someone calling out his name and I got up. I looked at him and he looked at me, and thus did our two souls meet ... my soul, which became lost at the edges of his imagination, which cried with him

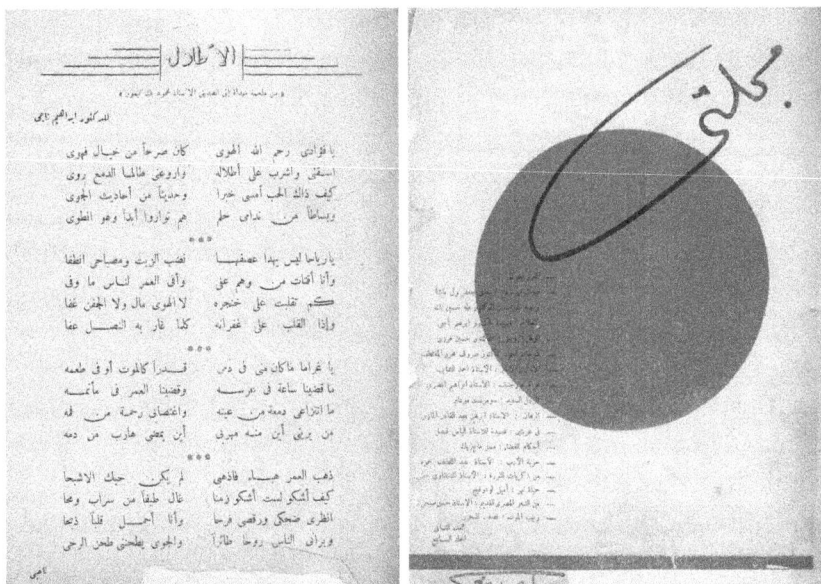

25. The first page of "al-Atlal" as published in *Majallati* magazine, 1937, and the cover of that issue of the magazine. Images courtesy of Sayed Mahmoud.

over his tragedies, and which joined him in song, and his soul, my twin, looking at me. In that moment, my soul was not sure which body it inhabited.

Ramy's deep understanding of Nagui at both the poetic and existential level meant that he was particularly well-equipped to intercede on his behalf with Umm Kulthum. Ramy was also very close to Umm Kulthum, for whom he prepared more than 147 poems and songs that she performed over the years, and was attuned to particular inclinations and capabilities. Ramy was very familiar with Nagui's poetry and had been a member of the committee formed by the Ministry of Culture and National Guidance to produce a collection of Nagui's work in 1960 (even if the committee encountered some difficulties in performing the task it was assigned). It was a trio—Umm Kulthum, Ramy, and Nagui—destined for success. The fourth member of this undertaking was Riad al-Sunbati, the unfortunate target of my childhood skepticism.

Ibrahim Nagui Superstar   127

Ramy's remaking of "al-Atlal" was based on his precise knowledge of the ins and outs of the poem and his great attachment to and faith in the edifice he was building. I imagine my grandfather sitting with Ramy—his soul's twin, as the eulogy put it—, choosing together the verses that Umm Kulthum would sing, looking through the other poems for stanzas that could fit with the verses that they had chosen, and eventually settling on adding in parts of Nagui's *al-Wada'*. I can see them deciding where to fit those stanzas in, and then turning to the even more delicate matter of poetic word choice (*lafz*), and touching up some of the verses so that they were ready to be sung. Then they would have showed it to *al-Sitt*, who gave it her blessing. "Al-Wada'" was also sung in full in 1954 by Nagat Ali, with music composed by Mohammed Fawzy, about a year after Nagui's death. It's a shame that, although both of these poems were well-known during Nagui's lifetime, it was only posthumously that Ramy undertook the labor of recasting "al-Atlal" for its second life off the page.

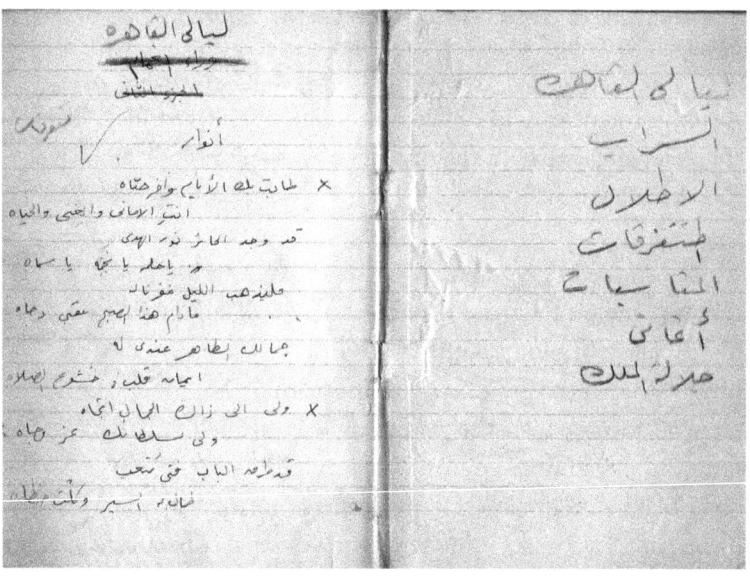

26. The first page of Nagui's notebook of poetry drafts.

In the second envelope that my aunt Dawheya inherited was an old lecture notebook containing handwritten drafts of poems. The 126-page notebook—which originally cost 10 piasters, according to the front cover—is still in remarkably good shape, considering it is more than eighty years old. These drafts likely date back to the early 1930s, although Nagui's second collection, *Cairo Nights*, was not published until about fifteen years later, in 1950. It seems from the first page that Nagui had intended to title his second collection *Behind the Clouds: Part 2* as a continuation of his first 1934 collection, and then crossed out this title (as is evident in the image of the first page of his notebook of poetry drafts) and changed it to *Cairo Nights*. The right side of the first page is also the inside cover of the notebook, and lists the titles of some of the poems that later appear in his 1950 collection.

It is clear that these drafts span more than ten years of writing and rewriting. They contain some handwritten verses that Nagui penned after a car accident in England in 1934 in which he broke his leg. He composed this poem—titled "al-Ruju'" (Going Back) in the notebook, although it was renamed "al-Ma'ab" (Heading Home) in his *Cairo Nights*—as the return boat from England approached the harbor in Port Said:

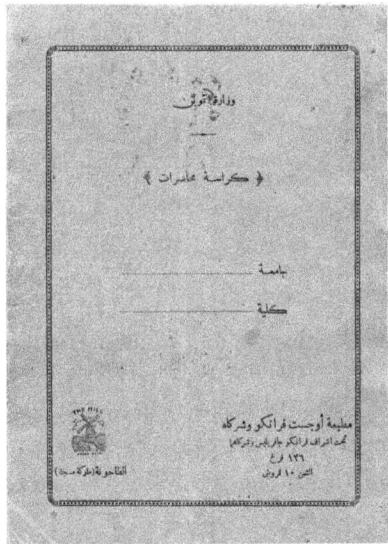

27. Nagui's draft notebook, containing some poems from his 1950 collection *Cairo Nights*.

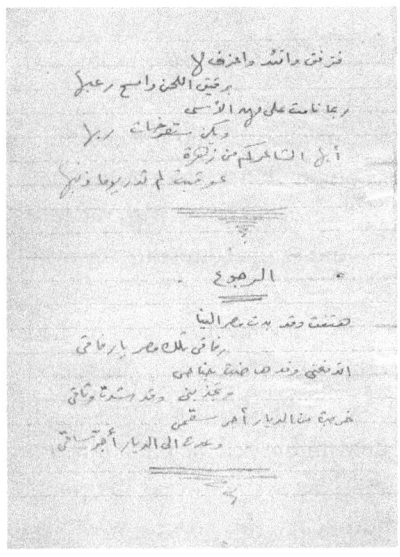

28. The verses that Nagui titled "al-Ruju'" (Going Back), which would later grow into the poem "al-Maab" (Heading Home) in his collection *Cairo Nights*.

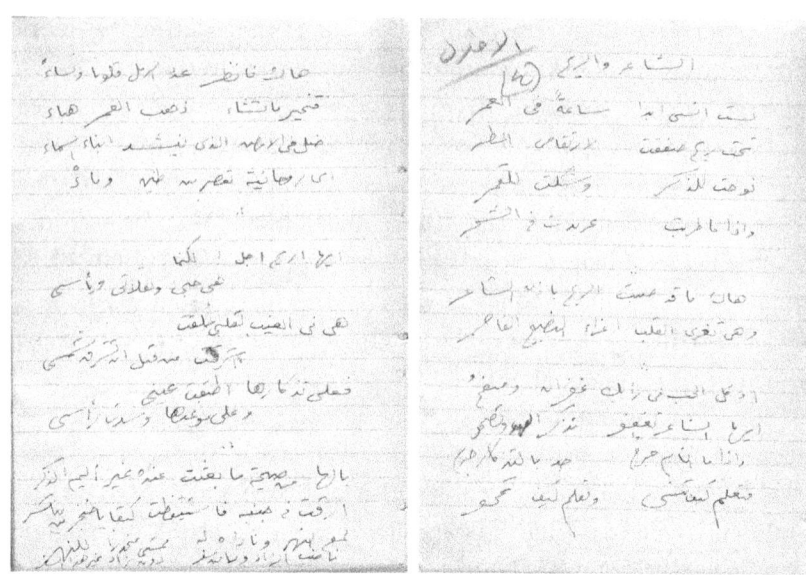

29. "The Poet and the Wind," the first section of "al-Atlal" in the draft notebook, labelled part IV since this section appears later in the sequence of verses in the full poem.

> I called out as Egypt came into view
> Look, my friends—Egypt!
> She gave me flight when my wings broke
> and pulled me free as my shackles grew tight
> I departed home with my miseries in tow
> And returned towing my own leg.

As luck would have it, I also found drafts of "al-Atlal" in this notebook! This was a fortuitous surprise because I discovered that these drafts did not entirely align with the "original" version of the poem published in his collection. These drafts provide a window on how Nagui composed his poetry, or at least one model for how he approached the process with his longer poems.

"Al-Atlal" appears in fragments throughout the notebook, its stanzas interspersed with parts of other poems. There are pages titled "al-Atlal," "al-Atlal II," and "al-Atlal III," handwritten so elegantly as to suggest these sections were copied from earlier drafts in other, no

30. The first page of the third section of "al-Atlal" in the draft notebook, labelled part V in the sequence of verses for the full poem.

longer extant notebooks. There are also sections written in a different, harried handwriting that more closely resembles that of his diary, with titles including "The Poet and the Wind" or "The Ruins: A Dialogue Between the Poet and his Demons." The various drafts of sections of "al-Atlal" do not appear chronologically in the notebook, but they are all numbered (I, II, III, etc.) according to where they would appear in the version of the poem that Nagui was preparing for *Cairo Nights*.[3]

The first part of the draft notebook is titled "The Poet and the Wind" (which Nagui labels "al-Atlal IV," since these stanzas actually appear later on in the published sequence of verses). This poem also works conceptually as a stand-alone *qasida*. In this section, the wind addresses the poet and pours into his ear "the enticements of its shameless counsel," reminding him of wounds that have never healed, and mocking his naivete in matters of the heart. The wind cautions that only those who are lost search for heavenly creatures, and derides his poetic endeavors ("for what heavens are wrung out of mud and water?"). The poet doggedly tries to respond to these accusations and describes his beloved and his devotion to her. Still, the wind's commentary leaves him raw, with "dagger shards" in his side. The poet hastens to the river's call, "provisions spent for the one road requir'ng none."

Nagui later made some changes to these verses for the final version, with regard to both stanza and word order. When Ahmed Ramy prepared the song for Umm Kulthum, he also replaced the word "poet" with "lover" in the line "Oh poet sleepless nights have slumber'd thee." Nagui also omitted eight verses from his original draft in the later version of the poem published in *Cairo Nights*, although he kept the famous verses which would eventually become part of the song, too:

> Oh dearest one we're in the hands of Fate,
> Our starts foretold we'd be unfortunate.
> Perhaps one day our destinies shall meet,
> Sometime when no reunion is decreed.
> Till one ignores the other when we meet,
> As strangers unfamiliar, cold receit.
> Depart we then, and each pursue his path
> We wanted not but fate desireth.

The last two lines were changed twice during these revisions. Originally they read, "Left we then, and each pursue the path/We never wanted, but faith desireth." This was changed by Nagui to become "Each pursued their path/Say nothing! But that faith desireth" in the version published in his collection, and then modified a second time by Ahmed Ramy to become the version in the song.

Among other changes as these drafts were revised into the poem and then transformed into the song was Ramy's omission of line 60 of the poem ("In nervous anticipation of the sound of footsteps"), which appears in both the published version and the draft of the poem. Meanwhile, verses 72 and 73 of the published poem are nowhere to be found in the draft notebook! Perhaps Nagui added them later from some other lost draft. There are also three additional final lines in the published poem (lines 77 to 80), which significantly magnify the poet's sense of despair.

It is also worth noting that the section that comes at the beginning of the published poem is missing here—verses 1–12—the first three of which also appear in the song in a slightly modified form. These were evidently derived from other lost drafts. In sum, Nagui had embarked on an immensely long and complex process of reworking draft upon draft of the poem that would later become the song that Umm Kulthum performed. In these many iterations of "al-Atlal," we see a different face of Nagui. Here, he belabors the process of composing and recomposing various segments of those 134 lines over an entire decade—a far cry from the popular image of the doctor-poet who could churn out verses for passersby as readily as he wrote prescriptions.

Finding these earlier drafts reminded me of an earlier stage of my own journey towards my grandfather when I was a master's student at AUC. In 1978, more than ten years after Umm Kulthum sang "al-Atlal," I was in my first year of a graduate program in English literature. At that time, there was a young American professor named Michael Beard teaching in the department at AUC. He was a great poet and guitarist and was obsessed with Bob Dylan. Michael was also a very capable translator and academic, and more importantly, a friend to his students. He invited his students over to his house to meet his small family and joined in our student gatherings. We therefore endeavored to be very studious in his classes, and he was kind and patient when we sometimes stumbled along the way.

Michael was the first to teach a translation studies seminar at AUC in 1978, a field we had not heard of before. This was also my first course in this field; I would later become the director of the Center for Translation Studies at AUC. I often think of my former professor when I am teaching or choosing from among theoretical texts that he originally taught us. I thank him for expanding my horizons in how I approach translation.

Michael (who preferred his students call him by his first name) had split this particular course into two parts: We read and discussed theoretical texts but also applied the theories we studied to a text of our choice, which we would translate into English.

At this point in my life, I was in my early twenties and had made my peace with Umm Kulthum, "al-Atlal," and many of her other songs. For my translation, I wanted to take on an ambitious project and decided that I would translate "al-Atlal" (the song) into English. I felt significant trepidation about embarking on this endeavor but I think that I wanted to be able to give the English text to my professor, who liked Arabic music and was just beginning to study the language. The translation was an enormous challenge for me and turned into much more than a course assignment. Michael Beard, without realizing it, became the first person to introduce me to my grandfather beyond the parameters of the portrait in my family home.

The process of translating "al-Atlal" required a huge amount of energy and time in getting to know the text, and my grandfather, more closely. I decided to challenge myself to translate the song with a certain rhyme and meter in English. I would also keep track as I translated of the choices I had made and the various steps of the translation process. First, I produced a very literal translation of the song. I listened dozens of times and learned it by heart until it inhabited me. Then I wrote my paper with a little background history on Nagui, the differences between the poem and the song, and also more background on how the song was written in very formal Arabic and used tropes from classical poetry, including the trope of stopping (and weeping) at the ruins. "Al-Atlal" is also written using one of sixteen Arabic classical meters. In Arabic poetry, meter is referred to as a *bahr* (literally, "sea"), and Nagui uses a simple metrical pattern known as *bahr al-raml* ("the sea of sand") in many of his poems. The poem does not have a consistent rhyme; the rhyming patterns shift every four verses. These general features of the poem helped me to decide how to translate the song into English.

In our translation studies class, we also learned that the translator can never reproduce the original text exactly, and that successful translation requires finding parallel tools in the target language and culture. As translators, we have to make informed decisions in carrying over the text and think flexibly about the new life that the text will take on in the host language.

In English, I wanted to use a rhyme and meter that could capture some of the cadence of the original—keeping in mind I was actually translating the song, and wanted to evoke some of al-Sunbati's music, which I could hear as I read. I drew upon the kind of early modern English one might associate with Shakespeare, and used iambic pentameter that felt similar to the *bahr al-raml* in the Arabic. I remember that in my paper for the class I also discussed the recurring but variable rhyme scheme I had used, as in the original, as well as word choice and imagery, and what I felt had been lost in translation. Unfortunately, although I am usually very good about keeping papers, I lost this particular project. I remember that Michael loved it and I still have a copy of the translation itself.

In 2010, thirty years after I translated "al-Atlal," and the year after I had founded the Center for Translation Studies at AUC in 2009, I decided to offer a seminar similar to the one that Michael Beard had taught back in 1978. This seminar, entitled "Translation Studies: Theory and Practice," drew upon various theoretical approaches to translation that Michael had taught us, as well as other developments and approaches to the field that had emerged during the intervening decades. I suddenly remembered my translation of "al-Atlal." I hunted for the three typewritten pages among the papers I'd kept as I moved between different homes in Egypt and the US: my family's home in Zamalek, the apartments I lived in as a student in Los Angeles, Tettu's house, where I lived when I came back to Egypt, then my family's house in Zamalek again, my apartment in Ithaca, New York, when I was working at Cornell, the apartment in Dokki once I came back to Cairo to work at AUC, and then the three other homes that I have since moved between within Zamalek.

I decided to use my own translation as part of the "translation in practice" component in the seminar I was teaching. In 1993, my former professor Ferial Ghazoul (who also keeps meticulous records!) had also sent me a full English translation of "al-Atlal"—all 134 verses of the original poem—which had been published in *al-Ahram Weekly* on the fortieth anniversary of my grandfather's death. It had been translated into English by Wadie Kirolos, and had been published in two parts in the 18 March and 25 March 1993 issues of the *Weekly*, since it was such a long poem.[4] This translation stayed closer to the literal meaning of the original, without translating the meter and rhyme, and used less archaic English. I thought these two translations might provide a framework for examining the different choices the translators had made, i.e., my approach to translating the song, and Kirolos's approach to translating the original poem.

For comparison, here are the lines of the first stanza of the poem translated by Wadie Kirolos and of the song, in my translation:

Oh heart! Ask not where love has wander'd to (SM)
Oh my heart, may God have mercy on our love (WK)[5]

'Twas Fancy's labour then today all lost (SM)
It was an edifice of illusions destined to collapse (WK)

Drink us together to this ruined woo (SM)
Let us drink over its ruins, and as long as tears (WK)

Tears have long remembered, heart retell (SM)
Continue gushing, you may recount on my behalf (WK)

How such love a memory has become (SM)
How our love became yesterday's news (WK)

Among the tales of true adoration (SM)
Mere talk of a tortured attachment (WK)

The song also would develop a fraught political afterlife that my grandfather, the so-called "delicate and sensitive poet," could never have imagined. Excerpts from the song appeared in this context in various works of literature during the 1960s, particularly in the wake of political detentions and torture during the Nasser era.

One famous story about the song appears in a book written by the late journalist Mustafa Amin called *Masa'il shakhsiyya* (Personal Affairs), which was published in 1984 by *Akhbar al-yom*. In the book, Amin tells the tale of how he came to know "al-Atlal" when he was imprisoned in the mid-1960s by Gamal Abdel Nasser; his assets were also confiscated. Mustafa Amin was very close to Umm Kulthum, who made every effort to get him released but was unable to do so. Amin explains in the book that he was summoned from his cell in the maximum-security prison Liman Tora when Dr. Abdel Qader Ismail, one of the top prison doctors at the time, asked to examine him in his clinic one Thursday. When Amin lay down on the examination table, the doctor whispered in his ear, "Umm Kulthum says to listen on Thursday, she's going to sing a poem with a few choice lines especially for you." That Thursday in 1966 was Umm Kulthum's first performance of "al-Atlal," to which Mustafa Amin dutifully listened, waiting for those auspicious lines. Amin writes:

> Suddenly I heard Umm Kulthum singing: "Give me my freedom, untie my hands! . . ."
> I sprung up from my bed when I heard those verses. I felt like Umm Kulthum was singing to me alone, that she was raising up my captive voice. She sang what I wanted to tell the whole world.
>
> It was as if Umm Kulthum had sent me a missive that had burst through the prison walls, shattered the walls of my cell, and broken my shackles and chains.
>
> Her voice stayed with me long after she sang those words, resounding from inside, whether or not I had a radio or record handy.[6]

The political afterlife of these verses also found its way into Ahdaf Soueif's epic first novel *In the Eye of the Sun*, written in English and published in 1992 by Bloomsbury in London. The novel's protagonist, Asya, who is a teenager at this point in the novel, recalls President Gamal Abdel Nasser attending an Umm Kulthum concert held in Festival Hall at Cairo University in 1966, during which Umm Kulthum sings "al-Atlal." Asya describes Nasser's arrival in the hall surrounded by guards and the media. The enormous crowd applauds and rises to its feet. Nasser turns around to greet the audience and then sits down. Umm Kulthum stands before them in a gray dentelle dress, holding her signature handkerchief in her hand. Asya is astounded by this enthusiastic welcome for the president and a voice in her head wonders about his policies of oppression and torture. But another voice enumerates Nasser's many accomplishments: liberating the country from colonial powers, nationalizing the Suez Canal, building the High Dam, undertaking agricultural reform. She tells herself that perhaps Nasser might not have known much about those repressive policies. As Umm Kulthum starts to sing, Ahdaf Soueif (through Asya's voice as narrator) translates several excerpts from "al-Atlal." This deliberately literal approach to translation, which we see throughout the novel, is intended to be disorienting for English readers. She begins:

> O my heart do not ask where is love,
> It was a fort of my imagination—and it fell.
> Let's drink together over its ruins
> Let's drink and let my tears slake my thirst—
>
> My yearning for you burns into my side
> And the seconds are live coals in my blood.
>
> Give me my freedom! Let loose my hands!
> I have given you my all and held back nothing.
> I ache with your bonds drawing blood from my wrists
> Why do I hold on to them when they have availed me nothing?
> Why do I hold on to vows you have broken
> And this pain of imprisonment when the world is mine?

Asya describes how the audience hesitates when Umm Kulthum performs these lines in front of Nasser, unsure how he will respond. The teenage Asya is impressed by how "audacious" Umm Kulthum is to sing these verses, even if "al-Atlal" is only a love song. In the end, Nasser applauds *al-Sitt*, the tension dissipates, and the audience cheers for more.[7]

I was several years older than Asya when I sat down to translate "al-Atlal" as a student at AUC. More than ten years had passed since this moment that Ahdaf Soueif's novel imagines in Festival Hall at Cairo University. For most of those years, my mother had been at the helm of the Nagui family, since her youngest sister Mahasen had died and Dawheya had emigrated, and my grandmother had recently passed away. Thus my mother became the official spokesperson for the family for all the media inquiries from radio, television, or newspapers that bombarded the family on Ibrahim Nagui's birthday, or the anniversary of his death.

When I translated "al-Atlal," my mother seized the opportunity to have me assist with these responsibilities. Although I had always strongly resisted, this time my pride let me finally concede to my mother's request: perhaps I could share a little of the spotlight. As it turned out, on this occasion my mother had been invited by the late TV broadcaster Amany Nashed to her popular program *Azizi al-mushahid* ("Dear Viewer") in March of that year, on the anniversary of my grandfather's death. For once, my mother didn't have to beg me; in fact, I was looking forward to being a guest on the show.

I remember how I picked out my outfit very carefully and looked over the translated text, running through all the questions that she might ask in my head. I practiced in front of the mirror over and over since we had been told it would be done live on air. On the day of the interview, my mother and I went to the Maspero television building. My mother had insisted firmly to the production team that I should be able to accompany her, and that Amany Nashed would be the first to report the news: Here was Ibrahim Nagui's eldest granddaughter and she had translated "al-Atlal" into English.

I felt a mix of terror and self-importance as we arrived at the studio. We sat waiting for our segment in the program. Then Amany Nashed came over to greet us and we took our seats: she in the middle, my mother on the left, and I on the right. I noticed that Amany Nashed did not look quite the same in real life as she did on television and I began to feel nervous that I too might look different on camera.

I searched at length for a recording of this program before writing this chapter, with the assistance of various friends, especially the journalist and critic Sayed Mahmoud and journalist Asmaa Ibrahim, but unfortunately we did not find anything. I had hoped to be able to more fully recall the galling details of this interview, which, rather than launching me into stardom, continue to haunt me until this day.

Amany Nashed treated me like a schoolgirl, even though I was already a graduate student. She affected the sweet voice people use when talking to a child, and asked me superficial questions even though I'd prepared as if I were about to defend my dissertation live on air. She barely spoke to me and talked primarily with my mother, asking the usual questions about Nagui the father, Nagui the husband, Nagui the doctor, etc. My mother gave the same responses she always did. She took my spotlight and I just sat there listening to those rehearsed answers I already knew by heart. I remember vividly how furious I was, waiting impatiently to vent all my anger to my mother, who had gotten me into this mess. I blamed myself for accepting the invitation, and waited as the ordeal under those infernal camera lights stretched on. My mother had elbowed me into the program, and so of course they had said yes, but in truth they had no interest in me at all.

Amany Nashed bid us farewell after the segment and we were escorted out of the studio by one of her staff. Before we could go, they asked us to wait a few minutes while they got the set compensation together. They insisted on keeping to procedure, even though my mother was entirely opposed to the idea. Finally, we were told to go to the cashier's office, where the man behind the counter handed us a receipt to sign, so we did. Then he handed us each LE5 through the little window! We left the money on the counter and took off feeling deeply insulted. My mother had never been offered monetary compensation for an interview before, and already considered this a great personal affront, even though she had been happy with the program itself. As for me, I was beside myself with fury, which my mother of course had to bear the brunt of. I didn't wait until we got home to make my feelings known but immediately set upon her while we were still in the taxi: "That is the first and last time you will ever ask me to speak about my grandfather!"

"Al-Atlal" had driven a wedge between me and my grandfather in the 1960s when Umm Kulthum first performed the song. I thought that my translation might help bring us together, but then along came Amany Nashed and sent us our separate ways again. Ibrahim Nagui remained the distant superstar, while I put my translation away in a drawer and with it any hopes to share his spotlight.

8

MY FRIEND SHAKESPEARE

My grandfather published an article entitled "Books that Shaped Me," on 16 February 1953 in the newspaper al-Gomhour al-Misri, a little less than a month before his death. In this article, Nagui writes at length about Charles Dickens, whose *Oliver Twist* and *David Copperfield* had been the two most important books of his childhood. He also pays tribute to prominent Lebanese poet and translator Khalil Mutran's collection *Diwan al-Khalil*. Mutran, a close friend of my great-grandfather Ahmed Nagui, had run the Apollo literary group after poet Ahmed Shawqi passed away. Ibrahim Nagui also sings the praises of Anatole France's "La Bûche" (The Yule Log)[1] and Paul Bourget's *The Disciple*—the story that Nagui had read with Alia al-Towayyer after teaching himself French. Finally, my grandfather pays his respects to Shakespeare, whom he calls his "beloved friend."

In this article, my grandfather tells a rather amusing story that captures some crucial elements of his ties to Shakespeare:

> Ten years ago, I was invited to give a lecture in Minya. When the time came, I realized I'd forgotten about it and hadn't prepared anything. I tried to write something on the train, but dozed off and only jotted down a few words that I couldn't make sense of later . . . When the lecture was about to begin, the head of the [British] Institute asked for a copy of my speech. I ruefully

informed him that I had only a few lines ready. The color drained from his face and he didn't say anything more. When he introduced me to the audience, he informed them of the truth: I'd forgotten to prepare my lecture.

It was a large audience—many were keen to hear the lecture that day, especially since some of them had heard of me before. I was unsure what to say, how to apologize. Finally, I turned to the crowd that had assembled and said: This was not a lapse on my part—I chose not to write about Shakespeare, because he's a friend of mine, a beloved friend. Since I am intimately familiar with his work and know every word he has written, it wouldn't be fitting for me to read to you from a prepared speech. I began to speak off the top of my head and just kept going. As I plowed on, the British director first looked aghast. But I finished to resounding applause and the fellow who had invited me rushed onto the stage to embrace me, lauding "the Egyptian who knew Shakespeare so well!"[2]

This is the same lecture Nagui recalled in his *Journal de vie* as a great success. He'd taken it upon himself to travel south to Minya as part of the Institute's assiduous efforts to promote British culture as widely as possible. Looking back, it's unclear whether he would have lectured in English or Arabic. I think he would probably have spoken in English because the head of the institute was able to understand and respond to the speech.

The eager crowd that day had heard of the literary prowess of this physician from Cairo, whose reputation had preceded him to Minya. Who would have come to hear my grandfather's lecture in English on Shakespeare in the mid-1940s and applaud so enthusiastically? What was the social makeup of that crowd in Minya in the first half of the twentieth century? These were important questions, but there was another I had decided to answer first: How did my grandfather become so closely acquainted with Shakespeare?

Nagui describes in "Books that Shaped Me" how this lifelong attachment began in school. He writes:

> Students hated being assigned [Shakespeare] to read—they memorized extracts against their will. But I liked memorizing and acting out his plays. For the baccalaureate exam at the end of high school, I memorized *Hamlet*. I recited it as if I were on stage. When my turn came for the oral exam, the British examiner asked me, "So what did you memorize?" "*Hamlet*," I said. "You may begin," he said. So I stood up to recite. I began to perform and forgot myself, and the examiner did too and lost track of the time—until with a start he suddenly noticed his watch. A whole hour had passed and there were people standing outside waiting and wondering why it was taking so long to test one student.
>
> Finally, the examiner looked at me and said: "Wasn't this supposed to be your baccalaureate exam? Very well done, go on now."
>
> Later I would read the rest of Shakespeare's work ... and began to give frequent lectures.[3]

This friendship began in my grandfather's youth and lasted through the end of his days. There are other anecdotes like this that often appear in writings about Nagui. This particular anecdote makes clear that Shakespeare and English literature were integral to school curricula, even in Egyptian national schools like the Tawfiqiyya School in Shubra that Nagui attended. Students were forced to memorize long extracts from Shakespeare, even if they couldn't relate to the cultural context or decipher early modern English. This colonial legacy continues to haunt private English-language schools in Egypt today, where students are still required to memorize long extracts from Shakespeare's plays.

The way that my grandfather's peers recoiled from Shakespeare reminds me of my own resistance to the Arabic assignments that I was given in school, when we too were asked to memorize without understanding. But unlike most of his peers, my grandfather had loved Shakespeare and learned his plays by heart, acting out the characters. I imagine my grandfather had been keen to learn this in school because he had already been exposed to English literature as well as classical and modern Arabic poetry at home from a young age, because of his father's expansive knowledge and library. Nagui was steeped in English literature and classical and modern Arabic poetry alike, and composed the first verses of his own at age thirteen. He also had an exceptional memory. All of this helped him feel closer to Shakespeare than his peers did.

It's interesting that Nagui had chosen *Hamlet* in particular to memorize for that exam, when he was not yet twenty. Was that why he took a particular interest in the young prince? Or was it because he'd always had a penchant for the more tragic side of literature, starting with Dickens? Did Nagui identify with Hamlet's pain about Ophelia because of his own anguished love story with Alia al-Towayyer? His youthful affinity with Hamlet later grew into an extensive study of Hamlet's character in Nagui's book *Kayfa tafham al-nas?* (How to Understand People), published by al-Maktab al-Thaqafi al-Dawli. The book is undated but was most likely published in 1945, based on the copy that Nagui gave to Wadie Filastin on 15 December 1945 (according to the book's inscription). That copy was then given to Hassan Tawfiq, the compiler of Nagui's complete prose and poetry works, and published in 2010 by Egypt's Supreme Council of Culture.[4]

How to Understand People contains various articles on psychology that Nagui wrote in Arabic, including one article entitled "The Oedipus Complex or the Psychology of Hamlet." Nagui writes:

> Prince Hamlet seems like an exemplary prince: sophisticated and refined, with all the usual qualities one might look for, as well as being a philosopher who appreciated music and the arts, a man with a shrewd understanding of human nature. When the curtain rises, we learn that he's finished his studies and that he's around thirty years old. These two points—his sophistication and his age—are of particular note. Hamlet becomes bitter about the world around him, and this vindictiveness casts a shadow over his character. Thus Hamlet's discontent begins to take restless directions.[5]

Nagui likely wrote this article in the early 1940s, when he had already lived more than a quarter-century in Hamlet's company. He'd memorized the play for his baccalaureate exam when he was, by his own reckoning, younger than Shakespeare's character, and continued to be preoccupied with the prince for years to come. Nagui eventually tried to psychoanalyze Hamlet near the end of his life—to understand *Hamlet*, but perhaps also to understand Shakespeare and to better understand himself. The Hamlet sketched above—an embittered man of letters—closely resembles Nagui. My grandfather, deeply discontented with the professional and cultural worlds he inhabited, endured his own internal psychological torments, even if his specific circumstances were quite different.

Nagui, influenced by Freud, read Hamlet's character as a reflection of Shakespeare's own psychology. He also saw himself pursuing a similar calling as the Bard, probing the depths of the human psyche through both poetry and prose. He extolled Shakespeare's "unique understanding of the human condition, which distinguished him from any other writer—past, present, or future."[6] Nagui drew parallels between Shakespeare and Hamlet, but also personally identified with both the Bard and the prince of Denmark on multiple levels.

My grandfather's teenage attachment to the prince of Denmark's story eventually developed into awe for Shakespeare as the quintessential symbol of the English Renaissance. Nagui was particularly interested in the Renaissance's focus on the forces within the individual mind and soul, which marked a departure from earlier ways of thinking.

In his article, Nagui examines the progression of other legends and literary works over the centuries that provided the inspiration for Shakespeare's Hamlet. Nagui makes reference to a similar hero featured in the work of sixteenth-century French writer François de Belleforest, and another in a play sometimes attributed to the English writer Thomas Kyd. He goes on to examine various critical approaches to *Hamlet*, from Johann Wolfgang von Goethe, to eighteenth-century French criticism, to Freud's interpretation that the prince of Denmark suffered from hysteria. Nagui concludes by explaining what made Shakespeare's *Hamlet* timeless, and celebrates the Bard's "master-stroke" in producing a play with dual resonance in literature and psychology alike:

Shakespeare was the first scholar of the psyche, which enabled him to deeply ponder the capacities and desires of the human spirit. He did so before Freud and his disciples, before psychoanalysis, because of his creative genius. Hamlet was more than a puzzle to unravel. For Shakespeare, Hamlet represented human nature in all its hidden intricacies, all its nooks and crannies. He delves into the recesses of the soul [. . .] If the earlier Hamlets savagely plotted murder without any pangs of conscience, Shakespeare's [Hamlet] is a considered man. In grappling with the question of revenge, the most significant obstacles Hamlet faces come from within—the entire tragedy is an internal affair.[7]

If *Hamlet* marked a shift in the dramatization of the inner workings of the psyche, Nagui also read the play as depicting certain turning points in Shakespeare's own life:[8]

[*Hamlet*] captures a moment in Shakespeare's life when he was shifting from a light-hearted, comedic Shakespeare to a darker, gloomier self. Shakespeare did not divulge in any other play what he laid bare in *Hamlet*. A look at Shakespeare's life suggests that *Hamlet* was written shortly after his father's death, and after his lover Mary Fitton betrayed him and left London for good. Mary Fitton—the "Dark Lady" of Shakespeare's sonnets—led him to be harsh on women in *Hamlet*. In the play, Shakespeare gives us a deceitful mother and superficial lover without any sense of self. Like all geniuses, Shakespeare was a sensitive soul. His own disappointments in love were etched upon his heart—and powerfully embodied in *Hamlet*.[9]

It is easy to see how Nagui, with his own troubled first love, found this reading of *Hamlet*—and of Shakespeare—appealing. For Nagui, Shakespeare wasn't only a friend; this was also a healing, therapeutic relationship. Reading and memorizing Shakespeare, and later translating nearly all of his sonnets, offered my grandfather a kind of creative catharsis.

When I told my mother this chapter was going to be called "My Friend Shakespeare," she didn't insist I read it to her, as I'd done with the previous chapters. She figured it would be "boring" and require too much concentration. So I spared her and found someone else to read this chapter to: my son Nadim, who only knew his great-grandfather through that photo on the wall of the family *salon*. This book became an opportunity for them to get to know each other and to introduce him to more of his family history as well.

The entire world came to a stop under lockdown as the COVID-19 pandemic began in January 2020. By March, Nadim was under lockdown in a little town in northern Scotland, while I was under lockdown in Cairo. We both endured long and solitary evenings. I suggested to Nadim that I could read him chapters of the book from afar. I'd send him a copy of the chapter in Arabic and then read to him so he could follow along with the written text. Nadim, who went to French schools in Cairo, never systematically studied Arabic in his formal education. He studied standard Arabic at home at various points over the years with Ustaz Mostafa, a kind and patient teacher who answered Nadim's endless questions and endured his resistance to the textbook *Selah al-telmeez* (The Pupil's Weapon). Despite years of these sessions, Nadim did not fully learn to read or write standard Arabic.

I read these chapters to Nadim, explaining some sections of the text, and translating others into English or French for him as we read. Nadim began to get to know his great-grandfather through these reading sessions and was open to continuing until we reached the eighth chapter.

I read the beginning of this chapter to him. By that time, he had come back to Egypt on a plane for Egyptians who had been stranded abroad during the initial lockdown. Nadim was very critical of how Nagui described Shakespeare. "What's this? It's so over the top, how Shakespeare is this timeless genius? As if he were a god or something." Why, Nadim wondered, did Nagui revere Shakespeare in this way? Why wasn't he more critical? Didn't he realize that Shakespeare's works were promoted by the British Empire as part of its imperial cultural facade in its (former) colonies?

I began to tell Nadim about how Nagui and his contemporaries saw themselves as literary modernizers and reformers building on the Arabic *nahda*. I explained to him that his critical perspective had formed long after his great-grandfather's time, and that Nagui's generation had not seen engaging with Western thought as an admission of intellectual inferiority. They saw themselves as approaching their literary endeavors as equal peers, brought up as they were by foreign teachers in national schools and universities, reading Western books in the original languages, and translating many of these works into Arabic. I told Nadim that we needed to situate these figures and moments in their historical context in order to understand them fully.

As I tried to justify why Nagui's generation had approached these questions differently, I was well aware that I was also defending myself and my generation. We were also the children of empire, reproducing that culture, all of us, friends of Shakespeare. Despite the emergence of postcolonial studies and critiques of Orientalism, we grew up studying Shakespeare in the same way my grandfather had, and I imagine this is still a problem in some Egyptian schools today.

We used to read abridged stories based on Shakespeare plays in school—as students still do today in similar schools—so that we'd get to know the plot and characters. When we got a little older, we'd be taught the full plays alongside lengthy explications to help make sense of the early modern English. Eventually we could read the plays without further aids and then we too had to memorize long extracts to recite in front of the class. At AUC, there were multiple English literature courses devoted solely to Shakespeare's works, which were also performed in the university theater. How could we not become lifelong friends of Shakespeare?

I told Nadim about my own experience with Shakespeare in school, specifically my affinity with the character Portia in *The Merchant of Venice*—"Porshia" as we said in our English classes, or بورسيا ("Porsia"), as Khalil Mutran transliterated the name in his Arabic translation of the play, favoring something closer to the Italian pronunciation. Not unlike my grandfather's relationship with Hamlet, I was captivated in school by Portia's wisdom, her ability to plead her case—disguised as a male lawyer—and most of all, her famous "quality of mercy" speech. I have always found this to be one of the most eloquent appeals to mercy and her words have stayed with me throughout my life:

> The quality of mercy is not strain'd.
> It droppeth as the gentle rain from heaven
> Upon the place beneath: It is twice blest;
> It blesseth him that gives and him that takes:
> 'Tis mightiest is the mightiest: it becomes
> The throned monarch better than his crown.
> His sceptre shows the force of temporal power,
> The attribute to awe and majesty,
> Wherein doth sit the dread and fear of kings;
> But mercy is above this sceptred sway;
> It is enthroned in the hearts of kings;
> It is an attribute to God Himself;
> And earthly power doth then show likest God's
> Where mercy seasons justice

As I went through Khalil Mutran's lengthy introduction to his Arabic translation of *The Merchant of Venice*, I could see he wrote about Shakespeare in the same way as my grandfather. Or more accurately, it was my grandfather who echoed Mutran's adulation of Shakespeare. Mutran's translation of the play was published in 1922, when my grandfather was in his early twenties, still a student enamored of Hamlet. Mutran writes:

> Whichever sources Shakespeare had drawn upon for inspiration for his plays, this unrivaled poet of the human nature conferred upon these tales his own genius of language and spirit, rendering them as universal masterpieces, far beyond the domain of everyday tales and stories.[10]

This is the same kind of language Nagui later employed. In other words, my grandfather did not have a unique obsession with

Shakespeare: this was typical of his day. Among the *nahda* generation of cultural reformers, Shakespeare was always placed on that pedestal.

Nagui's relationship with Mutran was just as important to him as his friendship with the Bard. Mutran was central to Nagui's developing poetic and cultural consciousness, and Nagui paid tribute to him and his book *Diwan al-Khalil* in his article "Books that Shaped Me":

> Khalil Mutran was a dear friend of my father and my late cousin Abdel Hadi al-Guindi. They were fond of spending their summers together in the al-Max neighborhood of Alexandria. I asked my father about why Mutran loved this place in particular, and he told me a great deal had happened near the boulder at sea at al-Max. Then he read me his legendary poem, "al-Masa'" [Evening]. I ventured to ask for a copy of *Diwan al-Khalil* and learned it was out of print, and that the only copy was in Abdel Hadi's library. So my cousin lent me this copy on the condition that I read and learn the poetry well [. . .] I don't know if I fulfilled my promise but I did memorize the whole book. As time passed I got to know Mutran better, and began to call him uncle. But people in Egypt forget quickly, and he wasn't well known during his final years. We were talking about this in his presence one day at a friend's house. Mutran was ill—he looked haggard and troubled. I tried to cheer him up and began to recite his poetry, starting at the beginning of that collection. Time passed and people were listening most attentively, rapt. When I'd finished reciting most of the poems, Mutran began to weep and rose to thank me, and told me he could now die happy.[11]

The relationship between Mutran and Nagui was more than that of teacher and pupil. They were also both founding members of the Apollo Group of poets, initially established by Ahmed Zaki Abu Shadi (1892–1955) in 1932, and which produced the *Apollo* magazine for just over two years. The group was first led by Ahmed Shawqi, "Prince of Poets," and then by Khalil Mutran. The group attracted a wide range of writers and poets from Egypt and other Arab countries, including

Ibrahim Nagui and a number of other leading Romantic poets: Ahmed Kamel al-Kayyali, Mostafa al-Rafi'i, Ali Mahmoud Taha, Hassan Kamel al-Serafy, and Saleh Gawdat, among others. The *Apollo* magazine became a forum for many poets, writers, and critics in Egypt and beyond. These included Shawqi, Mutran, al-Aqqad, and al-Rafi'i, as well as Ahmed Muharram, Zaki Mubarak, Mohamed al-Asmar, Ibrahim Nagui, Abdel Hamid al-Deeb, Sayyid Qutb, Mohamed Abd al-Mu'ti al-Hamshari, Mahmoud Ghunaym, the Tunisian poet Aboul-Qacem Echebbi, Iraqi poet Muhammad Mahdi al-Jawhari, Sudanese poet al-Tijani Yusuf Bashir, and Lebanese poet Elia Abu Madi, among others. Nagui's relationship with Mutran grew closer through the group and magazine, as well as through poetry readings.

I gave Nadim another example of how later interpretations of Shakespeare's work differed from his great-grandfather Nagui's approach. In Nagui's article on Hamlet and the Oedipus complex, it's clear that he understood the so-called "Dark Lady" of some of Shakespeare's sonnets to be a real woman in the playwright's life. Nagui unequivocally identifies this figure as Mary Fitton, whose affections were purportedly split between Shakespeare and Earl William Herbert, the English politician and nobleman who also founded Oxford's Pembroke College. It has also been alleged that some of Shakespeare's sonnets are dedicated to Herbert. This theory about Mary Fitton as the "Dark Lady" fell apart under closer scrutiny from various Shakespeare critics. Some argued the sonnets made reference to various other women, while other scholars contended that there was no such lady, and still others examined why some of the sonnets used a male pronoun. But in the 1940s, my grandfather took it for granted that the sonnets were written to Mary Fitton.

I am not a Shakespeare scholar, so after I had quickly read through some of these interpretations of his works, the authorship debates, etc., I called up my former classmate and now colleague at AUC, the late Mahmoud El Lozy, a professor of theater. Mahmoud and I had taken the same seminar on Shakespeare together back when we were students at AUC. I said to him, "Why didn't anyone raise these issues then?" We had a long discussion about what it meant to dissect and dismantle Shakespeare's work. Finally, Mahmoud said to me, "You know, the important thing is that we have the texts." We would remain friends of Shakespeare, come what may.

I turn now to my grandfather's translations of the sonnets and reread my aunt Dawheya's introduction to Nagui's unpublished translations. As discussed in chapter 3, Do did not originally realize what these "unmetered poems" were, or why there were numbers at the top of each page, but as she puzzled through the lines, she eventually found a sheet with the inscription "from Shakespeare to his love." She carefully checked each numbered Arabic page against the original English sonnet, and realized she had "stumbled upon a treasure."

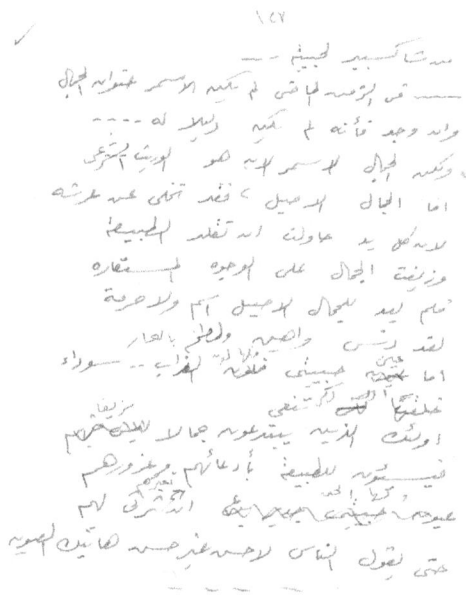

31. Nagui's translation of Shakespeare's Sonnet 127.

Do was seventeen when Nagui died. She had studied at the French lycée in Heliopolis and just started at the American University in Cairo. Do had been a voracious reader since she was little: She loved art and literature, and wrote and learned poetry by heart. Fortunately, she was the one who had inherited these inscrutable documents from her father, since my mother and her sister Mahasen were not necessarily as keen to delve into such texts.

Like her father, Do was fond of Shakespeare. She had read his plays and sonnets in English and attended productions of Shakespeare plays at AUC in English, and in national theaters, translated into Arabic. She says in the introduction that she was not aware she had inherited translations of the sonnets until four years after her father died, when she was still a student at AUC. Ibrahim Nagui had a different relationship with Dawheya than he had with her sisters because of their shared love of poetry and literature. He once wrote Dawheya a poem:

> O you who asked for poetry, here's one for you
> And all my love to my soul, *Dawheyati*
> Shall I elaborate when so much in one word is contained
> But poetry is the rose proffered—here's my flower, my verse
> Poetry is the meadow in full summer's fragrance
> Carried down to us from heaven's own perfumes
> And you are the loveliest garden of charms
> Shall a garden bestow its eloquence on another?
> This is for you, dearest daughter
> Most beloved of my heart
> A keepsake from your adoring father entrusted
> If you cherish this, that's all I ask
> For these verses are like paintings—if one day my ink
> Should fade, this vestige shall remain.

Do describes her attachment to poetry and Shakespeare in an interview with Egyptian journalist and television presenter Mufid Fawzy in 1999 at her home in New Jersey, which was later published in the weekly periodical *al-'Alam al-yom* on 31 May 1999. She explains:

> I inherited [Nagui's] love of literature, especially poetry. When I was thirteen, he enticed me to read Shakespeare even though I was at a French school. He said it was good to learn many languages. He taught me to read serious poetry before bed.

He'd recite the sonnets aloud for me so that I could hear their cadence and then wrote them out for me on the page. I'd wake up and hear his voice and listen.

Based on this interview, Nagui would have been "enticing" Dawheya to read Shakespeare at the same time that he was endeavoring to translate the sonnets. In an August 1944 diary entry in English, he wrote that he had signed a contract with Dar al-Nahda to translate Shakespeare's sonnets:

Wrote a contract with the Nahda [publishing house] for the translation of Shakespearean sonnets and "Venus and Adonis" for L.E. 70. Not started anything yet. When shall I?

Nagui later began the translation, which became—as he explains in "Books that Shaped Me"—a healing balm during his various health crises and setbacks. He died leaving this legacy scattered and incomplete, perplexing his daughter for many years to come.

Although Nagui's surviving translations reached her in this enigmatic form, Do was luckily very attentive to detail. She excelled at school and was a model of precision and order in her professional life. When her daughter Shahira and I were cleaning out her apartment in California after she died, we were amazed by how carefully she had kept her personal papers, water and electric bills, and taxes.

Do had decided to not work directly with the original documents she'd inherited from her father, whether the *Journal de vie* or the Shakespearean sonnets, in order to better preserve the texts. After the envelopes had finished their cross-continental tour first with Do, and then with me, through our various stages of life, I had found a photocopy inside of all the original manuscripts. I also found the notebook in which my aunt had transcribed the original English sonnets by hand to match Nagui's translations. Her handwriting was neat and elegant, and each sonnet was clearly numbered at the top of the page. I imagine she wrote them out like this in order to get to know the sonnets better herself before publishing the side-by-side translation.

Do held back for years on publishing—first because she'd realized Nagui's translation was incomplete, and then because she had married and emigrated to the US. She became caught up in her professional and family life, and had been reluctant to either fill in the remaining translations herself or to proceed with publishing the partial set. She writes in the introduction:

> There were forty sonnets total missing from the collection. I hesitated over this for a while, and wasn't sure what to do in order to come up with the missing translations. Sonnets 1–20 were missing, as well as Sonnets 51–59 and 143–154. I kept the manuscript and didn't do anything with it, because I felt that it couldn't be published without those forty sonnets.

Over the course of this long journey with the unfinished translations into Arabic, Do finally decided she would translate the missing sonnets. She explains that she tried to translate them but quickly changed her mind and opted to publish them as they were, deferring to her father's skill:

> In the end I decided against [translating myself] because Nagui's translation was exquisite, and my translation would not have been as good, no matter how hard I tried. [. . .]
>
> I hope that the reader will forgive me for not bringing the sonnets to light for such a very long time, first because I was young and inexperienced, and then because I was in the US and far removed from our literary world. I hope all of these reasons, which have prevented me from publishing this work until now, provide sufficient explanation for this delay.

But she still did not do it! She did not translate the remaining sonnets, nor did she publish Nagui's translations as they were. Yet she clearly had intended to: the introduction she wrote is proof of that. Do likely wrote her introduction in the late 1990s, based on another interview she gave in *al-Ahram al-Adabi* on 18 April 1995. In the interview, she discussed how she might publish her father's diary after redacting certain sections. She also spoke about publishing the translations of the Shakespearean sonnets in a separate book. The following week she sent *al-Ahram al-Adabi* three of the sonnets in Nagui's translation for an upcoming issue. However, due to space limitations for Sameh Karim's 25 April 1995 article "Tarjamat Nagui li-qasa'id Shakespeare al-ghina'iyyat: li-madha lam tunshar hatta al-an?" (Nagui's Translation of Shakespeare's Sonnets: Why Haven't They Been Published Before?), only a single line from each sonnet was included with the article.

The late Hassan Tawfiq undertook the enormous task of compiling and editing the complete prose and poetry works of Ibrahim Nagui—a tremendous labor of love. The collected prose works were published in Doha in 2001 at his own expense, and then by the Supreme Council of Culture (within the Egyptian Ministry of Culture) in 2010. In the introduction to the second volume of Nagui's complete prose works, Tawfiq tells the story of the three truncated sonnets:[12]

> I learned that Sameh Karim had received a fax from Ms. Dawheya Ibrahim Nagui. Sameh Karim was kind enough to get me a copy of the fax. Ms. Dawheya had sent the full translation of each of the three sonnets but since space was tight, Sameh Karim had decided to only publish the first lines of each sonnet. But I was able to access the full text from that fax [. . .]
>
> I should mention here that I have spoken on the phone with Ms. Dawheya Ibrahim Nagui several times. She is in New Jersey in the United States and I wrote to her in hopes that she would send me her father Dr. Ibrahim Nagui's translations of Shakespeare's sonnets. She apologized that she could not send them because she wanted to publish them in a separate book, after translating the sonnets that her father had not already translated himself.[13]

My aunt Dawheya was always a scrupulous guardian of the treasure that had fallen into her hands. She kept it hidden from the world's eyes, promising the journalists and scholars who pressed her that she'd share it later. But Do passed away leaving that envelope sealed shut until it fell into my hands. Although she'd decided not to translate the remaining sonnets, she wrote an unpublished introduction that reflected her deep attachment to the texts and their author. Do writes:

> I have been told that the beauty of these sonnets lies in their unmatched cadence, wit, and wisdom, that these are some of the most profound verses ever to be written. They are also among the most-read and oft-quoted poems in the world, and many authors have drawn upon the sonnets for the titles of their own works. The sonnets brim with profoundly personal emotions, and have often been the subject of critical analysis from those hoping to unearth more of their author's personal life [. . .]
>
> Over the centuries, many writers have tried to find out the truth of Shakespeare's personal life, to uncover the story of that handsome aristocratic young man and the mysterious lady who had inspired his sonnets.
>
> Others have argued that these sonnets might not have been drawn from Shakespeare's own life at all, and that this monumental poet conjured this wellspring of emotion from his own source and from his profound knowledge of human feeling.

Dawheya had read Shakespeare criticism from the 1990s by the time she wrote that introduction to Nagui's unpublished translations, which my grandfather had originally penned in the 1940s. Do had only the highest of praises for Shakespeare in her introduction, and was equally effusive about her father. But the important thing here is that Hassan Tawfiq was able to obtain the three sonnets from my aunt Dawheya's fax to Sameh Karim. These were sonnets 58, 92, and 116. Tawfiq also discovered that Sonnet 2 had been published in *al-Kitab* magazine (in its May 1953 issue), as he writes in his introduction to the complete prose works, and so these four sonnets became part of Nagui's published work.

As I was writing this book, my mother was following the terrifying news about COVID-19 and the growing number of deaths from the virus, including among our close friends.

"Aren't you done writing yet?"

"No, not yet, mom."

"Why are you writing all this? Who's going to read this book? Everyone is dead now anyways."

We both laughed, because laughter shielded us from the disastrous news coming in daily. I told her I was taking my time in writing precisely because of this. I began this chapter as COVID-19 began to spread in Egypt, and now it was the third week of June 2020 and I still hadn't finished the chapter yet. Sometimes it felt like what I was doing was pointless, but mostly I felt very grateful to my grandfather and Shakespeare and my aunt, who had whisked me away from the daily realities of the pandemic. I thought to myself: Here I am, doing what my grandfather did when he translated the sonnets. He also worked on the sonnets over long stretches of time, turning to this work during health crises and in moments of adversity. Nagui writes:

> The years passed and I grew old. As I was stricken with various illnesses and crises, I prescribed myself Shakespearean sonnets to read [. . .] I'd entertain myself with translating. Before I'd even finished, my body and soul were clear of all illness, and I was transported back to my youth [. . .] [thanks to] my friend Shakespeare.[14]

Perhaps writing this book as the COVID-19 pandemic spread throughout the world has been a similar process for me.

My aunt had initially struggled to identify the sonnets because, unlike my grandfather's other papers, they were not written in a notebook or planner, only on loose sheets—which is perhaps why some of them were lost, including the first twenty sonnets. Why would he start with Sonnet 21? Since Hassan Tawfiq later discovered that Sonnet 2 had in fact been translated and published in *al-Kitab* magazine, this suggests—as Dawheya had also supposed—that the first twenty translations had once existed. There are no such clues about the fate of Sonnets 51–59 and 143–154, but it does not seem that he omitted them originally. Nagui must have completed the full set in order to look back on a time "before I'd even finished," as he writes in the above passage.

32. Shakespeare's Sonnets 37 and 70 in Dawheya Nagui's handwriting and Ibrahim Nagui's handwritten drafts of an Arabic translation.

If Nagui had indeed finished the translation of the sonnets, one might ask why he didn't publish them himself. A quick look at the remaining papers provides an answer: the translated texts are handwritten in a way that indicates they were a draft and not a final copy. Many of the sonnets have sections and lines crossed out, with corrections added above or below the line. Nagui was evidently still mulling over the optimal translation. He had produced multiple drafts of "al-Atlal," first in a rushed handwriting, and then in a more polished script as he recopied the poem, changing certain details here and there. With the sonnets, Nagui did not reach this latter stage of the process—at least in the manuscript that I have.

Furthermore, since Nagui saw himself in a didactic role as a *nahdawi* translator, he would certainly have wanted to write an introduction and thorough study of the translated texts and to elaborate on his choices as a translator.

Nagui had previously translated poems from Charles Baudelaire's 1857 collection *Les Fleurs du mal (The Flowers of Evil)*. The book had caused an uproar in France upon publication and some of the poems were banned. Baudelaire was consequently fined 300 francs for "offending public morals." Nevertheless, he became a central figure of the French Symbolist movement, and *Les Fleurs du mal* was recognized as one of the most important works of poetic modernism.

Nagui's translation of this collection included an introduction and detailed study of Baudelaire and his life, a psychoanalysis of his character, and a critical reading of his work, which drew incisive connections between his life, milieu, and poetry. This introduction is quite similar to Nagui's reflections on Hamlet: Here he also applies the Oedipus complex to Baudelaire's work, and considers the latter's potential sadomasochistic tendencies. Nagui writes:

> Many of [Baudelaire's] contemporaries loved and related to him, and read him. This is because he was openly miserable, without any hypocrisy or duplicity. He described the wretchedness of this age in the most frank and honest terms, with all its iniquities and bare remnants of religious precept, and the futility of seeking to

rebuild the edifice of virtue. It is a portrait of the modern psyche—fraught, repressed, disturbed in every way. We read him to listen to his grievances, for these are the cries of every weeping man. And who among us does not weep or feel such pain? [. . .]

Why has our present century now turned back to this poet? Why have today's literati exhumed his grave and given his name new life?[15]

Nagui's answer to this question is that Baudelaire's star continued to grow because "his poetry served the needs of the modern age." That was also what Nagui aspired to do as a modernist poet, and his translation of Baudelaire was in pursuit of that aim.

Baudelaire was sometimes called the "last of the Romantics," because of how he developed and revitalized poetic forms like the sonnet, which he frequently employed in *Les Fleurs du mal*. The collection was bold in its choice of topics and in its interplay of the mystical and the tangible, the romantic and the symbolic. Nagui called Baudelaire a "first-rate poet . . . the cadence of his verses is unparalleled and his word choice is marvelous . . . it runs right off the tongue."[16] Nagui's translation similarly endeavored to modernize the host culture of Baudelaire's poetry, i.e., Arab culture.

Les Fleurs du mal contains Baudelaire's most famous work—a total of 163 poems. Of these, Nagui translated about fifty poems in addition to the poems that appear in his introduction, including "The Albatross," "A Past Life," and "Beauty." Nagui also translated parts of his autobiography, and Baudelaire's letters to his mother, whom Baudelaire adored (hence Nagui's Oedipal analysis).

One of the poems that Nagui translated is "The Albatross," which I have chosen to include here because it exemplifies the similarities between Baudelaire and Nagui as two poets plagued by a sense of failure and inadequacy. In this poem, the poet's situation is compared to an albatross, who descends from an elegant "sovereign of the skies" to a humble creature captured and mocked by the sailors on their boat:

In French, the original poem has a meter and rhyme which Nagui does not try to imitate in the Arabic. He translates it unmetered, as he does with the full set of translated poems from *Les Fleurs du mal*. Given that Nagui had translated other Romantic poets in rhyme and meter, I think that his choice to render Baudelaire in this way is closely tied to the Symbolist nature of these particular poems: the crux of this work was not necessarily its form, which is why Nagui was particularly careful about prioritizing meaning in the Arabic.

My son Nadim had studied some of *Les Fleurs du mal* in the French schools he attended. It was assigned too early, the same way Nagui's "al-'Awda" (The Return) had been imposed in my own education. Nadim knew that his great-grandfather had translated Baudelaire. He said that no one had understood why Baudelaire wrote so much about death and suffering, but that he'd liked "The Albatross," even though it might have had a greater impact if he'd studied it a few years later. When I told Nadim about what had happened to me in school with Nagui's "The Return," how I'd also struggled to understand the poem at that age, Nadim disagreed with the comparison. He said in his French school they'd been asked to analyze the poem based on their particular readings of Baudelaire. It was not like for you, he informed me, where you had to memorize someone else's explication, like in the textbook *Selah al-telmeez*. We were allowed to think and come up with our own interpretations, not just reiterate the same tired stuff.

But there was more I wanted to say to Nadim. I wanted to explain why my grandfather had translated Baudelaire, how "The Albatross" offered a window on the similarities between Nagui and Baudelaire as two poets who felt out of place in a society that did not understand their suffering. Baudelaire perhaps wrote about a great deal that Nagui did not express, and I imagine that translating him gave my grandfather the kind of solace and catharsis he had found with Shakespeare's sonnets. Nagui and Baudelaire were also both unlucky in love, physically ailing, financially unstable, and existentially distressed—but nevertheless loved beauty and life and were keen to express that in all its fullness. So it is not strange that my grandfather would have embarked on an in-depth psychological study of Baudelaire's works and life.

Nagui never had the opportunity to write the same kind of introduction for his translations of Shakespeare, although he did speak about the Bard in an interview with Sami al-Kayyali, founder of the magazine *al-Hadith* in Aleppo, who would later become the head of the Syrian Dar al-Kutub. This interview was published in January 1936, in the first issue of the magazine's tenth year—more than fifteen years before Nagui's later article "Books that Shaped Me."

Unfortunately, circumstances did not allow Nagui to develop this further. Even his translation of Baudelaire's poetry was only published posthumously, about a year after his death.

My grandfather's Arabic translation of *Les Fleurs du mal* contained a short dedication from Mohamed Nagui, his older brother, who had assumed leadership of the Modern Egyptian Literature Association, which Ibrahim Nagui had founded, after my grandfather's death. Mohamed Nagui writes in his 1954 dedication:

> We present this book to the esteemed reader, but this book, my dear brother, is yours and for you, from your beating heart and effervescent spirit. This book will live on after you into eternity, and I dedicate it to you who once dedicated your book *How to Understand People* to me. Today I dedicate your book on Baudelaire to you. This is the first of five books you spoke of printing and publishing when you were still with us. You often talked about Baudelaire. I thought you might first publish [. . .] *Qira'at Ahbabtuha* [Texts I Have Loved] or your third book-to-be, which will for the first time immortalize Shakespeare's sonnets in Arabic. I know how much his sonnets meant to you and how they once cured you of a most pernicious illness.[17]

When my aunt Dawheya realized while she was still a student at AUC in the 1950s that the loose pages of "unmetered poems" were in fact Nagui's translations of Shakespeare, she decided she had stumbled upon a "treasure." It really *was* a treasure because—as Mohamed Nagui explains—Ibrahim Nagui was the first to translate Shakespeare's sonnets into Arabic. Dawheya had been reluctant to act, as I too now found myself unsure what to do, for different reasons. I wondered what I should do with these drafts now. Was this still a "treasure"?

In the intervening seventy years, there have been various Arabic translations of the sonnets. The late Palestinian writer and critic Jabra Ibrahim Jabra published forty sonnets in translation in 1983. This was followed by a translation by the late Egyptian poet Badr Tawfiq in 1988, who also prefaced the work with a lengthy analysis of the sonnets. Later, in 2012, Syrian critic and scholar Kamal Abu Deeb published the complete sonnets in translation along with a thorough analysis of their historical context, and drew parallels between the literary form of the sonnet and the Andalusian *muwashshah* (ode). Another full translation appeared in 2013 by the Iraqi poet Abdel Wahid Lu'lu'a, published by Kalima in Abu Dhabi. In 2016, the General Egyptian Book Organization published a full metered translation by the late translator and scholar of English literature Mohamed Enani. There have been various selections of sonnets published by others, including the late Iraqi poet Sargon Boulous. No doubt there are others that I may not be aware of.

We can be sure that these retranslations of the sonnets into Arabic will continue. The debate over how to best translate the sonnets is evident even from their different titles in translation, which reflect their translators' divergent perspectives on the original. Translators into Arabic have variously titled the sonnets *aghani* or *ughniyat* (songs), *ahazij* (chants), *"sonetat"* (transliterated from the English, with the Arabic plural), or *ghina'iyyat* (lyric poetry). This matter remains unresolved, and a look at these different translations provides an interesting study in how the craft of translation has evolved. It is also illustrative of very different conceptions of translation, from a focus on literally reproducing the source material to a more creative approach in which the translator takes greater liberties in bringing the original work into another culture.

For example, we might consider the Arabic translation of Sonnet 55, which is one of Shakespeare's most famous sonnets, and is unfortunately missing from Nagui's manuscript.[18]

I have called the sonnets *aghani* here, because that was the word that Nagui used in his manuscript, even though I personally prefer either *ghina'iyyat*, the translation that Abdel Wahid Lulu'a uses, to highlight the sonnets' lyric qualities, or just to leave the word as is (*"sonetat,"* transliterated from the English), as Mohamed Enani and

Badr Tawfiq both chose to do, in order to acknowledge the particularities of the English sonnet as distinct from Arabic poetic forms. But I have honored my grandfather's choice.

Are my grandfather's first translations of the sonnets still worth reading now that the sonnets have been translated by several others? Nagui's translation is no longer the first, nor is it the most faithful or complete, but nevertheless this manuscript remains a "treasure" in its own right. Even if we think of these only as a set of first drafts which Nagui intended to develop further, they are valuable as a window on his process of writing and rewriting. They shed light on how an Egyptian Romantic modernist poet steeped in multiple literary traditions approached Shakespeare. Perhaps this manuscript also attests to the impossibility of translation with regard to how the translated work resonates in the host culture (Arabic, in the case of the sonnets) relative to the source culture.

Sonnet 55	Translation by Mohamed Enani (2016)
Not marble nor the gilded monuments	لن يصمد الرخام في مباني الملك والنصب
Of princes shall outlive this powerful rhyme,	حتى المزركش والموشى بالذهب
But you shall shine more bright in these contents	لصولة الزمان مثل هذه القصيدة العصماء
Than unswept stone besmeared with sluttish time.	وهكذا تزداد في هذي الحروف وهجا من ضياء
When wasteful war shall statues overturn,	يفوق أحجارا على قبر ترب
And broils root out the work of masonry,	ملطخ بما يلقي الزمان من وشب
Nor Mars his sword nor war's quick fire shall burn	وعندما ترى التماثيل قد انقلبت
The living record of your memory.	في غمرة الصراع في حرب ضروس
'Gainst death and all-oblivious enmity	وحين تجتث القلاقل الأحجار في مبان خربت
Shall you pace forth; your praise shall still find room	لن يستطيع مارس ربّ الحروب إن حمى الوطيس
Even in the eyes of all posterity	بسيفه وناره التي للتو قد توقدت
That wear this world out to the ending doom.	إحراق ذكراك التي تحيا بهذه الطروس
So, till the Judgement that yourself arise,	وسوف يستمر حطوك الوثيق ضو الموت للإنسان
You live in this, and dwell in lovers' eyes.	وكل عدوان يصيبنا من النسيان
	إذ سوف يستمر إطراء الجمال فيك جيلا بعد جيل
	حتى نهاية الدنيا وآخر الدهر الطويل
	وهكذا حتى تقوم للحساب يوم الدين
	تحيا بشعري دائما وفي عيون العاشقين.

I ask myself: Why was it important to my grandfather to translate the sonnets, apart from his friendship with Shakespeare, and the cathartic release this work provided? He must have decided to translate them because he was dazzled, as a poet, by the tight meter and rhyme, and the eloquent economy of language that captured such profound feelings and reflections on the human experience.

In other words, the fact that my grandfather was captivated by the sonnets must have been why he embarked on that almost impossible endeavor, like others after him. However, that fierce admiration and desire to transmit the source text into another culture can sometimes blind the translator to other issues in the process of translation that could better facilitate how the text is understood in the host culture.

Translators have two main responsibilities, since they cannot reproduce the original text exactly: to understand the text fully and correctly, and to exercise their own creativity in bringing the text into the host culture so that the work might resonate as it did in the original. Taking on this latter responsibility marks the difference between working in a subordinate role to the author while effacing their own capacity to engage with the text, versus acting as an equal peer in a creative process that harnesses the different potentials of the host language.

In this draft manuscript, my grandfather, like many later translators of the sonnets, falls into the first camp. In his literal translation, Nagui sacrifices meter for meaning. His subdued translations are sometimes clumsy in their Arabic word choice, which lack the kind of wordplay we see in Shakespeare's English. Nagui may have been captivated by the sonnets, but the Arabic reader can't necessarily relish Shakespeare in the same way in the language of Nagui's translation.

To be fair to my grandfather, it's true we're only looking at a draft translation here, and it remains unclear how this might have later evolved. Given more time, might he have developed a more poetic and less literal translation? It's certainly possible, based on Nagui's other published translations of English, French, and German poetry. When he translated the French poet Alphonse de Lamartine's "Le Lac" ("The Lake"), he rendered it in rhyme and meter in the Arabic.

The same is true of Nagui's translation of the French poet Alfred de Musset's "Souvenir" ("Souvenir") and German poet Heinrich Heine's "Ich war, o Lamm, als Hirt bestellt" ("Shepherd and Lamb"). Nagui also translated a great deal of prose and sometimes took creative license in these translations, as is the case with his translations of Italian writer Luigi Pirandello's short story "Notte" ("Night") and Gabriele D'Annunzio's "Campane" ("The Bells").[19] Nagui also published an abridged Arabic version of British author Charles Langbridge Morgan's *The Fountain*. All of these translations attest to the fact that Nagui was well aware of the process of how one might deftly adapt a poetic text into its new context.

Nagui also sometimes translated metered or rhyming English poetry into unmetered Arabic, including English Romantic poet Percy Bysshe Shelley's "Ode to the West Wind" and modernist poet T.S. Eliot's "The Waste Land." As with his translation of Baudelaire, here Nagui prioritized symbolic meaning over other elements of poetic translation. Perhaps Nagui hesitated on publishing the sonnets because he hadn't yet decided how best to translate them.

Most of the other Arabic translators of the sonnets also placed Shakespeare above themselves. This adulation of the original text led them to leave behind the lyricism of the original sonnets, one of the most important features of Shakespeare's work. I don't mean to blame any single translator, but I am struck by how consistent these choices have been in translations of poetry across generations and cultural contexts. I include in this critique most Orientalists, academics, and poets who translated Arabic poetry (whether classical odes or modern verse, including Nagui's poetry). These shining pearls of the Arabic canon unfortunately often lose their luster in English translation. Although there are many exceptions to this rule, a majority of translations of Arabic poetry are almost impossible to access in English because they lack the spark that originally attracted the translator. What the translator is able to do ultimately hinges upon their own positioning toward the text.

Among numerous exceptions, I think of Ezra Pound's translations of ancient Egyptian poetry, or the Irish poet Desmond

O'Grady, my former professor at AUC, who had translated the Arabic *Mu'allaqat* (the famous seven "suspended odes") into English. I imagine my grandfather being able to do the same—sitting down with the draft sonnets, putting aside his literal translation, and working on this instead as the veteran poet he was, with the confidence of a veteran poet.

There have been some translations of various Shakespeare plays into Egyptian ammiya, with the idea that these works were intended to be performed for a mass audience. Perhaps Shakespeare shouldn't be encased in classical Arabic's more formal lexicons. This brings to mind another poet I admire: the famed Egyptian colloquial poet and cartoonist Salah Jahin (1930–1986). What about translating the sonnets into ammiya or a more accessible register of Arabic? Do we have a contemporary Salah Jahin capable of such a task?

During the pandemic, I asked my students in a translation studies course to translate Sonnet 55 as a group exercise. They chose to translate the sonnet into Egyptian ammiya for the reasons described above:

لا رخام ولا تماثيل ملوك من دهب
حيدوموا أكتر من شعري فيك
إنت حتضوي في أبيات الأدب
أكتر من الحجر اللي عرّاه عُهر السنين
لما تقع التماثيل بعد الحرب العبثيّة
وتُطمَّس زينة الأنصاب المبنيّة
لا إله الحرب بسيفه المتين
ولا لهيب الحرب الهشيم
هيقدر يحرق ذكراك الخالدة
رغم الموت والنسيان وغدر الزمان
هتفضل ذكراك باقية
ولمديحك دايما مكان
في عيون الأجيال اللي جاية
لحدّ يوم الحساب هتعيش في أشعاري
وهتسكن سطوري وعيون العاشقين.

Translation: Aya al-Telmissany, Osama Amer, Bushra Hashem, Magda Ibrahim, and Mahmoud Kholeif

Mohamed Nagui writes in his dedication to my grandfather's posthumous translation of Baudelaire's *Les Fleurs du mal* that he had expected his brother to publish the sonnets in translation first. But Nagui had decided to publish the Baudelaire translation instead. He had put off the sonnets, and then Do had done the same, leaving me with this draft manuscript—perhaps to repeat the same cycle.

I pause here to reflect on what I should do with these translations—for Do and my grandfather's sake, as well as my own. I think that Nagui's translations should be published in their own book, as he and my aunt had wanted, not because it is the "treasure" that my aunt once stumbled upon, nor because it would necessarily add to the Arabic translations of Shakespeare we have now, but because it is a record of the process of translation itself, and would invite other translators and poets to engage with the complexities of this process. These papers are worth revisiting because they tell the unfinished story of my grandfather's lifelong friendship with Shakespeare.

9

THE FAMILY DOCTOR

On a small notebook with a pale green cover, my grandfather wrote: *Tabib al-'a'ila* (The Family Doctor), with the roman numeral I in the top left corner. When I first looked through this notebook, I thought it might be a draft of a book he later published under another title, but I couldn't find anything similar among his published prose works. Perhaps it was the first section of a longer project that he hadn't finished or which later developed in other directions.

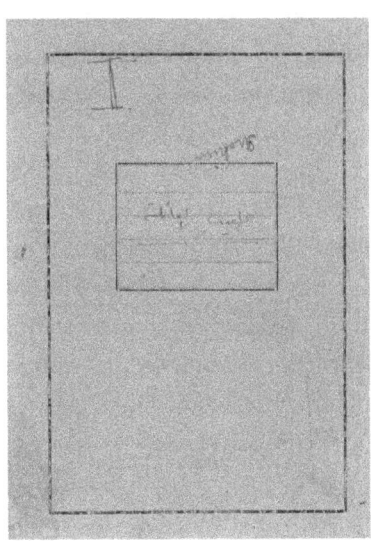

33. The cover of the notebook, titled *Tabib al-'a'ila* (The Family Doctor).

The notebook contained the outline of an ambitious book project, whose contents included the following headings:

Physiology and Anatomy
Immunity
Genetics
Discoveries of Modern Medicine
Endocrinology
On Various Diseases: Fevers—Heart Disease—Lung Disease—Liver Disease—Kidney Disease—Stomach and Intestines
Maternity and Pregnancy
Pediatric Medicine
First Aid
The Household Medicine Cabinet
Nutrition
Conclusion

I realized that this notebook—about thirty pages in all—contained the first chapter ("Physiology and Anatomy") of the book outlined above. Despite the headings, this was not conceived as a dense medical treatise, but rather an accessible reference work aimed at demystifying medicine for a household audience. In his introduction to the volume, Nagui outlines how he understood his role and responsibilities as a physician:

> This is a small volume that endeavors to fulfill a tremendous duty. We find ourselves now in an age of transformation and change. The new generation requires strong, healthy bodies, and it is incumbent upon parents to raise children of appropriately sturdy physique. How can parents carry out this task without sufficient knowledge of the necessary methods, or when they have only fragmentary information based on ignorant hearsay and anecdotal experience?
>
> There have been some useful books published on household medicine but they are generally lacking in two areas:

(1) Concise engagement with the topic at hand
(2) A brief explanation of the principles of medicine and how the body works

Household readers are not interested in pure medicine for its own sake: They want to know what to do when they cannot see a doctor. They need to understand how to prevent illness and to familiarize themselves with the basic tenets of human physiology that we all should know: what the heart is, where it is, and what it does, where the liver is and what it does, etc. Many of the conditions we treat in our clinics stem from ignorance, and from fear rooted in ignorance.

A patient may show up saying "the top of my heart" but they mean their stomach, or they say "my appendix" but they point to the left side of their intestines, or "my spleen" but gesture toward their liver. It is easy to dispel such concerns once I ask the patient, "And where is your spleen?" When they point to their liver, I let them know their spleen is certainly in fine shape because it is located elsewhere entirely. Ignorance begets fear, and so the physician can assuage these worries, aided by their own temperament and the treatment for the complaint.

I remain convinced that a great deal of physical and mental illness is the result of ignorance and confusion—of "misconceptions," as one says in English—and much of proper treatment depends upon overcoming this ignorance. But feigning knowledge is even worse than full ignorance. All too often, the physician enters the home only to find someone else already there—a relative or stranger trying to diagnose and prescribe in their stead. When the doctor tries to explain, the imposter will argue, and when the doctor leaves, this individual will give their two cents on the physician's credentials. Some of these people have memorized pharmacological information about prescription drugs. When I encounter one of these individuals, I always kindly listen to what they have to say, engage them in conversation, and then go over what they've said and help them see what they've left out. I calmly and firmly explain what they do not know, and that whatever they've pilfered from the pages of a book or the mouth of another doctor or pharmacist is not medicine. Medicine is something more profound—it cannot be quickly grasped in this way. If the imposter then saw his error, he'd step back—at least while I was there!—and let me determine what the patient needed and carry out my duties as proper medicine required.

These sorts of people likely get their facts from medical books written for general use—for doctors and non-specialists alike.

If a patient reads such materials, they make all kinds of self-diagnoses. If one of these stand-ins stumbles upon this information, they think they've understood medicine with a capital m, and administer their faulty knowledge until they are eventually forced to summon a doctor. By that time, the crucial window of opportunity may have passed. Once a woman came to me with her child who was already nearly strangled to death by diphtheria. She came too late. She'd consulted one of these healers, who told her "your kid's got a killer croup" but promised her that the child could not have real diphtheria since he'd been vaccinated against it. It was difficult for me to convince the mother that although the vaccine did provide protection, that didn't mean it prevented every case, and that only a doctor could evaluate that.

I've run into many other cases like this. That is what led me to try to put together a book that is as thorough as possible in providing all the medical guidance a family needs, without getting caught up in the finer points of medicine that don't concern the average household, so that they will not be subjected to the dangerous half-truths I have described above. I have endeavored to make this book very practical in hopes that it will be useful to families and helpful in times of need.

Perhaps I will be fortunate enough to succeed in this undertaking. But let me clarify once more that although this book aims to enlighten and guide, it is not intended to replace the medical advice of a physician.

It's surprising to me that my grandfather introduces this as a "small" undertaking, when it seems quite the opposite: No doubt the remaining chapters would have filled stacks of notebooks. The draft of the book's first chapter is undated, but inside the notebook I found a May 1947 letter to my grandfather from the Ministry of Education, asking him to proctor examinations for postgraduate certificate students at the School of Social Work in the al-Qarabiyya Public Primary School at No. 16 Sultan Hussein Street (currently al-Sheikh Rihan Street in downtown Cairo), next to the French lycée. I also found two electricity bills dated March and April 1947. It seems likely that my grandfather began this book project that same year. It also makes sense he would have begun the book late in his life, drawing upon his lengthy career and professional experience and knowledge.

We can see from this introduction how Nagui approached medicine as a "tremendous duty," as he put it. He saw this as more than a material livelihood or professional obligation. For Nagui, this was a social responsibility to the family unit as the foundation of society so that parents could "raise children of appropriately sturdy physique." Nagui's language here is not unusual; it builds on the discourse of *nahda* reformers on proper upbringing, the cultivation of sound bodies and minds, and the obligation to rescue society from "ignorant hearsay." As postcolonial scholars and historians have noted, this discourse mirrored Western discourses about the modern family and molding modern minds and bodies.

Nagui's unfinished volume resembles many other household medical manuals written for a mass audience since the nineteenth century, particularly in Europe and the US. These kinds of publications were very popular and certainly had counterparts elsewhere. There is also a long and rich legacy of medical writing in Arabic, but Nagui sees himself here as engaging primarily in a modernist *tanwiri* project.

34. The two electric bills found in the book, dated March and April 1947.

I remember that when I was in middle school, we used to seek out a popular magazine called *Tabibak al-khass* (Your Private Doctor), which is still published by Dar al-Hilal today. We'd furtively buy these magazines as teenagers in order to find answers to the many questions that some of us were embarrassed to ask our parents, especially about puberty and sex. We'd go off to read in little groups, hidden away in the corners of the schoolyard, laughing over what we learned from those forbidden pages. These publications had a social and educational function and remain very readily accessible.

We know from Nagui's published and unpublished writings that he approached his book from his longstanding sense of social responsibility as a physician, as is clear from various aspects of his medical practice. Because of this, my grandfather needed to connect with non-specialist readers—they were his first priority. He wanted to provide "all the medical guidance a family needs, without getting caught up in the finer points of medicine that don't concern the average household," and planned to produce a manual that would be "very practical in hopes that it will be useful to families and helpful in times of need." Nagui promised his reader a brief and concise overview of relevant medical knowledge, with the aim of dispelling "ignorance" and "fear rooted in ignorance."

In this introduction, Nagui's literary capabilities served him well. Not all doctors can write clearly, but Nagui's introduction is fluently written and easy to read, with none of the jargon of medical annals. He draws upon literary techniques instead, personifying and personalizing abstract topics by narrating his own experience as a practitioner. The text is light and conversational. Nagui sees himself as embodying some of the characteristics that are crucial to successful medical practice: "I always kindly listen to what they have to say, engage them in conversation, and then go over what they've said and help them see what they've left out." As a negative counterexample, Nagui tells the story of the child who has almost suffocated from diphtheria to illustrate another kind of doctor, whose careless haste is ruinous for the patient, and who does not take the time to gently listen, engage, and explain.

Nagui thus sets forth two competing visions of the profession: those physicians who embrace this responsibility to society and those who only see medicine as a lucrative occupation at their patients' expense. These themes reappear throughout Nagui's articles and stories. In the early 1950s—not the mid-1930s, as Saleh Gawdat, Wadie Filastin, Hassan Tawfiq, and others have claimed—Nagui published a monthly periodical entitled *Hakim al-bayt* (The Household Doctor). *Hakim al-bayt* ran for three years and initially had a similar focus as this unfinished manuscript. The editor's note from one 1951 issue of *Hakim al-bayt* lays out the magazine's philosophy. Sayed Mostafa, the editor-in-chief, writes:

> Leave no stone unturned! We live in an age of specialization . . . Everyone has something they do best and to which they devote themselves fully [. . .] Still, there is some knowledge that should be shared among all educated people. In other words, every man should partake a little in each branch of learning. Perhaps most important in this regard among all the arts and sciences is knowledge of physical health, because a healthy body is key to achieving a good life. Do not hesitate to expand your knowledge of health and medicine as much as you are able.[1]

The rest of this issue continues in a similar vein. The periodical clearly reflects Nagui's didactic concerns with educating the reader as well as his efforts to work beyond the parameters of specific fields. Those parameters were a hallmark of his age, and produced the kind of closed circuits that Nagui himself became fenced into within his professional life. By contrast, the table of contents of *Hakim al-bayt* includes articles from prominent Egyptian doctors working in a variety of medical fields, as well as translations of Western medical scholarship. Some are more specialized medical treatises and others have a more literary bent.

The opening article, "Mushkilat al-taghdhiya al-haditha" (Problems in Modern Nutrition) is written by Nagui and proposes changes to the dietary recommendations for kidney disease patients, offering alternatives with greater efficacy in managing the disease. Nagui once again draws on his personal experience with patients to craft an engaging narrative accessible to the everyday reader:

> I remember there was a patient who came to the hospital with both feet swollen and a great deal of albumin in his urine. He'd undergone stringent treatment abroad. His diet consisted only of milk and he was very weak and didn't seem to be making progress. When he came to us, he was in dire straits. As he was served lunch, he looked at it incredulously and said to me, "With my kidneys, how can I possibly eat all this?" I replied, "Leave it to us: This is indeed a generous lunch—but without any salt, and that's what you need."[2]

The patient gets better on this new diet and leaves the hospital on his feet and in good health. This is one of many anecdotes about individual patients that Nagui uses to illustrate the effectiveness of new approaches that depart from conventional medical practice at the time.

There are several excellent articles in this issue of the periodical, including a translated piece entitled "Circus Doctor" by J. Y. Henderson, chief veterinarian of the Ringling Bros. and Barnum & Bailey Circus, who wrote a series of entertaining articles about his experience treating various animals. These articles were later collected in a 1951 book of the same name *(Circus Doctor)*, which became a classic. One of Henderson's articles appeared in the 5 December 1951 issue of *Hakim al-bayt*. The fact that the Arabic translation was published the same year as the original attests to how closely Nagui was following Western medical literature—and literature about medicine. In *Hakim al-bayt*, Nagui provided a range of doctors' writings in translation for his Arabic audience, as part of his efforts to employ translation to enrich and modernize various spheres of Arabic culture, and to make medicine accessible to a wider readership beyond the confines of a single field.

These were questions that had preoccupied Nagui throughout his life. In a July 1949 article that Nagui published in the ninth issue of the journal of the Egyptian Medical Syndicate, he wrote about how he had seen medicine and literature as two sides of the same coin since he was a student in medical school:

> I began to study medicine from an artistic angle. I'd illustrate the material for my friends, inventing mnemonic devices to help them memorize the content. I've continued to do that my whole life. I practice medicine as an art, and I write literature scientifically, with attention to logic, specificity, and clarity.

Even the young Nagui was cognizant of how literary "illustration" could aid students of medicine in memorizing abstract theoretical concepts. Although he continued to pursue this interplay between medicine and literature throughout his short life, his efforts in this regard remain marginalized, even intentionally blotted out.

When Saleh Gawdat wrote about *Hakim al-bayt*, he not only placed the publication in the wrong decade, but also misinterpreted how this periodical fit into the broader trajectory of Nagui's life:

> In his free time, which had been occupied by writing poetry, Nagui published a monthly magazine entitled *Hakim al-bayt*, which proved an immediate success because of its innovative approach to household health. However, its popularity faded quickly, for the magazine inevitably foundered when it strayed

into literature. Most of the contributors to the magazine were writers, and so there was talk of lovers' reunions and parting rifts, instead of rheumatism and coughing fits.³

I reread that paragraph and said to myself: My poor grandfather! Even Saleh Gawdat, who claimed to know you well, clearly didn't understand at all. You did so much for the periodical—gathering medical scholarship from both the Arab world and the West, searching for articles that would take the reader beyond the narrow strictures of specialization. You located texts from other cultures which would further that vision, and you translated to illustrate the intersections between medicine, literature, and knowledge in multiple contexts. How, after all this, could Gawdat claim the journal was just a distraction to occupy spare hours? Not to mention that Gawdat incorrectly claimed you published the periodical in the 1930s, after you "pretended" (in Gawdat's words) to abandon verse following Taha Hussein's attacks on your poetry in 1934. How could Gawdat have attributed the end of *Hakim al-bayt* to its "straying" into literature instead of medicine? Wasn't he aware you were reaching out to literary minds on purpose, that you saw your professional and cultural duties as one and the same? Didn't he know about the grueling responsibilities you bore, or the financial crises that you endured in order to continue your literary projects? The Modern Egyptian Literature Association that you established in 1945 only "foundered" after seven years because of a lack of resources.

Wadie Filastin's recollections of Nagui cast my grandfather in a different light. Filastin had been the deputy head of the Literature Association for all its seven years. He wrote:

> The Literature Association was a true school for literature, and our head teacher was Ibrahim Nagui. He was a doctor and scholar with an incredible capacity to forge connections between science and literature. He'd sometimes speak to us about what literature had to do with psychology or sex, or about how health and illness figured in the lives of writers, or why poetry should be considered

a psychological phenomenon, and so on. He usually gave his lectures off the cuff and rarely read from a prepared text. Even one of these lectures would have required dozens of references, but he had all the sources ready to go in his keen mind.[4]

Filastin's account is crucial in correcting the narrow, one-sided vision of Nagui as a "delicate poet of love," as Hassan Tawfiq described him. But if Gawdat incorrectly assumed that Nagui turned toward translating and writing articles and stories to fill his "free time" after being driven away from poetry, Tawfiq was much closer to the mark:

> Nagui's legacy is not limited to poetry alone. This delicate poet of love was also a prolific writer of prose, which has often been denied the same attention as his poetic work. Nagui's interest in writing prose did not develop in response to Dr. Taha Hussein and Abbas Mahmoud al-Aqqad's brutal attacks on his poetry, as some who have written about Nagui have imagined, including Saleh Gawdat [...]
>
> Hussein and al-Aqqad launched their attack on Nagui after he had published *Behind the Clouds* in 1934, by which point Nagui had in fact already published various prose articles [...]
>
> Nagui was just as engaged with prose as he was with poetry, and indeed his interest in prose went beyond many poets of his generation [...]

Nagui published his first collection of poetry, *Wara' al-ghamam* [Behind the Clouds], in 1934 and his first book of prose, *Madinat al-ahlam* [City of Dreams], in 1935. During his lifetime two collections of Nagui's poetry were published—*Wara' al-ghamam*, and *Layali al-Qahira* [Cairo Nights]—but seven books of prose: *Madinat al-ahlam, Kayfa tafham al-nas?* [How to Understand People]; *Tawfiq al-Hakim: al-fanan al-ha'ir* [Tawfiq al-Hakim: The Artist's Dilemma], with Dr. Ismail Adham contributing most of the book's chapters; *Layali Finisia* [Venice Nights], co-written with two other authors; *Adrikni ya duktur* [Cure Me, Doctor]; *Risalat al-haya* [The Meaning of Life], and *'Alam al-usra* [Family Matters].[5]

Hassan Tawfiq, the editor of Nagui's complete collected works, is right that Nagui had been just as immersed in prose as poetry. He was perhaps even more broadly committed to prose given his sense of societal responsibility to contribute to modernist efforts in diverse fields of study including psychology, sociology, philosophy, and classical and modern Arabic, and Western literature (whether in English, French, Italian, or German).

Tawfiq is also correct that Nagui wrote prose of his own accord throughout his life, and not in response to Hussein and al-Aqqad's criticism of his poetry. The dates of publication for these prose works are consistent with Tawfiq's claim. More than twelve years after his first prose book *City of Dreams*, Nagui started to draft *Tabib al-'a'ila* (The Family Doctor).

Nagui begins the draft chapter of *The Family Doctor* on physiology and anatomy with a clear and well-organized description of the tissues of the human body, which he divides into four categories: epithelial tissue, muscle tissue, nerve tissue, and blood tissue. To illustrate how the nervous system, brain, and spine function, Nagui explains:

> This system is a whole network of wires. We can clearly see how they work: Each movement of the body is wired to an alarm that receives these messages. As with a telephone, first someone has to place a call. The brain receives this incoming request and transmits it to the right part of the body to respond to the signal. For example, suppose you see an apple. Your optic nerves will send a message about this to the brain, which processes the signal . . . and you can move your hand (positive feedback) to pick up the apple.

It's also clear from the draft that Nagui is drawing from many different sources for this chapter. In his marginal notes opposite each page of the text, Nagui writes certain terms in English. The idea of using telephone wiring to represent the human nervous system is not Nagui's own invention: He has written "switchboard" in the margin and seems to have taken this metaphor from an English text. Nagui again moves between medicine, literary technique, and translation, Arabizing an English medical metaphor for his audience in unobtrusive prose. Nagui also employs these techniques in other prose works, including *How to Understand People*, *The Meaning of Life*, and *Family Matters*, as I will explore below.

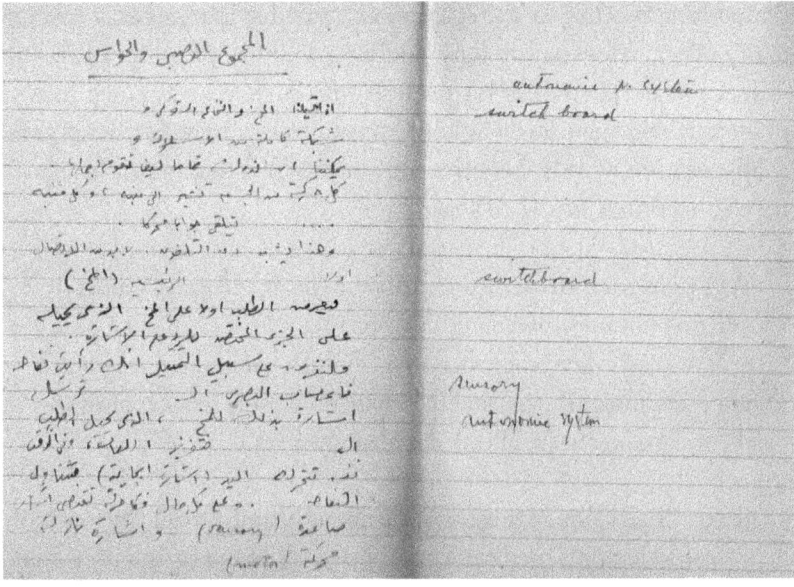

35. A page from *Tabib al-'a'ila* (The Family Doctor) in which Nagui compares the nerves connected to the brain to telephone wires, with corresponding notes on English terminology on the opposite page.

As I was writing this chapter, I felt I had taken on Portia's mantle. Clearly, injustices had been done to my grandfather which need to be remedied. How could I not defend him at this stage in my journey, just as he had advocated for and upheld medicine in its broadest and most inclusive sense? The key question here is why biographers and editors writing about Nagui's life, even Hassan Tawfiq, have treated his prolific and expansive prose works as of secondary importance to his poetry. They tend to run quickly through this material, listing the books one after the next (with wildly inaccurate publication dates), only to return once again to his "delicate" poetry. They forget or overlook that Nagui was also a physician. Why did they want him to be only a poet? For Nagui's biographers, he was a poet first and foremost, and a doctor in the narrowest sense of practicing a trade. Other physicians, meanwhile, brushed aside his encyclopedic contributions because these were understood as being beyond the scope of his professional credentials as a doctor of internal medicine. They treated him as a cog in the system, and saw his lectures and articles in any other field—psychology, sociology, philosophy, literature—as evidence of dereliction of his professional duty. He was hewn in two even after he'd spent his whole life trying to sew together those artificially severed worlds. Nagui writes in the introduction to his short story collection, *Cure Me, Doctor:*

> Yet I was born with two hearts: a doctor's heart and a poet's heart—one that fills up with feeling, and one that releases it. Thus I have experienced everything twice over: Human pain finds a resounding echo in my ribcage, and the images my soul's lens captures of the waking world are always double exposures.[6]

It's true that some of those writing about Nagui did quickly touch on the human side of his medical work. Nearly all of the stories they mention were originally tales he told to his friends, or related in his prose writings, whether in personal anecdotes, short stories, magazine and newspaper articles, or introductions to his books. For example, I often heard the story "al-Farkha" (The Hen) told as a child. Sami al-Kayyali includes this story in a postscript to one of Nagui's poetry collections, published by Dar al-Awda in Beirut in 1980. Al-Kayyali writes:

> [Nagui] was a very compassionate doctor, and often paid out of his own pocket for the medical care of his destitute patients. I once heard a funny story from him about this [. . .]

One day a patient came to him in his clinic. The man was poor and didn't pay the usual fee. The poet sat him down for the examination and could not find anything wrong except hunger. He took a pound from his pocket and gave it to the man and said: Take this pound and buy a pair of chickens and eat them, and God willing, you'll be cured.

The man got up and wished him well. A week later he crossed paths with the same man in the street and asked him:
"How are you doing now?"
"All's well, doctor."
"Did you eat those chickens?"
"No, doctor."
"What did you do with the pound then?"
"I went to a doctor who cured me of my disease!"

Wadie Filastin tells another story about Nagui's generosity as a doctor:

[Nagui] opened a private clinic on Ibn al-Furat Street in Shubra above the pharmacy run by the renowned Dr. Niqula Haddad, who translated Einstein's theory of relativity into Arabic. Nagui and Haddad had a "gentlemen's agreement" that if Nagui examined a patient who was poor, the patient wouldn't have to pay anything, and when they went down to Haddad's pharmacy, the prescription would also be free. Nagui paid the pharmacy bill from his own pocket at the end of each month.[7]

This second story could have been loosely adapted from Nagui's own account of this arrangement, as narrated in the short story "Dada Halima" in the collection *Cure Me, Doctor*. In this very brief tale, a young doctor rents a clinic in Shubra from an "elderly pharmacist" who is a friend of his father's and refuses to take any rent for the clinic room. The old pharmacist tells the protagonist, "Just send me your patients, and we'll settle up at the end of the month. Go on, my boy, get working, and may God bring you success."

The story "Dada Halima" is clearly drawn from Nagui's life, like the other stories in the same collection, as Nagui mentions in his introduction to the book. This particular story is one of the most moving because it depicts the bond between Nagui and his underprivileged patients. The protagonist describes the first day in his new clinic as follows:

> The next day I started working—I sat down to see what was going to fall from the sky. The *bawab*, a pleasant and well-spoken black man, came up to the clinic and we got to talking. I learned that he wanted to circumcise his boys and various nephews. So I said: Bring them all here tomorrow [...]

> The next day he arrived with a huge number of boys with their hands painted with henna. The women let forth their *zagharid* and the whole building stopped what they were doing to see the festivities. The operations were over quickly. The bawab kept coming with other relatives each day so they could undergo their "change," and the furor began again for all the neighborhood to see. Amm Hassan would not stop going on about the clinic and it quickly filled with patients. There were even patients standing in the stairwell, and I had them take a seat in the in entryway leading into my one-room clinic.[8]

Dada Halima herself, the eponymous character, is described by the narrator as "an elegant black woman, who looked as if she had once been prosperous, and carried about her the scent of musk particular to royal palaces." Dada Halima comes to the clinic after hearing about it from the head vendor at the vegetable market. However, the doctor-narrator's neighbor, who specializes in immunizations, tries to steal the new patient away from the young doctor. Amm Hassan, the bawab, intervenes to rescue her from the older physician, scolding him: "Shame on you! You've been in the building for twenty years, and this new doctor's only been here a month."[9]

The young physician reassures the woman and takes her to the clinic. The narrator explains:

36. Ibrahim Nagui in his clinic.

I was in the habit of becoming friends with my patients. I'd quickly shift from talking about the patient's illness to their personal circumstances and sufferings. I learned from Dada Halima that she had been working in the palace of Ratib Pasha and then married [. . .]

We became closer and I began to visit her in her little room and drink coffee with her. Sometimes she'd spread out a clean blanket on the floor so we could rest a while during the day. Her adorable young grandson Saad, the child of her late daughter, would amuse us [. . .] He had smooth ebony skin, wide eyes, and a wonderful smile. He'd throw himself at me when he saw me and burst out laughing. She'd say, "If you need an assistant at the clinic, Saad will be your *tamargi* when he's older."[10]

When the syndicate of newspaper sellers decided to republish *Cure Me, Doctor* after Nagui's death in 1953, the book was published with a postscript from the head of the syndicate, Abdel Hamid Amer, entitled "A Note of Gratitude":

> Dr. Nagui—may God rest his soul—was a spiritual father to us. He often rendered medical services and would treat us without asking for payment. He made similar arrangements with an optometrist in Sayeda Zaynab to treat us there as well, and with the lawyer Dr. Khalil Atallah who defended us in our legal cases. We now publish this collection of short stories that this generous doctor gave us, and pray he might be showered with every mercy, May God rest his pure soul and reward him with goodness.[11]

It is not surprising that Nagui would devote his "spare time" to studying psychology and immersing himself in this relatively new sphere of knowledge, even publishing a full book in this field *(How to Understand People)*. Freud, as much as Shakespeare, captivated Nagui throughout his life. In his introduction to Nagui's complete prose works, Hassan Tawfiq describes this volume:

> *How to Understand People* contains a series of articles and studies from the strange and unfathomable realms of psychology, including industrial psychology, medical psychology, psychology of character, child psychology, adolescent psychology, communal psychology, women's psychology, the Oedipus complex and psychology of Hamlet, and the psychology of love.[12]

In Nagui's collected prose works, Hassan Tawfiq lists the chapter titles above, provides a relatively long excerpt from Nagui's introduction, and then leaves it at that! No one has addressed how this book fits into Nagui's trajectory or examined his abiding interest in psychology given his regular commentary on the physician-patient relationship and the importance of not treating patients as sterile cases. In addition to other oversights, Nagui's biographers and editors have neglected to critique the political ramifications of this work, perhaps taking Nagui and his generation to task for imitating the West and eagerly embracing each new scholar, for so keenly shepherding these texts into Egyptian cultural spheres. Did Nagui's work in psychology matter? Who was he addressing? What "family" did he have in mind? This text raises many questions worth thinking about that have thus far been overlooked.

The introduction to *How to Understand People* provides a comprehensive outline of the historical development of modern psychology, which Nagui considers to be the most contemporary of sciences and the most deeply embedded in various spheres of life. He traces the Greek etymology of the English word "psyche" and examines how psychology offers a more precise lens for understanding the psyche— "that thing that inhabits the body and makes it alive." Nagui begins with classical philosophers such as Plato and Aristotle (and his treatise *Peri Psychēs/De Anima* [*On the Soul*]), before continuing onward to the seventeenth-century thinker Descartes, Kant in the late eighteenth century, and finally to the most recent contributions regarding the concrete questions of behavioral psychology. Nagui concludes:

> When psychology solidified into its current form, it gathered momentum and began to branch out like a tree after it has set down its roots. The study of normal behavior provided a window onto understanding many complex psychological and intellectual processes. This was soon followed by research into abnormal behavior, based on what Freud and his followers had theorized about the unconscious mind and repressed instincts and impulses. This is why modern psychology is considered to be "psychodynamic," compared to earlier notions of a more static psyche. In order to understand people—in order for you to understand yourself—normal and abnormal behaviors must be studied together, so that we can come to understand how the healthy psyche becomes sick, and how the sick might become healthy.[13]

Despite Nagui's efforts to trace these developments across various fields of psychology and to translate and explain the key theories and terminologies—and despite Hassan Tawfiq's efforts to locate a copy of *How to Understand People* to include in Nagui's collected works—there were unfortunately many major English spelling errors printed in that edition of the book.[14] It saddens me that such errors were made after my grandfather took such painstaking care with the research and writing. To get an idea of the extent of these errors, I have listed some of them below:

English term	Spelling errors that appear in Nagui's *Complete Prose Works*	Nagui's translation into Arabic
anxiety neurosis	anviety nevais	القلق العصبي
vocational guidance	vontional guciace	التوجيه المهني
paranoia	pargnoia	جنون العظمة
superego	superwgo	الذات العليا – الرقيب
regression	rehression	تراجع باطني نحو الماضي
adolescence	dalescence	المراهقة
behavior	behavriour	السلوك الإنساني
sense of judgment	senes of judgement	سرعة حكم الحواس
psychoanalysis	psycho aualy sis	التحليل النفسي
cultural deprivation	cultural prisction	الحرمان الثقافي
conscious	coiscious	العقل الواعي
unsublimated expression	unsublimeted cxprcssion	النوع التعبيري الذي لم يتسام به

These spelling mistakes obscure key terminology in the text and should have been rectified, not only out of respect to Nagui's memory but also to the reader and Arabic cultural heritage in general. Equally appalling errors appear in Nagui's English bibliography for the book, including the names of authors listed in those references. The same is unfortunately true of Nagui's poetry collections, which have been published and republished with the same errors and omissions, as Hassan Tawfiq explains in his introduction to my grandfather's complete poetry works.

If the unfinished manuscript of *The Family Doctor* reflected Nagui's interest in the physiological health of the family, Nagui took up the family's psychological health in *How to Understand People*. As described above, the book included chapters on child psychology, adolescent psychology, women's psychology, and the psychology of love, including marital and sexual relations. As with *The Family Doctor*, these questions reflected Nagui's preoccupation with his social and professional responsibilities as a physician. These concerns were not limited to a single article or chapter, and were also abundantly present in his short stories, as described above, and in his psychoanalytical interpretations of literature, as we saw with his analysis of Shakespeare and Baudelaire. To this we might also add that Nagui published a study on the psychology of Tawfiq al-Hakim, whose plays and stories he admired immensely, drawing on their close friendship and al-Hakim's literary production to paint a detailed portrait of his character.

In Nagui's short story "Tahlil nafsi" (Psychoanalysis), the narrator explains to his mentor, who is a prominent doctor, why he—the young man—has been so successful after only just starting out with a modest clinic. The young doctor explains, "You write your prescriptions, but I treat their inner souls."[15] Unfortunately, the real-life Nagui did not receive credit for these efforts; instead, they cost him his career.

In 1947—the same year that Nagui began the draft of *The Family Doctor*—Nagui published another book, *'Alam al-usra* (Family Matters). This volume brought Nagui's work on household medicine full circle in focusing on the cultivation of the individual within the family unit. In the introduction, Nagui summarizes the central question of the book with his usual eloquence:

> There was once a father who wanted to test his son's intelligence. He gave his son a map of the world that had been torn into pieces and asked his son to put each piece back where it belonged. In only a few minutes the boy had put the map back together—without a single mistake. The father was stunned, for he knew his son did not have the capacity to fix the map so quickly and accurately on his own. He cried out: How did you do it? The boy said: There was a drawing of a man on the map, and he was torn into pieces. When I put the man back together, the map was in order too.[16]

Of course, the moral of the story about the father and son is that change starts with the individual (in the story, the figure on the map) and that reforming the individual is what mends the world—not the opposite, as in the task the father originally sets. This is why Nagui devotes a book to the environment in which the individual is raised and to the family's responsibility in this process. Nagui's insistent focus on the centrality of the individual and family raises questions about his modernizing reformist discourse, and how this discourse might or might not have been reflected in broader Egyptian society—especially given that it was coming from *tabib al-ghalaba* ("the poor man's doctor"), as Nagui was called. The world of his characters—Dada Halima and her grandson Saad, or Amm Hassan the bawab—seems far removed from this lofty discourse about cultivating the individual within the family. The family that Nagui was constructing and the precepts that he was recommending excluded most of Egyptian society, for whom this world was out of reach. We might read this excerpt from *Family Matters* in that light:

> The family charter should be grounded in principles governing health, ethics, and the mind and psyche. Matters of health include sustenance, shelter, clothing, exercise, and spare time. The second category (ethics) pertains to traditions and customs, and the duty to embody and instill them. The third requires knowledge of the principles of psychology [. . .]
>
> These three charters constitute the "book" that every family should consult regarding all matters concerning the Eastern man, Eastern family, and Eastern society. I use "Eastern" here because that is who this book is for, keeping in mind our particular traditions and customs, including the progress made in recent years.[17]

It is evident from Nagui's writing that the audience he imagines for this text is a reader very much like himself, settled within a modern bourgeois family. All the examples Nagui goes on to provide in the book regarding diet, housing, clothing, household medicine, physical exercise, marital relations, and childrearing are consistent with this vision of life. Nagui states in his introduction that he is writing this book for an "Eastern family." In addressing this audience, he produces a table listing common ingredients in Egyptian cooking with corresponding nutritional values so that "anyone" could create a well-rounded meal. He observes that the chart reflects how "Egyptian products, according to the most recent analyses, are nutritionally rich, especially in vitamins."[18]

With regard to Nagui's overarching concern with the psychology of the family and its members, he argues that a sound family unit requires at least basic awareness of psychological principles:

> We don't need to delve deeply in the philosophy of [Alfred] Adler and Freud to raise our children and build strong families. However, the charter of the mind and psyche set forth in the pages of this book contains several articles, and failure to learn these principles will not spare the reader the consequences of their ignorance, or exonerate them from their crimes.[19]

Nagui goes on to affirm the importance of a correct understanding of psychological matters, and condemns the lack of this knowledge in Egyptian society. He had himself been reproached by prominent doctors for his insistence on studying psychology. Nevertheless, he believed it was foundational for any doctor regardless of their particular specialty:

> I don't know why we open clinics to prevent disease when there are no similar clinics opening to prevent dangerous social problems, namely the disintegration of family ties.[20]

By way of example, Nagui drew on his own experience treating a pregnant mother to illustrate how the social context of the family shaped the mother's health:

> Ten years ago, the writer of these lines was a doctor in a pediatric clinic at the Railroad Authority. He sought to avoid a narrow focus on the specific diseases afflicting pregnant women and children, but rather believed it was important to examine the conditions of ignorance and poverty that affected these cases. This doctor wondered:

What is the point of prescribing medicine to a sick child if he's nursing day and night? And what will the mother's milk do if she is destitute and can hardly find anything to eat herself?

This doctor followed the practice of the late Dr. [Richard] Cabot at Harvard, who opened a social clinic next to each medical practice or surgery. Dr. Cabot believed that the social condition of the family should be addressed alongside any medical treatment. No doubt by "social condition" he was referring to education and material means, or what we here would call curing ignorance and poverty.

This is what I was doing in my pediatric clinic. I would teach the mother first, and if she came again, I'd have her repeat what she'd learned to me before I'd prescribe any medicine. I'd copy out the instructions and distribute them to whichever women knew how to read. I'd tell pregnant women that their own good health during pregnancy would ensure a strong and healthy child . . . These recommendations included seven points [with regard to] exercise, hard work, and traveling long distances. [I would ask]: Could she use a sewing machine? Did she have a place to bathe in the summer? What maternity clothes did she have? Peace of mind for pregnant woman—was it necessary? What about protecting her breasts during pregnancy? What should pregnant women eat and drink? Was she seeing the doctor regularly?[21]

Perhaps this sounds like an unremarkable description of bourgeois domestic life during that era, but Nagui was writing this out in 1947 in order to provide a new approach for his colleagues and peers working with patients who were expecting. He drew on what he saw as cutting-edge practices, in this case from a prominent American physician.

Nagui's interest in enlightening and guiding others extended beyond his family medical practice to the Modern Egyptian Literature Association, which he founded and led until his death. He saw this association as a logical extension of the family and of his preoccupation with nurturing and guiding the individual within the family unit. This was especially true with regard to Nagui's efforts to assist the younger members of the association, which Wadie Filastin recalls at various junctures in his book. In one of these passages, Filastin writes:

> Although dozens of people attended the Literature Association's weekly meetings, Nagui sought to create "family gatherings" [within the larger group], in which all the participants had a chance to get to know each other. This aimed to bridge the gap between old and young and to foster a more intimate literary community, which was an important part of Nagui's life purpose.[22]

Wadie Filastin describes how Nagui used to take on the role of teacher with new generations, which were in "dire need of someone to direct and guide their path ... and Nagui, for his part, was glad of the youth gathered around him." He would alternately encourage and challenge the younger members, and sometimes point them toward worthwhile books and lend them volumes from his private library. Nagui even went as far as to "sort out their juvenile difficulties and treat them if their health went off course, and would include the members of their family."[23]

Nagui's prose works and his approach to these various avenues of family medicine deserve serious study, beyond the scope of my own journey with my grandfather. For my purposes in this chapter, it is enough that I began to get to know him as a scholar, translator, physician, and didactic teacher. He sought to immerse himself in diverse fields of learning, and in many cases Western scholarship, and to find accessible methods to circulate complex, specialized knowledge to a mass audience as part of his generation's efforts to enlighten and instruct. This chapter might serve as a first step toward a more critical engagement with Nagui's prose work—for better or for worse—putting to rights what has not stood the test of time, and finding due remedy for the severed halves of Nagui's legacy. I hope that my defense of my grandfather as a physician has brought him some joy even if he and I have very different conceptions of "enlightenment" and "guidance." A little disagreement will not detract from the affection that has grown between us over the course of my journey through the chapters of this book.

10

FAREWELL

My time has come and the omens foretell
What lies in store at journey's end
The days have run thin and my vigor is spent
I close where I began

—Ibrahim Nagui, "The Farewell"

"Mom, what happened the day that my grandfather died? How did you find out? Who told you?"

I'd never asked this question before. It had never occurred to me to ask. No one had ever talked about the details of that ill-fated day in front of us. All of us grandchildren and great-grandchildren had been left with only that portrait in our homes, peering at us in silence.

My mother was taken aback by the question. "Why do you have to bring this up, Samia? Why are you asking me this now?"

"Mom, it's important to me. You've never told us exactly what happened."

At first, my mother didn't want to talk about it. She looked troubled and claimed she couldn't recall the details, that she didn't want to remember. When I insisted, she began to speak—reluctantly at first, but then she quickly took up the threads of the story.

"I was home with my sisters. Mom was out. The woman who worked for Tante Bahia, our upstairs neighbor, came by to tell me that someone wanted me on the phone."

"Why did they have to call you at the neighbor's? Didn't you have a phone?"

"Yes, but it wasn't working. The line had been disconnected for a while because Papa had refused to pay the bill. It was LE40, which was really a lot of money, and we used to go on too long on the phone. Not just us girls but also our friends and the people staying with us for weeks at a time. So when they disconnected the line, he let them do it. We gave people our neighbors' numbers: Tante Bahia upstairs and Tanta Zakiya downstairs. They'd send for us and we'd go pick up the phone. That day it was Tante Bahia, so I went up to see who was calling since Mom was out.

When I picked up the receiver, a man I didn't know offered me his condolences and asked when the funeral for Dr. Nagui was going to be. Naturally I cried out, "What are you talking about?" Tante Bahia got up and took the receiver from me. My head was spinning and I couldn't believe what I'd just heard. Tante Bahia hung up and tried to calm me down and assure me that the man had been confused and was speaking nonsense. Of course, the truth soon became clear. Everyone had already heard by the time we got that call. He'd passed away in his clinic, so all of Shubra knew before the news reached us by phone from someone who'd probably been a colleague of his at the Ministry of Endowments.

Mom got the news as she was coming back into the building. We were all in a state, wailing and crying, and we girls had to be distributed among the care of the neighbors: Dawheya had fainted, and Suna was still young. All the neighbors were standing about us, and Farah the *sofragi* was in floods of tears. No one could believe what was happening.

Eventually our uncles went to the clinic to get him. They brought him home and that moment was incredibly difficult—for us, for the whole building, for the whole street. We were wailing, "What are we going to do without you?" and Mom was saying: "*Ya habibi ya Ibrahim.*"

The whole street had gathered, not just our building, and his sisters and my mom's brothers had of course come too.

They decided to lay him on his bed until morning when the corpse washer would come. They wanted his body to be washed at home. He lay in that bed until morning. It was very hard to feel that he was in the house with us but no longer there. We didn't sleep that night, and for a long time after Mom slept with us in our rooms. She couldn't sleep in that bed anymore."

My mother suddenly remembered that she and her sisters had found my grandmother in her room a week before my grandfather's death, pensive and tearful. When they'd asked what was wrong, my grandmother had said:

Oh girls, your father kept me up weeping all night. Things were weighing on him and he said to me: Souma, I feel like I'm going to die this week. When I go, what are you and the girls going to do without me? I tried to comfort him and hugged him close. I told him not to say things like that—none of that thinking.

My grandfather knew his time had come, and that he'd soon slip away and leave them unprepared for what was to come. Although they were stricken by his death, my grandmother, who had nursed him through his health crises, including chronic diabetes and the tuberculosis he'd miraculously survived, knew the end was coming. But even she hadn't imagined that it would be as brutally sudden as all that. My mother continued:

"After they washed the body, they got ready to take him down. The funerary procession began in front of the house. It was really quite a funeral. The whole neighborhood walked together in that procession, as well as neighbors from his clinic in Shubra, his patients—rich and poor alike—, his doctor colleagues, colleagues from the ministry, his students and acolytes, and various other friends: artists, intellectuals, poets, government and party officials, magazine editors, members of the Literature Association, plus all our relatives and neighbors. It was huge. We girls bid him farewell from the balcony, sobbing and wailing. We felt terribly vulnerable and adrift. All I could say was, 'What are we going to do without you, Papa?' Douha had fainted; she was too fragile to bear these kinds of situations."

If Do hadn't been able to bear that moment, she was still the one who took it upon herself after the funeral to collect a great deal of what was written about my grandfather after his death: eulogies, poetry, short articles from dozens of newspapers, and all the many condolences from various friends, colleagues, and institutions that were published at the time. She also took care to document the funeral and who had attended, and left behind an entire file of papers with those details. As with the other documents, Do had made photocopies of everything in the file to preserve the originals.

When I first began to write this book, I hadn't paid close attention to this particular set of papers—I knew how Nagui's daughters had idolized him, and I imagined this was more of the same. I could see that these papers documented how his sudden death had reverberated among the medical and literary community in Cairo, and the kind words that were heaped upon him, recalling the doctor, man, and poet he had been. This further solidified the legend that his daughters had created: Nagui loomed ever larger in their minds. The more time passed, the more pristine their memory of his life and legacy became.

But when I'd come further in this journey, I began to look through this file again. I realized that it was full of important material that I'd only half seen before. One newspaper clipping described how then-Prime Minister (and later President) Major General Mohamed Naguib had selected Salah al-Shahid, master of ceremonies in the Council of Ministers, to attend the funeral service for the late Dr. Ibrahim Nagui. Former Prime Minister Mostafa al-Nahhas Pasha was also reported to have sent one Mostafa Abu Alm to attend Nagui's funeral. As I pored over these clippings, I remembered that Salah al-Shahid, who had worked in the royal court and then with the Free Officers, was close friends with my grandfather and grandmother. I later met his daughters, because they and their mother remained part of my grandmother, mother, and aunt's lives. This clipping prompted me to delve further into Salah al-Shahid's life and the role that he had played at this moment of transition after the 1952 revolution. I was also surprised that al-Nahhas Pasha was referred to as "al-ra'is" in the other clipping, even though it was about eight months after the 1952 revolution, and al-Nahhas was no longer prime minister. Moreover, the Free Officers had placed him on their arrest list until Mohamed Naguib intervened and got his name off the list. However, al-Nahhas would still be arrested later in 1953 under duress, along with his wife Zainab al-Wakil. These two clippings are only a few lines long, but shed light on a crucial moment in Egyptian national history, whose twists and turns we briefly glimpse through these funeral arrangements.

37. Obituary notices for Ibrahim Nagui published in *al-Ahram* on 23 March 1953, from the folder of newspaper clippings collected by my aunt Dawheya.

Reading through these clippings brought to mind an important article by the historian Hussein Omar, a friend and colleague. He wrote about how obituaries can serve as a source for social history, and how historians of modern Egypt might utilize this material to understand how individuals imagined their social worlds.[1] I also thought of Egyptian writer Sonallah Ibrahim's novel *al-Lajna (The*

Committee), in which the narrator is asked to present a report to the Committee and decides to research a figure only referred to as "the Doctor." When the narrator is unable to find anything in the official archive because this material has been censored, he tries to glean information about the Doctor through reading the obituary page in the newspapers. This enables him to uncover information about the Doctor's network of social, political, and economic ties which he could not access through official archives. The narrator produces a detailed account of various facets of the Doctor's life, which is at odds with the image the Committee wants him to present. The obituary pages become an important archive and key source in uncovering who the Doctor is.[2]

I go back to reread the papers from my aunt Do's file with Hussein Omar's article and Sonallah Ibrahim's narrator in mind. As discussed in chapter 5, Hussein Omar had sent me a copy of an obituary for my grandfather from *al-Ahram* several years before as an entry point to documenting the ties between our two families, between my grandfather Ibrahim Nagui and his first muse, Alia al-Towayyer, who was Hussein Omar's great-grandmother. I asked myself as I went through these clippings: Who were all of these people mourning my grandfather? How were they connected to him? Why were all the newspapers concerned with acknowledging his passing? Was it really because of the depth of their sorrow at his death? Or was this a way for the obituary writers to broadcast their own social and political status?

In his book on Nagui, Wadie Filastin writes that my grandfather had visited him several months before his untimely death. Filastin's account of that visit reflects the immense gulf between the genteel discourse of newspaper eulogies and the private burden of marginalization that my grandfather bore in his later years. Filastin writes:

> The last time I saw Nagui was in August 1952. Nagui had been unjustly and cruelly dismissed. The Literature Association had fallen apart as the number of literati in its ranks thinned, and others began to take their place. I had won a Spanish medal along with several other Egyptian journalists. Nagui came to visit me in

my office at the paper where I was working. He took out a piece of paper and scribbled some verses on it to congratulate me on the award. But soon after he began to weep. He was wracked with sobs over his misfortunes. [Nagui] bemoaned how all had wanted was to bestow knowledge, learning, and health upon others, but in return he received only suffering and hardship, and had his name dragged through the dirt. He greeted people with love, and they were accusatory in reply. For the goodwill he offered freely, he was subjected to trenchant attacks and iniquity.

I didn't know what to say to this magnificent soul except to console him by telling him he was no less tremendous for his troubles and travails, as is true of all great men.

He embraced me, and we planned to meet again, although we did not set a date. But fate rushed onward and chose a means of departure that would restore his honor, so to speak. He died carrying out his vocation, among his patients at his clinic. He lived and died a noble soul, and his poetic instincts were just one aspect of that incredible generosity of spirit.[3]

It's clear from Wadie Filastin's poignant recollections that my grandfather felt that he had been backstabbed unexpectedly, that everyone had abandoned him at the end of his life. But the obituary clippings contain none of the harsh sentiments that Filastin mentions. Nagui's well-wishers have only kind words as they mourn "the great human being, Ibrahim Nagui" (Zaki Talimat), "the poet we've lost" (Saneya Qoraa), "a wonderful human being," (Gamil al-Rafi'i), "the romantic poet," (Abdel Ghani Salameh), "the late exemplar of medicine and poetry" with his "radiant smile" and "quick wit" (Salama Moussa), "may God bless his grave" (Galila Reda). He was mourned by many, and a look at the names of these obituary writers helps fully map out my grandfather's social network and interests. There is much that can be said about the tone and style of each of these different notices, each of which capture a different relationship with my grandfather. Delving into such obituaries further could be a project for other researchers who, like Sonallah Ibrahim's narrator, are keen to see what might emerge from these backdoors of history.

I was particularly surprised by one obituary published in *al-Ahram*, the morning after my grandfather's death, because it seemed to be trying to belatedly clear his name, though without regard for the facts of what had happened (or at least, my grandfather's version of the facts). Although Nagui had been dismissed from his government post, the obituary reported that he had "resigned" from that position:

> The literary and medical world was shaken yesterday afternoon by the unexpected news of the death of poet and physician Dr. Ibrahim Nagui, who is solemnly mourned by his friends and those who knew him.
>
> The deceased had dedicated his life to medicine and literature. He excelled in both fields, and put his abilities to use in the service of humanity and the greater good. His medical practice was a haven for impoverished patients and those in need, and his poetry was resplendent with sincerity of spirit, which illuminated the manifest Truth for those who might otherwise go astray.
>
> Dr. Nagui had been employed as a physician by the Railway Authority, the Ministry of Health, and the Ministry of Endowments. He resigned from government service two months ago, after leaving an indelible mark everywhere he worked. By all accounts, his work was highly regarded and much appreciated, and no one who knew him will forget his gentleness and humility, his gracious spirit, or his sense of duty. May he rest in peace, and may God ease the sorrows of his family and friends.

I read this obituary and thought: Perhaps these sentiments are best summed up by the popular saying: "Once a man's in the hearse, the sun shines out his arse." Popular sayings are uncomfortably straightforward. These pithy expressions put all their cards on the table and say it like it is, unlike that ostentatious and misleading prose that masks a certain violence and shame.

In any case, the hullaballoo quickly subsided. After all these lamentations for "the late exemplar of medicine and poetry," none of the literary and cultural organizations in Egypt went out of their way to organize a memorial service, with the exception of Nagui's pupils and friends in the Literature Association. The Association held a relatively belated service on 9 May 1953, in which his "soul's twin," Ahmed Ramy, read the following elegy:

O all who have left us
We've woken while you're still sleeping
I arise in the morning, my mind befuddled
Where do you slumber, O dust-dwellers?
Friend after friend fades away
All too soon this race is run
And one dear to me, who yesterday
Filled my ears with a familiar nectar
Now departs with the phantoms
Breath dissolving into harmonies
Extinguished like the meteor that cuts through the
Night, only to disappear into shadow
Vanishing like the nightingale fluttering upon the branch
Confiding in the sky and shepherding the clouds
Fatally struck by an arrow in the throat,
Ephemeral, now returns to dust.
A transitory soul, a hidden spirit
In the life of illusions we lead—
O Nagui, when I heard of your death
The tears poured forth in floods
You filled life with gladness and good cheer
With harmony and gentle elegance
A poet endowed with a magical gift
And a doctor who eased pain
Flitting here and there like a bird

On the water, melodious and resonant
Captivated by creation's beauty
Weak-kneed before the world's charms.
Abidingly loyal in love
A true prince of fidelity
You've left me now but still your voice
Echoes in my ears, words there entrusted
The beauty that beguiled you
Calls to me in confidence like a besotted lover
And the heart that was wont to gladden and
Make wretched in turns, now stands at destiny's door
Companions intent on remembering
Your nights as a bard, reciting
The rhetorical flourishes spun into your poetry
For each soul, transcendent
The stranger's lament in a distant land
The bereaved mother's keening, the orphans' tears
With such tenderness, cascading
Melodies rendered as exhalations
O my dear, the creek's now run dry
Yet the aroma of lavender still hovers on its banks
You have not perished, for you dwell in our hearts
Ablaze with yearning
You're here among us, reflected in our eyes
Brimming with reveries and dreams.

Another particularly remarkable memorial notice in the newspaper *al-Sabah* was entitled "Ta'bin Nagui fi Amrika" A Tribute to Nagui in America:

> The Minerva Society for literature will hold a memorial for the late poet Dr. Ibrahim Nagui on the evening of 20 April [1953] at Columbia University in New York. The prominent Mahjari writer Abd al-Masih Haddad, founder of the famed Pen League [al-Rabita al-Qalamiyya], noted that the Society had taken on the

mantle of the Pen League and reinvigorated Arabic literary life in America after most of the League's members had passed away. The Minerva Society has also counted leading Arabists among its members. Hence the Egyptians in the Society appreciated the group's efforts to commemorate the late Egyptian poet [Ibrahim Nagui]. The Society is currently led by the well-known Mahjari poet Neama al-Hajj, with the esteemed Egyptian poet Ahmed Zaki Abu Shadi (professor of Arabic literature at the Asia Institute[4] in New York) acting as secretary. We have learned that Abu Shadi will open the evening with a eulogy for his dear friend, and which we will publish as soon as it reaches us.

This was really a nice gesture on the part of the Minerva Society. In addition to remembering Nagui, the announcement evidently also served to broadcast the activities of the Society and its Arab Mahjari poets, including Ahmed Zaki Abu Shadi. Abu Shadi had been the founder of the Apollo Group of poets in Egypt as well as the *Apollo* magazine that the group published from 1932 to 1934. Abu Shadi was close friends with his colleague Nagui, a founding member of the group and a regular contributor to the magazine, along with various other young poets. It is widely known that Abu Shadi was also a physician—in fact, no less than the deputy dean of the Faculty of Medicine at Alexandria University—who loved poetry and literature. Like Nagui, he was influenced by the Romantic poetry movement in the West and sought to revitalize and modernize Arabic literature. Abu Shadi's 1934 collection *al-Yanbu'* (The Wellspring) was harshly criticized by conservative poets, especially Abbas Mahmoud al-Aqqad, not unlike Nagui's first collection *Wara' al-ghamam* (Behind the Clouds), which was published that same year. The criticism that Abu Shadi was subjected to was reportedly what led him to emigrate to the United States, where he set aside his medical practice and worked instead in teaching, radio broadcasting, and journalism. Abu Shadi helped found the Minerva Society to modernize Arabic poetry in the diaspora and to engage with the modernist poetry movement in the Arab world. My grandfather and Abu Shadi had a special bond and wrote introductions to each other's poetry collections. They kept up their friendship through correspondence even after the latter emigrated, so it's lovely that Abu Shadi would have opened the memorial service held at Columbia for my grandfather. The eulogy he read was as follows:

> Go ask the pale moon
> the weeping blossoms
> the diffident stars
> the circumspect sun
> Go ask the faint light, roving
> the despondent river, quavering
> Go ask that love which bow and arrow
> have passed over
> Go ask the meek and the good, lost or gone astray
> what here shook soul and stone
> How did death so suddenly snatch him and flee?
> How—when his only sin was writing poetry?

Abu Shadi was guilty of the same "sin" as my grandfather, and the two men had suffered similar rejection and exclusion in their lives. In Abu Shadi's case, he responded to the pressure by emigrating to the United States. This was something that Nagui held against his friend. Before his death, my grandfather wrote:

> I blamed my friend Dr. Zaki Abu Shadi for letting his frustrations about life in Egypt get the better of him. The government kept passing him over for promotion until he finally became fed up and emigrated to America. I reproached him for giving in to his weariness. I told him that we have a duty to the people and a responsibility to see that through no matter what. But he despaired and left. I'd been tempted by the thought of emigrating too from time to time, but then I'd remind myself of what I'd said to Abu Shadi. I told him I'd taken up the pen to fulfill my duty to the people of this nation.[5]

I wondered about Abu Shadi's own passing abroad. Who was there to mourn him, with Nagui gone so early? I remembered something Hussein Omar had told me when we first discussed this book—that Abu Shadi had a granddaughter in the US, who, like me, was in the midst of writing a book about her grandfather, whom she had never met. The only difference was that Joy was writing her text in English; she'd been raised in the US and didn't write fluently in Arabic. All Hussein Omar had told me was that Abu Shadi's granddaughter's name was Joy. I tried to find her on the internet, which was difficult, because her last name was different from her grandfather's—as is also true of me. I followed the trail through the Abu Shadi family papers which Joy had donated to NYU Abu Dhabi and found out who I needed to speak to. Her name was Joy Garnett.

I wrote to her and heard back right away. Joy told me that Hussein Omar was a mutual friend and had told her about my book on Nagui. He had already suggested to her that we have a chat. Joy told me that she had spent more than ten years putting together the Abu Shadi archive and organizing his papers into more than forty separate boxes. Since she was busy with her own professional life—she was a painter and writer—she decided to donate the papers to the NYU Abu Dhabi library. She then embarked on a literary memoir about her grandfather rather than writing an academic book on the topic. Her project was very similar to mine: She was trying to follow her grandfather's footprints to understand his legacy, which she had only come to know through her mother and her maternal aunt and uncle's recollections.[6]

I was hoping that Joy might still have letters exchanged between our grandfathers that would have documented their transnational correspondence and friendship. She said that if such letters existed, they were tucked away inside some box in the NYU Abu Dhabi library. Joy suggested wishfully that we might try to meet there after the COVID-19 pandemic had abated. We'd have coffee, talk about our grandfathers, and look for those letters together. Until that future meeting, Joy was kind enough to give me two photos of Nagui, with an inscription from him to his dear friend Abu Shadi.

 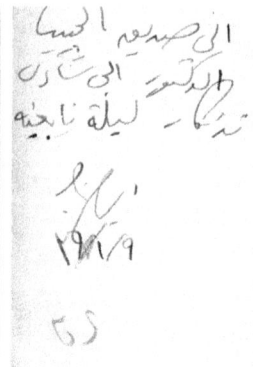 

38. Ibrahim Nagui as a young man. The text on the photograph on the left reads: "To my dear friend Dr. Abu Shadi, 11-2-1933." The center image is the inscription on the back of the photograph on the right: "To my dear friend Dr. Abu Shadi—for a memorable evening,[7] 9-1-1936." Images courtesy of Joy Garnett, granddaughter of the poet Ahmed Zaki Abu Shadi.

My mother continued her story of the day that my grandfather died:

"My aunt Leila brought over the calf. They butchered it in front of the building. Part of it was distributed to the needy and the rest was for the mourners who were eating meals with us during those first days. Every day the dining table was laid and everyone ate. Farah was serving us and looked at us in anger and disgust. He couldn't believe that we had any appetite when Dr. Nagui had just died. Farah wept for forty days. For forty days he didn't shave his beard or cut his hair or change his clothes. He wouldn't take any food, he just wept.

During one of these days when people were coming to pay their condolences, a relative of ours who was also one of Papa's colleagues from the Ministry of Endowments came and sat down next to me. He said to me, "By the way, another woman's holding a funeral gathering up the street." Of course I said, "What are you talking about?" He said, "Come with me now and you'll see for yourself." I told him I didn't want to see any such thing. We never did look into what was going on, and no one ever came asking for an inheritance or anything."

I wanted to hear more about this story from my mother, because I had read before about this "Zaza" who appeared in my grandfather's later years. It was not really a secret within Cairo's cultural scene, at least.

"Was it Zaza who organized that other memorial? Did you know about her before or just find out then?"

My mother began to speak about this for the first time. After everything we'd covered in the course of writing this book, she finally let that mulberry leaf fall.

"Of course we knew," she said. I was truly surprised at her answer and asked her to elaborate.

"Did Tettu know too? How could she stand it? Didn't it bother her?"

My mother came to my grandmother's defense: "My mother was a rational woman. There was an unspoken agreement between all of us not to mention it. Everyone knew, she knew, us girls knew, her brothers knew, but no one talked about it. My mother was the eldest sister, and because of that her younger brothers had to comply with her wishes. More than once they wanted her to get a divorce. We also gave her grief for going along with it. But my mother always said, 'Divorce him? And then where would we all go? You need to understand that despite everything, your father is an angel. Do you understand what I'm saying? He's an angel.'"

My mother continued, "Anyways, Papa was never gone overnight. He'd come back as late as he wanted, but he always slept at home. And he never neglected us. He wore himself out to make us happy.

We knew what was happening because Zaza was our neighbor down the street. She was much younger than he was, and she was living with her siblings. We'd see her sometimes on account of being neighbors. She was young and beautiful.

Sometimes we'd be sitting at the breakfast table in the morning, and find someone at the door who'd come on her behalf saying, 'Dr. Nagui, *Sitt* Zaza would like you to come see her because she's a little tired.' When this happened, Papa would leave his food and get up in a hurry. We'd look at each other in silence because we understood what was happening, but no one wanted to confront him.

So when that relative sat down and told me that there was another lady mourning Nagui up the street, I wasn't really that surprised. I guess I didn't understand why it was in his interest to say anything. Anyways, what's done is done."

I thought to myself: Zaza is an unusual name. I wondered if she was really called Zaza or if it was a pet name. And what was her last name? I didn't know, and no one else seemed to either. Perhaps the nickname was to avoid a scandal, even though the affair was more or less out in the open. She remained only "Zaza" in the poems that Nagui wrote for her. My grandfather's sole novel *(Zaza)* also bore her name. It was no secret then: This wasn't like with Alia al-Towayyer, his first muse, who had remained A. M. forever, even after his death. In the case of A. M., no one had been able to correctly identify who she was, or the nature of that bond, until Hussein Omar finally told me the full story last year.

I looked for Zaza in the writings about my grandfather. I found that Saleh Gawdat had written about her in his book *Nagui: His Life and Poetry*:

> As for Zaza . . . I wouldn't be missing the mark in saying that she was the only woman who truly loved that poet. She was young, attractive, and elegant, and fond of both modern and classical poetry. She'd learnt a great deal of poetry by heart and had no special designs as some ladies might.
>
> All she wanted from life was to spend time with a poet she loved and who loved her. Zaza had played an important role in the lives of three poets prior to Nagui, all of whom were well-known writers. She eventually settled on our poet here, in whom she found something that had been lacking in the poets who had previously fallen for her. [Nagui] was devoted: She was the only thing on his mind for entire days at a time. Unlike the others, he sought the mind over the body. I knew her well, and she was a rare sort of woman who seduced him with something other than her body [. . .]
>
> Zaza remained at his side until the last days of his life, having given herself to him as a young woman, when he was nearing sixty. He was also rather unlucky in matters of beauty, wealth, and

virility, not to mention being ill with pneumonia—so evidently she must have been attached to her ideal of him without any other motive save love itself.[8]

What a strange saga this was! There's no doubt that Zaza was a real person, and that she had a relationship of some kind with my grandfather—since even his daughters and my grandmother knew of her—but Saleh Gawdat's overwrought, circuitous, and callous version of events does little to clarify matters: When did this relationship begin, and what had led my grandfather to seek out this kind of connection in his final years? Who was the girl who'd stolen his heart? Did he actually marry her, as Gawdat claims later on in this text, without any proof of such a union?

I turned to Nagui's novel *Zaza*, which was among the prose texts collected and edited by Hassan Tawfiq. This novel appears alongside Tawfiq's analysis of the book in a separate volume along with three other stories (beyond the two volumes of Nagui's complete collected prose works). I wanted to look at the novel in order to get a sense of Nagui's relationship with this young woman in her fictional guise. Like any novel, *Zaza* is not necessarily a full rendering of the truth, but rather a selection of fragments that sometimes resemble the truth, and at others stray from, stretch, or twist it. Nevertheless, my grandfather did title the book *Zaza* and wrote it specifically during that period of his life.

The cover of the novel is a painting of a sleeping woman in a brilliantly colored dress, resting upon darker red draperies on a marble bench. The image is English painter Frederic Leighton's *Flaming June*, a famous late-nineteenth-century work inspired by Michelangelo's statue "Night." It's a pretty tasteless choice. It certainly offers some variation on the same portrait of Nagui that appears on all his other book covers and all the books written about him. Still, the cover staring back at me now is unnecessarily sexualized. The sheer red dress (orange in the original painting) both conceals and reveals the woman's body, her white cheeks are flushed, and her eyes are closed to whoever is sneaking a glance at her.

39. The cover of Ibrahim Nagui's novel *Zaza*.

I am not against artistic portrayals of the sensual, but Saleh Gawdat's account of Zaza's bond with my grandfather does not suggest that sensuality was a central aspect of their relationship. Nagui, in Gawdat's telling, was a wizened man of almost sixty, and "unlucky in matters of beauty, wealth, and virility, not to mention being ill with pneumonia—so evidently she must have been attached to her ideal of him without any other motive save love itself." The image of the young woman on this cover is also at odds with Gawdat's physical description of Zaza, whom he claims to have known well—just as he claimed to know A. M. (In the latter case, it became clear to me that Gawdat was not personally acquainted with Alia al-Towayyer after all.) Gawdat says that Zaza was a "rare sort of woman who seduced [Nagui] with something other than her body." Why then choose a cover that suggests quite the opposite? This choice of cover is part of the commercialization of books that entirely disregards the actual text and content. The cover also promoted the book with the statement, "A heretofore unknown novel by the poet of 'al-Atlal,' Dr. Ibrahim Nagui."

In any case, what does this "heretofore unknown novel" in fact contain? Hassan Tawfiq writes in his introduction that the person who brought his attention to the book was Farouk Khorshid. Tawfiq explained that he'd been able to obtain information about the magazine in which the novel was serially printed with the help of Dr. Ali Shalash's 1988 book *al-Majallat al-adabiyya fi Misr – tatawwuruha wa-dawruha* (The Development and Role of Literary Magazines in Egypt), published by the General Egyptian Book Organization. Tawfiq discovered over the course of his search for *Zaza* that Nagui had published serial excerpts in *al-Qissa* magazine, which ran two issues every month from 1949 to 1955. The magazine was in fact edited by Nagui himself until just before his death. My grandfather published the first installment of the novel in the 20 December 1949 issue, and the last on 20 May 1950. Tawfiq described how difficult it was to find these issues, and that he had bought some beat-up copies of the magazine from the used book market Sur al-Azbakeya for LE10 per issue when the original magazine had cost only 10 piasters.[9]

In reading Hassan Tawfiq's introduction to the novel, I tried to follow the series of dates he gave in order to piece together some of the key details. My grandfather began to serially publish the novel in December 1949, so he must have met Zaza at least a year before that in order to have had some material to write about. We also know that Nagui ended his *Journal de vie* in October 1949, the same year he embarked on the novel about Zaza. His last diary entry on 4 October 1949 is his briefest entry, but also one of the most telling, though it shuffles around the truth:

> Almost a year has passed in which I have not penned a single line. It felt like a decade. It has been a year of tremendous happiness and misfortune both. I regained my health and felt like a young man. I came to know A. M. . . .

In the image above, the last "M"— the Arabic letter *meem* م on the left of the final line of the diary entry—appears to be written over another letter, as if to cover up what had been written originally. Perhaps the original letter had been a "Z"— the letter ز —and Nagui had decided to change the initials of the woman with whom he'd experienced "tremendous happiness and misfortune both"? Did this emotionally-charged entry initially make reference to Zaza, especially since he began writing the novel around the same time he wrote this in his diary? If so, their relationship would have mostly taken place during 1948, the year that "felt like a decade," in which he didn't write anything in his diary. It certainly doesn't make sense that he would have "come to know" A. M. that year, since Nagui had known Alia al-Towayyer since they were children. Why would he have "felt like a young man" again, when Alia would

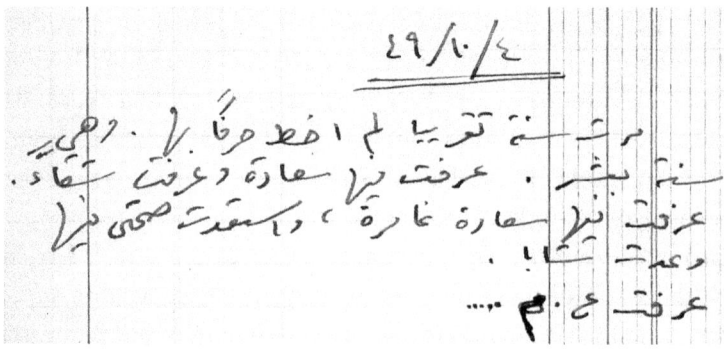

40. Nagui's final diary entry, dated 4 October 1949.

have been about his age (forty-nine years old to be exact, since she was born before 1900). If the letter "Z" was hiding behind that "M," what does this mean about my grandfather's connection with both of these women during the final years of his life?

I looked at this cross-out for a long time while I was writing the chapter about my grandfather's diary. It's hard to make out that letter clearly. After several attempts to decipher it, I gave in to what was written there on the page: A. M. But later, when I heard my mother's story about Zaza and what that relative had told her as they gathered to mourn my grandfather, I went back to the diary page again. If this entry really was about Zaza, then why did my grandfather try to cover up her initial? Can we understand more about his relationship with Zaza based on these small clues?

Some answers can be found within the text of the novel Nagui wrote. I will not delve into the book in detail here, but it is worth drawing some parallels between the fictional text and the events of Nagui's life. The novel's two protagonists are friends: the lawyer Hussain Nani and the doctor Albert Fanous, who represent different sides of Nagui. Hussain Nani has an exhaustingly turbulent relationship with a young woman named Zaza—who is neither white like the woman on the cover, nor a sleeping beauty. The character Zaza is tall, slender, and brown-skinned, with a high brow. She is described as "an artist both strong and kind, noble of character, but surrounded by wolves—indeed, she herself liked to spar with them." The narrator describes Zaza as:

A stunning picture of beauty, struggle, and anguish ... She silently chafed against the destiny that had laid its hands upon her liberty and shackled her and her proud head. So Zaza had bent down with a strange humility [...]

She was a lively woman overflowing with youthful vigor, and she was bound by a secret that she did not understand and whose nature had not yet become clear, to a man upon whom the curtain had nearly fallen. His heart had turned to ashes, and his back was already bowed by long years and disease.[10]

This description of their relationship indicates the obstacles and, indeed, impossibilities they were encountering. The character Zaza is evidently tormented by her love for Hussain Nani, and is in conflict with herself for ending up in a relationship in which she has reluctantly relinquished her freedom. For their part, Nani and Fanous are middle-aged men who have experienced their share of professional successes in their younger days, but are now in the midst of psychological and financial collapse and marginalization. The narrator says of Nani and his relationship with Zaza:

When the two met, his lease on life was running out, and he was getting his affairs in order, like a bankrupt man preparing his shambles of a budget [...]

The office had been bustling with customers, and he'd known fame, glory, and money, until failure conspired against him and left him forsaken. These trials escalated until Nani found himself sick in bed with a dire illness, which wore on and eventually robbed him of any remaining hope.[11]

The novel depicts Nani's anguish as Zaza quarrels with, criticizes, and ignores him. She is involved with other men, but agrees to become engaged to one "Baagar Efendi"—literally the "flabby" *efendi*, as Nani sometimes wryly refers to him, referencing a recurrent caricature from the Egyptian satirical press. Zaza accuses Nani of being overly romantic, eventually leaves him, and he ends up in the hospital. His sole friend, Albert Fanous, arrives to tell him some good news in an effort rescue his twin soul from this crisis. It's unclear to the reader if Fanous is conveying actual news or inventing something to cheer up Nani. The novel ends with Nani alone and ill, feeling depressed that Zaza has left him:

> Albert sat down and began to tell Nani the good news. The big job that he'd been promised had come through—it was indisputably his.
> The Academy of the Arabic Language had decided to give him the prize. Glory awaited him—money, too.
> The whole world was calling his name.
> He needed to get well soon to enjoy these things.
> Nani smiled a wan smile.
> Everything had come too late. What was the point in living, even if he'd finally got his due? What did all that matter if Zaza was gone?[12]

The novel's subtitle ("the faithful lover") is also an unlikely choice given that the character Zaza does not seem to be faithful at all. I don't know if Hassan Tawfiq was the one who added the subtitle, since he mentions in the introduction that he decided to add chapter titles. Or perhaps my grandfather had hoped Zaza would prove "faithful" at the beginning of their relationship, and so these wishes were also reflected in initial chapters of their fictional bond. When things suddenly turned in a direction that Nagui had not anticipated, the novel concludes with the end of their relationship. The fictional Zaza, and likely the historical Zaza, both disappeared.

The similarities between the novel's protagonists and the real-life Zaza and Nagui suggest to me that their tumultuous relationship had in fact ended by the time that my grandfather was writing the final installments of the novel. If the affair wasn't already over, it was entering a crisis that continued unresolved as Nagui finished writing. This context perhaps helps explain that final diary entry, in which my grandfather crossed out the "Z" and wrote the letter "M" on top, and added an "A" to the right, so that the entry appeared to refer to Alia al-Towayyer instead of Zaza.

Hassan Tawfiq raises a crucial point in his introduction to the novel regarding the reemergence of "A. M." in this relatively late stage of my grandfather's life:

> Nagui had dedicated his celebrated second collection of poetry *Cairo Nights* and his book *The Meaning of Life*, both published in 1950, to his great love, A. M. This is perhaps surprising given that he wrote his only novel, the one now in your hands, in late 1949. He began to publish the first installments of the novel on 20 December 1949 and the last on 20 May 1950—the same year that he dedicated a poetry collection and a book of prose to his first love, A. M. Was he still thinking of his first sweetheart even when he was deep in love with the "faithful" Zaza?[13]

The answer to Tawfiq's question is clear from my grandfather's diary. Saleh Gawdat's false claims, later taken up by other writers—that Nagui's affection for Alia was unrequited, or that she had disappeared from his life and left him pining for her—are all untrue. What Nagui recorded in his diary disproves those allegations: Alia sometimes reached out to call him later in their lives, and he continued to visit her (according to her daughter Amira, as previously described). The fondness between them endured, despite their separate married lives, and persisted throughout the period of time in which Nagui embarked on his tumultuous affair with Zaza. Contrary to what Tawfiq suggests, there is really no reason to be surprised. It seems clear to me from these small clues which allow us to reread and reexamine Nagui's life, that my grandfather meant to cross out that "Z" from his diary because Zaza had dramatically exited his life and he was nursing his wound by thinking of his first muse.

Despite the undeniable similarities between the end of Zaza and my grandfather's fictional relationship and their real-life affair, which is also alluded to in his diary, there is still the question of the comment to my mother about the second memorial for Nagui up the street. If Zaza had held this memorial, it would suggest that there was still something between them when he died, and that they perhaps had even been married. This is also the version of events that Saleh Gawdat and Hassan Tawfiq offer:

> There is a story that has been passed down among a narrow circle of people, but which has not been verified, that the poet [Nagui] had married Zaza during his final days. It is said that their marriage remained a secret concealed in a document only shared between them. Zaza did not disturb the poet's memory after he died. She never bothered the family about an inheritance, if there was one, and let the story to be forgotten.[14]

No one has been able to verify the tale of this secret marriage. If true, was Zaza really mourning Nagui? How did she bid him farewell? Again, Saleh Gawdat's account proves unsatisfying and unsubstantiated:

> When [Nagui] died, Zaza did not mourn him [. . .] She didn't wear black. This was not because she was insensitive, but rather because of her higher convictions and her belief that the poet had not died. For her, he'd simply gone without leaving an address [. . .] as she wrote in a letter to the poet Ahmed Ramy.[15]

A strange end to Gawdat's impossible story.

I reread this chapter, and wondered: Why did I ask my mother this question that brought us to where we are now, and required unearthing all these stories? Why was it suddenly important to me after all these years to know how my grandfather had died? I didn't ask before because we didn't know each other, my grandfather and I. He didn't know me and I didn't know him. There was nothing between us except that portrait hanging in the family *salon*, gazing into the distance, whose presence I had tried to ignore. I had not been among those mourners, stricken and weeping after his sudden death, because I was not yet born. But after such an intimate journey with him, I suddenly felt that I needed to bid him farewell in order to bring this journey to a close. That is why I asked my mother, even though it was difficult for her to talk about. All of those who loved him and eulogized him, who criticized him and mistreated him: those newspaper clippings and articles laid out before me became feelings and moments in his life, and in mine too.

For a whole week, I hesitated before saying farewell. I'd begin to write and then leave off, knowing well what I wanted to say, but not yet saying it. I wanted to continue to stay in his company, like a guest who lingers too long and doesn't want to go home. I spent years preparing for this moment and being frightened of it at the same time: What did those envelopes from my aunt hold? How would I read them with him? Then the fateful day came, during a yearlong sabbatical when I immersed myself in this journey toward my grandfather. And what a year it turned out to be! Hardly the peaceful year I had expected: a global pandemic, war, loss, destruction. Not a day passed without terrifying or grim news. I took refuge in my grandfather's company. I'd take him to the sea far away from news of contagion and death, where we got to know each other in peace, at first haltingly, but quickly we became close. A friendship began to emerge, with plenty of mischief and revelation. I spent long hours talking with him and asking him questions, criticizing him, quarreling with him, sometimes getting exasperated. He encouraged me, pushed me to continue. I'd imagine him looking over my shoulder as I wrote, agreeing and disagreeing in turns. I let him into my world sometimes and ignored his presence at others.

I said to myself: At the end of the day, he's my grandfather and I'm his granddaughter, and now we've become friends. Even if we differ or disagree, there's no turning back. I know him now in a way all those mourners did not. I was entrusted with his papers and have shared them, unembellished, with those who loved him, without any qualms, without holding back any secrets—for these are the papers of a man who was not ashamed, who did not embellish, and who had no secrets. Writing this now, ten years older than he was when he died, I am certain that I have done what he would have wished me to do. And if I once took offense that Gamal al-Ghitani had seen a resemblance between my grandfather and me, now—after this much-belated trip—I take pride in having assumed even a wisp of his mantle.

NOTES

Note on the translation
Any errors in excerpted texts or archival documents that appear in Arabic have been preserved to maintain the integrity of the original text.

In keeping with the light footnotes in the Arabic, this edition likewise includes only brief references, rather than identifying all public figures or encumbering the reader with a lengthy glossary.

English transliterations of Arabic names are in accordance with the author's preferences and family usages.

Chapter 1
1. Ahmed Abd al-Maqsud Heikal, introduction to *Diwan Ibrahim Nagui* (Cairo: Ministry of Culture and National Guidance, 1963), 31.
2. Ibrahim al-Masri, *Sawt al-jil* (Voice of a Generation) (Cairo: Maktabat Saba, 1934), 139.
3. See Latifa Zayyat, *The Search: Personal Papers*, translated by Sophie Bennett (London: Quartet Books, 1996). (Latifa al-Zayyat, *Awraq shakhsiyya: hamlat taftish*, Cairo: General Egyptian Book Organization, 1992).

Chapter 2
1. Ibrahim Nagui, "Madinat al-ahlam" (City of Dreams), in *Madinat al-ahlam* (City of Dreams) (Cairo: Matba'at al-Tawfiq) 5.

Chapter 4
1. Saleh Gawdat, *Nagui: hayatuhu wa-shi'ruhu* (Nagui: His Life and Poetry) (Cairo: Supreme Council for Arts and Letters, 1960), 55.

2   Mohamed Ahmed Ghoneim, *Jama'at al-ghina' wa-l-tarab: dirasa anthrubulujiyya bi-madinat al-Mansoura* (Troupes of Singers and Musicians: An Anthropological Study of the City of Mansoura) (Cairo: Dar al-Ein for Human and Social Studies, 2006), 55.

3   Mohamed Ahmed Ghoneim, *Souq al-khawagat bi-madinat al-Mansoura: dirasa fi al-anthrubulujiyya al-iqtisadiyya* (Mansoura's Souq al-Khawagat: A Study in Economic Anthropology) (Cairo: Dar al-Ein for Human and Social Studies, 2006), 15.

4   Hani Saad Salem Ahmed, *Rasd wa-tahlil al-mabani al-tarikhiyya wa-dhat al-qima al-mi'mariyya bi-madinat al-Mansoura* (An Analysis of Historical and Architecturally Noteworthy Buildings in the City of Mansoura), Master's Thesis, Department of Engineering, al-Azhar University, 2004.

5   The name spellings in this French letter are Nagui's own, and reflect the Francophone spelling of the family name and an alternate spelling of Souma; Translation from French into Arabic by Nashwa al-Azhari.

6   The title of the short story that Nagui uses in his letter (written in Arabic) is the title of the English translation of the original Italian story ("Le Tentazioni," or "Temptations").

Chapter 5

1   Wadie Filastin, *Nagui: hayatuhu wa-ajmal ash'aruhu* (Nagui: His Life and Selected Poems) (Cairo: Dar al-Mustaqbal, 1987), 28.

2   Saleh Gawdat, *Nagui: His Life and Poetry*, 101.

3   By his own account, Tawfiq was close to Gawdat, and had asked the latter in confidence who had inspired Nagui to write his famous poem, "al-Atlal" (The Ruins). Gawdat explained to him that Nagui had written his masterpiece for his first love, Anayat Mahmoud al-Towayyer, not for any of the various actresses who had claimed to have been his inspiration. After Gawdat died, Hassan Tawfiq tried to confirm this this story with Ibrahim's younger brother, the late Hassan Nagui, who allegedly told him Gawdat's version was accurate.

4   Ibrahim Nagui, "Tasdir: dhikrayat wa-wada'" (Preface: Memories and a Farewell), in *City of Dreams* (Cairo), 2.

5   Enas al-Assal, *Nagui: 'ashiq al-hurriyya* (Nagui: Lover of Freedom), television screenplay, unpublished, 5–6.

6   Ibrahim Nagui, Introduction to *Adrikni ya duktur* (Cure Me, Doctor) (Cairo: Dar al-Jihad, 1953), 4.
7   Ibrahim Nagui, "Safhat gharam" (A Tale of Love), in *Cure Me, Doctor*, 53.
8   Nagui, "A Tale of Love," in *Cure Me, Doctor*, 57–61.
9   Nagui, "A Tale of Love," in *Cure Me, Doctor*, 57.
10 Ahmed Abdel Muti Hijazi, *Ibrahim Nagui: Dirasa wa-qasa'id mukhtara* (Ibrahim Nagui: Studies and Selected Poems) (Beirut: Dar al-Adab, 1971), 17.

Chapter 6

1   Ibrahim Desouky Abaza Pasha, who was minister of transportation at the time.
2   Ibrahim Nagui, *Cure Me, Doctor*, 3–4.
3   Lajnat Nashr al-Thaqafa al-Haditha, or the Committee for Spreading Modern Culture, a leftist group during this period which briefly published the magazine *al-Fajr al-jadid* (The New Dawn).
4   Wadie Filastin, *Nagui: His Life and Selected Poems*, 11.
5   Filastin, *Nagui: His Life and Selected Poems*, 12.
6   Robert F. Jardine (OBE), the Director of Land Settlement and Water Commissioner in Palestine, and W. J. A. Livingstone, Administrative Officer for the District Administration of the Galilee District.
7   Literally, "seeds to crack between his teeth" (*qazqazat al-libb*).

Chapter 7

1   The southern province of Dhofar, part of present-day Oman. For more on the Dhofar rebellion (1963–1976) and the war in Oman during this era, see for example Sonallah Ibrahim's novel *Warda*.
2   Translation by Samia Mehrez, 1978.
3   For a fuller discussion of the composition of the poem "al-Atlal" and of the evolution from poem to song, bilingual readers may wish to consult chapter 7 in the Arabic edition of this book, which we were unable to include in its entirety here.
4   Please see appendix for Wadie Kirolos's full translation of the poem "al-Atlal."
5   Note that the differences in the first line of these translations also reflects differences in the original Arabic in the poem versus the song.
6   Mustafa Amin, *Masa'il shakhsiyya* (Personal Affairs) (Cairo: Akhbar al-Yom), 90–92.

7   Ahdaf Soueif, *In the Eye of the Sun* (London: Bloomsbury, 1992), 62–63.

Chapter 8

1   The first of two stories within Anatole France's novel, *Le Crime de Sylvestre Bonnard* (*The Crime of Sylvestre Bonnard*, 1881).
2   Ibrahim Nagui, "Kutub aththarat fi hayati" (Books that Shaped Me) in *al-A'mal al-nathriyya al-kamila* (Ibrahim Nagui: The Complete Prose Works), volume 2, edited by Hassan Tawfiq, first edition (Doha: al-Raya, 2001), 263.
3   Ibrahim Nagui, "Books that Shaped Me," 259.
4   Hassan Tawfiq, Introduction to *al-A'mal al-nathriyya al-kamila* (Ibrahim Nagui: The Complete Prose Works), volume 1, edited by Hassan Tawfiq (Cairo: Supreme Council of Culture, 2010), 13.
5   Ibrahim Nagui, "Murakkab Udib aw sikulujiyat Hamlet" (The Oedipus Complex or the Psychology of Hamlet), in *Kayfa tafham al-nas?* (How to Understand People), in *Ibrahim Nagui: The Complete Prose Works*, volume 1 (2010), 221.
6   Nagui, "The Oedipus Complex or the Psychology of Hamlet," 224.
7   Nagui, "The Oedipus Complex or the Psychology of Hamlet," 226.
8   Freud wrote: "Of course it can only be the poet's own psychology with which we are confronted in Hamlet." See footnote on p. 225 of Freud's *The Interpretation of Dreams* (trans. A.A. Brill, New York: MacMillan, 1913).
9   Nagui, "The Oedipus Complex or the Psychology of Hamlet," 227–28.
10 Khalil Mutran, *Tajir al-bunduqiyya* (*The Merchant of Venice*) (Cairo: Hindawi Foundation for Education and Culture, 1922), 10.
11 Nagui, "Books that Shaped Me," 258–59.
12 Hassan Tawfiq classifies Nagui's translations of the sonnets and of Charles Baudelaire's *Les Fleurs du mal* as part of Nagui's "prose works," because he renders them as prose poetry, as distinct from the metered poetry translations discussed on p. 193. Nagui's prose poetry translations can be found in a chapter entitled "Qasa'id mutarjama nathran" of the second volume of Tawfiq's 2001 compilation of Nagui's complete prose works (p. 219–252). Prose poetry in Arabic is unmetered but does not necessarily refer to a lack of line breaks as in English. Readers interested in Nagui's metered poetry translations may wish to consult Hassan Tawfiq's introduction to that chapter (p. 219–222) for a list of other publications in which individual translations

appeared; these metered poems were also collected in Nagui's 1934 collection, *Wara' al-ghamam* (Behind the Clouds).
13   Hassan Tawfiq, Introduction to *Ibrahim Nagui: The Complete Prose Works*, volume 1 (Cairo: Supreme Council of Culture, 2010), 23.
14   Nagui, "Books that Shaped Me," in *The Complete Prose Works*, volume 2, (2001, first edition), 261.
15   Ibrahim Nagui, *Azhar al-sharr*. Arabic translation of *Les Fleurs du mal* (Beirut: Dar al-Awda, 1977), 27.
16   Nagui, *Azhar al-sharr*, 65.
17   Mohamed Nagui, "Dedication," *Azhar al-sharr*, 7.
18   For those interested in additional Arabic translations of this sonnet, translations have also been published by Palestinian writer Jabra Ibrahim Jabra (1919–1994), Iraqi translator and scholar Abdul Wahid Lu'lu'a (1931–), Iraqi poet and journalist Sargon Boulous (1944–2007), and Egyptian poet and translator Badr Tawfiq (1934–2014).
19   Luigi Pirandello's short story "Notte" ("Night") was first published in 1912. Gabriele D'Annunzio's "Campane" ("The Bells") appears within his 1882 short story collection *Terra Vergine* (Virgin Soil). Nagui likely read these in English translation.

Chapter 9

1   Sayed Mostafa, "Editor's Note," *Hakim al-bayt*, no. 11, year 1 (15 December 1951), 2.
2   Ibrahim Nagui, "Mushkilat al-taghdhiya al-haditha" (Problems in Modern Nutrition) in *Hakim al-bayt*, no. 11, 4.
3   Saleh Gawdat, *Nagui: His Life and Poetry*, 49.
4   Wadie Filastin, *Nagui: His Life and Selected Poems*, 10.
5   Hassan Tawfiq, "Introduction," in *Ibrahim Nagui: The Complete Prose Works*, vol. 1 (2010), 10–12.
6   Nagui, *Cure Me, Doctor*, 3.
7   Filastin, *Nagui: His Life and Selected Poems*, 27.
8   Nagui, "Dada Halima," in *Cure Me Doctor*, 8.
9   Nagui, "Dada Halima," in *Cure Me Doctor*, 9.
10   Nagui, "Dada Halima," in *Cure Me Doctor*, 10–11.

11 Abdel Hamid Amer, "Kalimat wafa' wa-'irfan" (A Note of Gratitude), in *Cure Me Doctor*, 100.
12 Hassan Tawfiq, "Introduction," in *Ibrahim Nagui: The Complete Prose Works*, volume 1, (2010), 13–15.
13 Nagui, *How to Understand People*, in Hassan Tawfiq, ed., *Ibrahim Nagui: The Complete Prose Works*, volume 1 (2010), 130.
14 This refers to the edition of Nagui's complete prose works published by Egypt's Supreme Council of Culture in 2010.
15 Nagui, "Tahlil nafsi" (Psychoanalysis), in *Cure Me, Doctor*, 14.
16 Nagui, *'Alam al-usra* (Family Matters), in *Ibrahim Nagui: The Complete Prose Works*, volume 2 (2001), 25.
17 Nagui, *Family Matters*, 26–27.
18 Nagui, *Family Matters*, 44.
19 Nagui, *Family Matters*, 26.
20 Nagui, *Family Matters*, 35.
21 Nagui, *Family Matters*, 71.
22 Wadie Filastin, *Nagui: His Life and Selected Poems*, 9.
23 Filastin, *Nagui: His Life and Selected Poems*, 8.

Chapter 10

1 Hussein Omar, "'Snatched by Destiny's Hand': Obituaries and the Making of Class in Modern Egypt," *History Compass*, volume 15, no. 6, (June 2017): https://doi.org/10.1111/hic3.12380.
2 Sonallah Ibrahim, *al-Lajna (The Committee)* (Beirut: Dar al-Kalima, 1981).
3 Wadie Filastin, *Nagui: His Life and Selected Poems*, 13.
4 A now-defunct institute of art and archaeology which existed under various names and was directed by of Arthur Upham Pope, first in New York (1928–1966), and later in Shiraz, Iran.
5 From Nagui's article "Dardasha adabiyya," (A Literary Chat), in *al-Gomhour al-Misri*, published in Naamat Ahmed Fuad, *Nagui al-sha'ir* (Nagui the Poet) (Cairo: Modern Egyptian Literature Association), 132.
6 E-mail communication with Joy Garnett, 18 and 19 August 2020.
7 A *layla nabaghiyya*, a reference to the sixth-century pre-Islamic poet al-Nabigha al-Dhubyani.
8 Saleh Gawdat, *Nagui: His Life and Poetry*, 129–132.

9   Ibrahim Nagui, *Zaza: al-ashiqa al-wafiyya* (Zaza: The Faithful Lover), edited and with an introduction by Hassan Tawfiq, (Beirut: Mu'assasa al-Rehab al-Haditha) 2011, 5–14.
10 Nagui, *Zaza*, 18.
11 Nagui, *Zaza*, 18.
12 Nagui, *Zaza*, 124.
13 Hassan Tawfiq, Introduction to *Zaza*, 8.
14 Tawfiq, Introduction to *Zaza*, 6.
15 Gawdat, *Nagui: His Life and Poetry*, 132.

Appendix

1   This change in line breaks is consistent with the version published in *al-Ahram Weekly*. In the Arabic version, there are no four-line stanzas.

APPENDIX

The Ruins
By Ibrahim Nagui

Translated by Wadie Kirolos and originally published in two installments in the 18–24 and 25–31 March 1993 issues of al-Ahram Weekly. *Used with kind permission.*

> O my heart, may God have mercy on our love; it was an edifice of illusions destined to collapse,
> Let us drink over its ruins and, as long as the tears continue gushing, you may recount on my behalf
> How our love became yesterday's news, mere talk of a tortured attachment.
> A texture of dreams woven by drinking companions, who have disappeared for ever, and it has disintegrated too,
>
> O wind whose roaring never slackens, the oil in my lamp is finished and my light has been extinguished,
> I fed on an illusion that has been shattered, showing loyalty for a lifetime to a person who was never loyal,
> How often have I tossed over the dagger but my love never swerved and my eyelids never enjoyed the comfort of sleep,

The deeper the edge of the dagger delved, the more forgiving my heart became

That love was like destiny in my blood, like death or the taste of extinction,
We spent barely an hour in its wedding and the remainder of a lifetime in its funeral,
Of what import is wrenching a tear from an eye or wrestling a smile from the mouth
For where is my escape, how can a man escape from his own blood?

How can I forget you, having heard your sweet summons coming forth from a tender mouth,
A hand stretched out to me, like a hand extended through the waves to a drowning man,
You are the target toward which my feet walk, though they may complain that the road is strewn with thorns,
A flashing light to which the night traveller yearns; oh, how do I miss that light in your (beautiful) eyes!

How can I forget you after you showed me the way to the sublime heights and I became addicted to ambition,
You were a spirit in my sky toward which I fluttered aloft, as if I were pure spirit too,
O the summits where we met and exchanged our secrets,
Getting a glimpse of the unknown on the peaks and beholding people as if they were shadows down below

You are beauty in its prime, but my heart is filled with the sorrows of sunset,
The remaining shadows of a departed caravan, the threads of light from a vanishing star,
I view the world with the eyes of boredom, the ghosts of ennui around me
Dancing over the dismembered body of love, wailing over the graveyard of hope

My life has been in vain; so you go away too for your promise was nothing but a phantom,
A page which was folded by Time, a page on which love was scribbled and then erased,
Look how I laugh and dance for joy although I carry a heart that has been slaughtered,
People regard me as a fluttering spirit, although my tortured love is crushing me like a millstone

You were a statue constructed by my imagination and then it came down; thus Fate decreed, not I,
Woe to it, it did not know what it destroyed; it smashed my crown and pulled down my temple,
Now begins the life of a desperate and lonely man in an uninhabited desert,
A scorching desert without companions, the silence of eternity

How do I miss my charming beloved, her nobility, majesty and bashfulness
Confident of her step, she walks angelically, her beauty oppressive, her pride delectable,
Her magic as fragrant as the breath of the hills, her look as pallid as the evening dreams,
Her face shining, talking the language of light, the expressions of heaven

How do I miss your company, the enchantment is complete, the brightness overwhelming,
And I am the embodiment of love, a throbbing heart, a perplexed butterfly drawing closer to you,
Longing is like an emissary going back and forth between us or a drinking companion who served us wine,
As we drank, we shuddered for a moment because we were touched by worldly dust

We came to know the despotic power of the body which rules over humans and reigns in their blood,

A scream we heard, thundering like an executioner's whip, the torture inflicted by a god,
It commanded us but we disobeyed, refusing that our foreheads be bent by humiliation,
The tyrant issued his verdict; we were found to be rebellious and expelled beyond the walls of life

O for two exiles who lost their way in the wilderness, their feet bloodied by thorns and rocks,
Whenever the nights became cruel, they tasted the glory of suffering in their undefiled banishment;
Robbed of their big dream and ousted into the darkness of misfortune, the blackness of night,
They derived light from their souls whenever the world was miserly with light

You have transformed my life into something strange indeed; though the birds of the hills flutter around me galore,
My heart refuses to sing except for Leila,
Curtains have fallen, blinding my vision to all sights except your eyes which are my sole target,
It was you who pulled down those blinds; so don't claim they were brought down by me

O how many times did despair incite me to remove them, but mocking Fate would tell me: Let them be;
What a blind scheme; had I any vision, I would never have become its victim,
Woe to me if I responded, and woe to me if I did not comply,
It bent my head, but should all forces vie to buy my pride, I would not sell it

O for a beloved whose orchard I once visited, flying with longing, singing my pain,

You were coyly tardy with your largesse, displaying the cruelty of the powerful and potent,
My yearning for you inflames my bones; the seconds are like burning coals in my blood,
As I wait anxiously in my position, hearkening to the sound of footsteps

A step advances, my heart beats like a wave advancing towards its shoreline too,
O despot, for how long, by God, will I shed tears over the marks left by those footsteps,
You are the embodiment of mercy, so why can't you show mercy to an estranged or a thirsty soul,
You are the cure of my soul, but my soul complains to its Maker of the injustice shown by its healer

Give me back my freedom, set my hands loose, for I have given all, withholding nothing,
O your fetters have bloodied my wrists; why should I keep them though they proved untrue?
Why should I keep a covenant which you have broken; why should I remain in captivity when I have the rest of the world!
So, I have dried my tears; please forgive them for, before you, they had not been shed for a living soul

The bird has flown your nest, the fountains have dried and the snow has set in,
This world is made up of frozen hearts; the flame is waning, the live coals are dying,
So, if my heart tries to kindle fire from ashes tomorrow, don't ask how it is faring,
Don't ask but remember the sufferings of a man seeking warmth who blows at ashes and gets no flame

May God withhold His blessing from a cruel evening that showed me that all my dreams have been in vain,

And showed the heart whom I worshipped make a mockery of my tears
    as if he were an enemy;
Who knows the events that took place, imprisoning your soul into a solitary dungeon,
Your soul has rusted in its darkness, for souls too can be covered with rust

Now I view the universe as a narrow grave where despair and silence
    prevail unchallenged,
My eyes have beheld the falsehoods uttered by love, they are as brittle as
    the threads of a spider,
You would have shown compassion, sympathising with my pain, were it
    possible for a mute statue to commiserate with tears,
At your feet, a world ends, at your door, hopes perish

You used to call me a child whenever my love was aroused and my eyes
    became wet with tears,
You were right, for love inhabited my soul like a child who, though growing, did not become rational,
I see the stab which you delivered delving madly to a kill,
It struck the child, piercing his heart, and also wounded the man's pride

I said to myself as we crossed beyond the narrow passage: hurry up for a
    firm resolve is of no avail if it advances slowly,
Leave the flaming temple behind you for its fire to eat up those who are
    kneeling and bowing inside,
But my loyalty wishes that I go back, and yet my wounded love refuses;
In relation to the raging flame, I am like a wooden branch that is being
    used to feed the fire

I will never forget an hour in a lifetime
In which the wind clapped, as the rain poured down,
Lamented the memories, complained to the moon,
And, becoming festive, raced unchecked through the trees;
Here is what the wind poured into the poet's ear
As it attempted to seduce his heart with impious eloquence:

"You poet, keep alive the memory of the covenant in your sleep and your vigilance,
And whenever a wound heals, another wound is opened by the hand of memory,
So, learn how to forget, learn how to erase,
Or is all love in your belief a matter of tolerance and forgiveness?
Look, there are as many hearts and women as the grains of sand,
So choose whom you wish, for life has been in vain,
He is lost who searches on earth for the sons of heaven,
What spiritually can be squeezed from a mixture of water and mud!"[1]

Yes, O wind, but she is my love, my excuse, my despair,
She was created in the unknown for my heart, shining for me before my sun rose,
On her promise, I folded my eyes, on her memory, I rested my head

The wind went mad and he was summoned by the demons of darkness;
Is this the conclusion! How can we possibly begin with the end?
O you injured man who surrendered his wound to his beloved, only to have it reopened by her,
You would not weep if the bearer of the news of death brought you this message,
You powerful man, would you be felled to the ground for the sake of a woman?

It was a cry that only revived his painful memories,
They were brought back to life like the remains of a broken dagger,
The river glistened and called for him, so he went down to the river,
Devoid of provisions, and this is the only trip that requires no provisions

O my beloved, everything is decreed by Fate; we were made unhappy but not by our own hands,
Perhaps we will be reunited by destiny one day, though a reunion had seemed unlikely,
So if friends deny each other and our meeting is the encounter of strangers,

Each going his own way, don't say that we had willed the past into existence
but say it was a stroke of luck
You who wish to celebrate eternity have wasted your life composing
songs for mortals,
None among the living hears us, although we are not singing for stones,
Or inanimate objects that have no consciousness or worn out corpses in
their holes,
Yet sing it and your song will rise, showing compassion to the chanter
and shedding tears for the strings

Whenever I issued my call, it was returned back, defeated, thwarted by
bad luck,
And my songs of hope came back to me as lamentations and regrets,
A statue of beauty and light revealed itself to me at a time when life was
full of grief and injustice;
The tune, unaware that this is stone-deaf beauty, hurled itself, kneeling
down at the feet of the statue

The night is calm; it has no heart to sympathise with your dilemma, you
who are keeping vigil,
Pick up your lyre, O poet, sing your sorrow, pour out your tears,
Perchance the star would dance to your music; perchance it would penetrate the clouds and dissipate the planets,
So sing it until the curtains of darkness are torn apart by the new dawn

And should some flowers panic and you see their hearts anguished by
terror
Be patient and kind and play them tender tunes that would take away
their fear,
Perhaps they had slept in the cradle of sorrow, tearfully supplicating their
God,
O poet, how many flowers were punished, without knowing what they
did wrong!

Printed in the USA
CPSIA information can be obtained
at www.ICGtesting.com
JSHW011726061124
72888JS00001B/1/J